Beyond Concord

Selected Writings of David Atwood Wasson

Beyond Concord

SELECTED WRITINGS OF

DAVID ATWOOD WASSON

EDITED WITH AN INTRODUCTION BY

Charles H. Foster

1965

Indiana University Press

BLOOMINGTON

FOR DORIS

ACKNOWLEDGMENTS

Since David Atwood Wasson is so little known, I have not had the usual advantage of discussing my subject with friends and colleagues nor have I had the benefit of their criticism during the writing and rewriting of my study. But I must thank Herbert Ross Brown, Newton P. Stallknecht, Allen Tate, and Mildred Wasson for their interest and encouragement and most of all Robert C. Albrecht of the University of Chicago for undertaking the very considerable labor of compiling a bibliography of Wasson's writings. The extent to which Mr. Albrecht has expanded the knowledge of Wasson may be estimated immediately by noticing that the only other bibliography, that by O.B. Frothingham, accompanying his collection of Wasson's work, *Essays: Religious, Social, Political* (1889), lists only fifty items.

I am indebted to the librarians of the University of Minnesota, the Minnesota Historical Society, Bowdoin College, Harvard University, the American Antiquarian Society at Worcester, Massachusetts, and the Concord Free Public Library for making rare and sometimes unique items available. I particularly thank Mr. Russell Fridley, director of the Minnesota Historical Society, and Mrs. Marcia E. Moss, reference librarian at the Concord Free Public Library. In addition to finding documents pertaining to the Concord School of Philosophy, Mrs. Moss discovered the photograph of Wasson prefacing this volume.

vii

Finally I thank the University of Minnesota for a single quarter leave in which I studied the *Radical,* the *Index,* and other periodicals illuminating the second cycle of American Transcendentalism.

For permission to use copyrighted or otherwise restricted materials I am grateful to the following: Concord Free Public Library for the photograph of David A. Wasson; Mildred Wasson (Mrs. David A. Wasson) for quotation from a letter in which she recalls William James's appraisal of her husband's grandfather; Harvard College library for quotation from a letter of David A. Wasson to T.W. Higginson; Odell Shepard for quotations from *The Journals of Bronson Alcott* (1938); Alfred A. Knopf, Inc., for quotations from *The James Family Including Selections from the Writings of Henry James, Senior, William, Henry, & Alice James* (1947), edited by F.O. Matthiessen; Rutgers University Press for quotations from *The Widening Gyre: Crisis and Mastery in Modern Literature* (1963), by Joseph Frank.

C.H.F.

University of Minnesota

Contents

❧❦

Beyond Concord

Selected Writings of David Atwood Wasson

A Study of
David Atwood Wasson

DAVID ATWOOD WASSON

(1823–1887)

I

Anyone who reads the essays here reprinted for the first time will find it natural that Alcott, Emerson, and William James should have praised David A. Wasson.[1] Wasson is an extraordinary figure in American intellectual history, claiming and holding our attention by his very modern responses and reactions to nineteenth-century thought. Some of his writings, admittedly, are reaffirmations of standard Transcendental teachings, but characteristically he is a critic of and a corrective to Emerson and Thoreau. In his insistence on open relations with opposites, in his recognition of evil, and in his assertion that individualism is a half truth, he advances, in fact, so far beyond Concord as to join hands with Irving Babbitt and T.S. Eliot. Yet Wasson is for most students of American thought no more than a name among the post-Civil-War American Transcendentalists.

Why he should have faded from notice becomes immediately clear when we realize that the bulk of his work was published once and once only in the *Atlantic Monthly,* the *Christian Examiner,* and such little known and seldom consulted periodicals as the *New Englander,* the *Radical,* and the *Index.* During most of his life Wasson suffered from ill health and never found the time and energy to revise and collect his essays and poems into books. Consequently, while he could impress his contemporaries, who had felt the immediate impact of his personality and writings, subsequent readers had no firm grounds on which to con-

3

sider him. His image was so broken and scattered as to give no
true sense of his achievement, and his cause was quite as much
harmed as it was helped by those unsatisfactory posthumous volumes, *Poems,* collected and edited by Ednah D. Cheney in 1888,
and *Essays: Religious, Social, Political,* edited with a long "Memoir" by O.B. Frothingham in 1889.

In his will Wasson confided to Mrs. Cheney the task of collecting his poems, and with more enthusiasm than literary discretion
she took him at his word, printing every one of his poems she
could lay her hands on.[2] This was unfortunate. Unrevised poems,
several of them much too long, which Wasson presumably would
have chosen to forget, draw our attention away from the sonnets
and the four or five lyrics such as "All's Well" and "Seen and
Unseen" which have an interesting particularity of vision and
phrase. Furthermore, Wasson was only incidentally a poet, and
to make his first book a collection of his poems was a step which
could lead only to misunderstanding. Wasson is a good enough
poet to merit the honor Emerson awarded him in printing two
selections in his anthology *Parnassus,*[3] and Alcott was perhaps
justified in turning Ellery Channing out of his study for failure
to appreciate Wasson's sonnets.[4] But Wasson is, when all is said
and done, definitely a minor poet, and the *Poems* give the unwarranted impression that we need not investigate him further.

The essays Frothingham collected in *Essays: Religious, Social,
Political* indicate, on the other hand, an original and penetrating
thinker. But if Mrs. Cheney offended by publishing too many of
Wasson's poems, Frothingham offended in precisely the opposite
fashion by publishing too few items to make for genuine understanding. For the most part he brought forward hitherto unpublished pieces, which Wasson wrote late in life, and we need to
know Wasson's earlier work to read them with full intelligibility.[5]
In his 123-page "Memoir," Frothingham should at least have
called our attention to "Mr. Buckle as a Thinker," "Modern
Speculative Radicalism," and "Epic Philosophy," but they go
unnoticed.[6] The most we grasp from Frothingham's "Memoir"
is that Wasson was in some sense a Transcendentalist and at the
same time a political conservative, even a reactionary. The image

Frothingham creates through his comments and choice of readings is in many respects self-contradictory, and we are likely to dismiss Wasson from our minds as a provocative thinker who is unusually hard to follow and whom it is scarcely worth our time to try to follow.

There is thus no puzzle in Wasson's present lack of reputation: his writings simply have never had their proper chance with posterity. To give them their full chance now, after the passage of almost a century, they must be read not only in the light of the biographical details in Frothingham's "Memoir" and the only other important source of information, F.P. Stearns's essay in *Sketches from Concord and Appledore* (1895); [7] they must be seen in the context of New England intellectual history as an unfolding pattern of concern and comment, in which Wasson emerges as both like and unlike his notable contemporaries.

II

We begin to delineate Wasson when we think of him as the Orestes Brownson of the second cycle of American Transcendentalism. Like Brownson, who was born in Vermont in 1803,[8] Wasson, born 20 years later in Brooksville, Maine, was a product of rough northern New England. The son of a farmer and shipbuilder also named David,[9] young Wasson was combative and intransigent from birth, and his inclination toward the sturdily masculine may have been intensified by the early death of his mother.[10] Much of Wasson's mature life was marred by various illnesses, poor eyesight, nervous disorders, and trouble with his back, possibly traceable, as O.B. Frothingham supposed, to a wrestling match brought on by a political dispute in 1840.[11] But Wasson's vigor and impulse to combat were undiminished. Characteristic of his stance in the world of ideas is his writing in an open letter to Thomas Carlyle in 1864, "Give me leave to 'wrestle a fall' with you on this theme. . . . For I must wrestle to-day in earnest!" [12] And wrestle in earnest Wasson did, not only on this occasion but throughout his career, in a muscular prose, consequential and logical, in which he repeatedly downed, or gave the appearance of downing, the illusions, delusions, and even personalities of his softer contemporaries.

Like Brownson again, Wasson swung from orthodoxy through radicalism back to orthodoxy. His "Autobiography," incorporated by Frothingham in the "Memoir" prefacing *Essays: Religious, Social, Political,* is a bitter complaint, almost a wail, against the provincial Calvinism of his childhood and its concomitant doctrine of perpetual work preached and enforced by his father, a man, Wasson declared, with four eyes and six hands.[13] But the "Autobiography" is, I suspect, a product of Wasson's radical period and reports only the negative aspects of his immersion in village Puritanism. Ultimately, in any case, he would be a defender of the ancestral spirit if not its creed; and if, like Brownson, who left the Presbyterian Church after only two years, Wasson also "signed off" from Puritanism, he, again like Brownson, owed a lifelong debt to its discipline. This Emerson himself perceived, as we may read in his *Journal* for 1862: "The Unitarians, born Unitarians, have a pale, shallow religion; but the Calvinist, born and reared under his vigorous, ascetic, scowling creed, and then ripened into a Unitarian becomes powerful, as Dr. Channing, Dewey, Horace Mann, Wasson, Garrison, and others." [14]

I think it is something better than an educated guess that Wasson's ripening into a religious liberal and a Transcendentalist began at Bowdoin College, which he entered in 1845 after training at Phillips Andover Academy. The great man at Bowdoin in those days was Thomas C. Upham, Professor of Mental and Moral Philosophy, and Upham's books, *Principles of the Interior or Hidden Life,* and its supplement, just off the press, *The Life of Faith,* might well have inspired a young man weary of Calvinism to move from the faith of the fathers to the faith of Alcott and Emerson. By intention Upham was reinvigorating Edwardsean Calvinism, but in his advocacy of the inner light and of union with deity he drew so close to the Concord Transcendentalists that in 1844, one year before Wasson entered Bowdoin, Alcott's friend Charles Lane wrote approvingly in the *Dial* of *Principles of the Interior or Hidden Life.*[15]

All of this looks very promising in terms of Wasson's later development. I find, however, no references to Upham in Wasson's essays or letters. Furthermore, Wasson did not stay long enough at Bowdoin to take classes in philosophy with Upham; they were reserved, as the college catalogues indicate, for juniors and seniors. We are on safer ground if we suppose that Bowdoin instilled in Wasson, as dissolvent of Calvinism, an admiration for Greek and Latin literature. Xenophon and Livy, Homer and Horace, the authors Wasson read in his freshman and sophomore years, certainly do not appear dangerous reading for a young Puritan from Brooksville, Maine, but this further training in the classical languages ultimately had surprising results. We have, I believe, an important clue as to what Bowdoin unintentionally taught Wasson in the recommendation in the "Autobiography" that Plutarch be substituted for the Bible in the education of the young, followed by Epictetus and Antoninus, the New Testament to be added only when "those were well digested." [16]

We must not, however, exaggerate the liberalizing influence of the training in Greek and Latin which Wasson received at Bowdoin. Greek and Latin literature—Plutarch in particular, it would seem—helped disenchant Wasson with American and French democracy. As early as 1854 we find him writing in a letter: "I have cast aside democracy and every one of its axioms . . . God be thanked!" [17] Wasson is not only a later Brownson; he is also an earlier Irving Babbitt, finding a motto for his own practice and that of others in a favorite quotation from Schiller: "He who would do benefit to the age in which he lives must bathe deep in the spirit of classical antiquity and then return to his own time to be in it, but not of it." [18]

Early in his sophomore year Wasson left Bowdoin, never to return. F.P. Stearns's version of the separation is that Wasson refused to inform against fellow students who had set the college woodpile afire, whereupon he was suspended by the faculty and in indignation withdrew from Bowdoin.[19] This may have been the truth behind the scenes but it is not borne out by the faculty minutes. There we learn that in October, 1846, Wasson and another sophomore named Ten Broeck were "suspended for two months of the next term" for being "actively concerned" when the upper classmen tried to block the exit of the freshman and sophomore classes from evening chapel. It is easy to understand Wasson's entry into such an engagement. Given his disposition, his size (he was almost six feet tall) , and his prowess as a wrestler, Wasson was not the man to push around in collegiate horseplay. He was not, furthermore, the man who would endure an injustice, and he would quite naturally have regarded his suspension for involvement in a ruckus he did not begin as a flagrant injustice. I suppose that here was reason enough for Wasson to quit Bowdoin for good in 1847, though the woodpile does glow temptingly as an explanation.

After leaving Bowdoin, Wasson began the study of law only to desert it after a year on the ground of conscience. In his subsequent groping he bought a copy of Carlyle's *Sartor Resartus* at a country store, and this book, which he had tried unsuccessfully to read earlier, inspired him to study for the ministry at the theological seminary in Bangor.[20] Thanks to Abbie Smith, whom he would marry in 1852 and who had influential relatives in Groveland, Massachusetts, Wasson was in 1851 installed as minister of the Congregational Church and Society of Groveland.[21]

Wasson's ministry, lasting less than a year, confronts us with one problem after another. Nothing in Wasson's career suggests the slightest taint of duplicity. It is simply impossible to suppose that to secure a position he would subserviently commit himself in public to a body of belief for which he did not expect to hold himself fully accountable. But Wasson's integrity seems called in question by his *Confession of Faith,* published by the Groveland Church after his dismissal. We have here, if we are to believe our eyes and the deacons of the Groveland Society, Wasson's unequivocal commitment at his ordination to all the central doctrines of Calvinism: the Scriptures as the revealed word of God, the Trinity, the atonement through Christ, the fall of all men in Adam, the necessity of regeneration, and the election and sanctification of the saints. Furthermore, we are called upon to believe that having given this public endorsement of faith, Was-

son then completely repudiated it in practice. As the "Notice,"
vindictively furnished by the Groveland Church, explains: "The
Congregational Church and Society of Groveland, having lately
dismissed their Minister, Rev. David A. Wasson, after a connection of but one year, and he having published a farewell discourse, which will sufficiently justify that separation to every
candid and serious mind; it is felt that the only question which
it is necessary for us to answer is, How we ever came to settle him?
In reply to which, it should be known that he came to us from
an Orthodox Institution, well recommended by Orthodox Professors, and gave in at his Ordination the following Confession
of Faith." [22]

When we turn for help to the "Farewell Discourse," signifi-
cantly entitled "Religion Divorced from Theology," we are further baffled. Wasson makes it clear that his whole ministry has
been devoted to preaching not the letter but the spirit of Puritanism, which he finds to be "fidelity to the inmost law of our
souls. . . ." Why, if he had acknowledged orthodox doctrines at
his ordination, should he then so rashly have aligned himself in
his subsequent preaching with Emerson's position in the "Divinity School Address" and with Theodore Parker's in "A Discourse
of the Transient and Permanent in Christianity"?

There may be an explanation for all this if we suppose that
Wasson was a rock-ribbed Calvinist at his ordination and then
experienced an immediate and almost total theological change
of heart and mind. But of this Wasson makes no mention in his
"Farewell Discourse" or elsewhere. The most probable explanation of the mishap at Groveland is a series of misunderstandings.
In the "Farewell Discourse," Wasson writes that his Transcendental program is a renewal of Puritanism in its vital phase
before theology strangled it. Such a distinction becomes marvelously obscure the more we reflect on it, since Puritanism is in-
sistently theological, and the orthodox at Groveland were not
unusually obtuse if they came to the unwarranted conclusion
that Wasson was in fact a thoroughgoing Calvinist or at least that
he claimed to be one. What actually happened at his ordination
we cannot know, except that there was confusion about those

articles of faith subsequently printed in the *Confession*, and that this confusion was deepened by a split in the congregation. Not all of Groveland was orthodox. After being dismissed from the Congregational Church, Wasson established an independent religious society at Groveland with some members of his former parish, and he emerged as a notable member of the movement party. His preaching before this independent religious society won the attention of Thomas Wentworth Higginson, minister of a similar church in Worcester, Massachusetts, and resulted in Wasson's becoming Higginson's colleague in 1856, after a year as his substitute.[23]

To appreciate how thoroughly Wasson now belonged to the avant-garde, we need only read a letter of 1857 from Lydia Maria Child to her friend Lucy Osgood. As an abolitionist, Transcendentalist, and liberal theologian, Mrs. Child stamped her *nihil obstat* on Wasson with these words: "I have seldom had such a day as the delightful one passed with you and David Wasson. I have marked it in my pilgrimage by a golden pillar, hung with amaranth garlands. I said he was poet, philosopher, and priest. During the evening that I subsequently spent with him I found he was also full of fun. I might have known it, indeed, by those eyes of his, that look out so smiling upon the world. It is many a day since I have met with such a real child of God and Nature. He will not be popular, of course; for

'Souls are dangerous things to carry straight
Through all the spilt saltpetre of the world!' "[24]

Mrs. Child's poetic flourish was apt. At Worcester in the 1850's saltpeter was figuratively spilling in the streets. Higginson's failure in 1854 forcibly to free the fugitive slave Anthony Burns from the Court House in Boston had by no means dampened his antislavery ardor. Now, three years later, he held in Worcester a State Disunion Convention, advocating the separation of the free and slave states. Wasson, who regretted that ill health had kept him out of the Burns affair, must have attended this convention and listened as his ministerial colleague reported among other resolutions: "That the sooner the separation takes place, the more peaceful it will be; but that peace or war is a *secondary consideration*, in view of our present perils. Slavery must be conquered, 'peaceably if we can, forcibly if we must.' " [25] Wasson was also aware, of course, of Higginson's support in 1858 of John Brown's warfare in Kansas, and in 1859 he must have learned, if he had not done so earlier, that Higginson was a member of Brown's secret council of six abetting the Harper's Ferry raid.

Worcester did not mark the limit of Wasson's involvement with radicals. In the late 1850's he moved to the old Thoreau house in Concord, where, as Wasson's son recalled, Henry himself once came to fix the pump in the kitchen sink.[26] It is easy to see the impact of Concord in that bright essay, "The New World and the New Man," published in the *Atlantic Monthly* in 1858. Wasson there recapitulates much that is familiar in his Transcendental elders. Indeed, the ideal citizen, whose organization is "that of the seer, the poet, the spiritualist, of all such as have an eye for the deeper essences and first principles of things," turns out at the close of the essay to be realized in Emerson himself because of his "sight and insight" and poetic-prophetic genius.[27] As interesting as the mention of Emerson is the omission of Thoreau, which may not have been accidental. I think there is good reason to suppose that while Emerson attracted Wasson more deeply into Transcendentalism, the personal encounter with Thoreau was an important fact in Wasson's ultimate rejection of Transcendentalist individualism.

In his essay of 1862, "Individuality," Wasson is close to Robert Frost's sentiment in the line, "Keep off each other and keep each other off." [28] He too believes that we must not bare ourselves completely to the inspection or invasion of others, nor must we impose upon them any excessive individuality. Singularity to Wasson is as shallow as the shallowest conformity. "In particular," he writes, "I make occasion to say, that those oddities, whose chief characteristic it is to slink away from the habitations of men, and claim companionship with musk-rats, are, despite Mr. Thoreau's pleasant patronage of them, no whit more manly or profound than the average citizen, who loves streets and parlors, and does not endure estrangement from the Post-Office." [29]

In phrasing this objection Wasson seems to make Thoreau simply the sponsor of eccentricity, but passages in other essays indicate that it was Thoreau himself whom Wasson had in mind. On one occasion he offers Thoreau as exhibit A representing those who in reaction to eighteenth-century conformity cry out, "Leave behind all formal civilization; let us live only from within, and let the outward be formless,—momentarily created by our souls, momentarily vanishing." He grants Thoreau's purity, his moral steadfastness, which he admits is, indeed, unsurpassed in his observation; he recognizes the priceless gift of his imaginative sympathy with outward nature. But Thoreau, he notes, was obliged to omit marriage from his scheme of life; in fact he compared it to a carrion-flower, and there was a fundamental deception in his whole revolt: "The civilization he slighted was an air that he breathed; it was implied, as impulse and audience, in those books of his, wherein he enshrined his spirit, and whereby he kept its health." [30]

In another essay Wasson recalls Thorcau's once telling him, doubtless during the Concord residence, of finding remnants of Indian tobacco pipes and broken pottery in the neighborhood. "When I come upon these things," Thoreau had said, "I feel that I have indeed found something! This is genuine and unmistakable; there is Nature in it, no cant, nor artifice, nor make-belief; it is solid and real as rock; and with such relics before me I could lose the houses of the village, the shops, the churches, and the post office, without missing them." Wasson's countermove was to praise the Westminster catechism: "Here," he told Thoreau, "are arrowheads of another sort, weapons used in a warfare with the embodical principle of evil,—quite as primitive in their way as those of your Indians, and somewhat *harder* than flint, I think. Here is the smoke of the bottomless pit rather than that of a tobacco pipe, suggesting a narcotic for nerves finer and more vital by far than those affected by the Indian weed. Broken pottery? Think of that cup of communion which men once quaffed, verily believing that they drank the blood of God. There is broken pottery for you! Broken, hopelessly broken, I admit; but suggesting such memories, such thoughts not to be spoken!" [31]

We find on the first page of Wasson's *Ice and Esquimaux,* the report of his excursion to Labrador in 1864, the observation that it was only in the North that one could find the Wild unless one invented it as Thoreau did. Morover he laughed off the notion that Thoreau, now dead two years, had actually found it in Concord: "Talk of finding it in a ten-acre swamp! Why, man, you are just from a cornfield, the echoes of your sister's piano are still in your ears, and you called at the post-office for a letter as you came! Verdure and a mild heaven are above; *clunking* frogs and plants that keep company with man are beneath. But in the North Nature herself is wild." [32]

It is unjust to interpret Thoreau, as Wasson does here, as a backyard primitive. "Ktaadn and the Maine Woods," published in 1848, and "Chesuncook," published in 1858, report encounters with the truly wild, and there are few passages in *Ice and Esquimaux* more evocative of the completely untamed than Thoreau's account of "Vast, Titanic, inhuman Nature" on the summit of Katahdin.[33] But in his chapter "Autochthones" Wasson does damage badly Thoreau's idea that primitive man in America "begins where we leave off. It is worth the while to detect new faculties in man, he is so much the more divine. . . ." [34] Measured by his own standards, the life of the Eskimo was, indeed, a piece of perfection; and if one looked at him through the eyes of a fox or a wolf, he was a marvelously skilled and even beautiful being as he handled his kayak and cared for himself and his family in the Arctic waste. Through the eyes of civilized man, however, the Eskimo's life was simply a response to his physical environment; he had stopped short of ideas even to the extent of having them in his blood and imagination. Since history and civilization began when man responded to himself and built "architectures" out of his own spiritual activity, the Eskimo was actually pre-historical, "pre-Adamite." From his position Palestine and Greece, Moses and Homer seemed wild dreams, impossible fancies, and the best advice was "Go, spear a seal, and be a reasonable being!"

Alcott, with whom Wasson as an acquaintance of Emerson and Thoreau would inevitably have become conversant early in his Concord residence, was a more compatible figure than the ex-sage of Walden Pond. In 1858, when Wasson had settled or was just about to settle in Concord, Alcott recorded in his *Journal:* "1 P.M. comes Emerson and asks me to accompany him home to tea. We talk late on intellect and individualism, discriminating the latter from Personality." In a footnote to this passage, Odell Shepard quotes a letter of Alcott's written in 1868 making clear that Alcott's discrimination involved that which separates man from, and that which unites him to, his fellows.[35] This discrimination approximates very closely Wasson's doctrine in "Individuality," that the individual, the particular man or woman, the biped atom, must always be subordinated to the "person," the universal nature which makes all men one inseparable humanity. It seems very likely that whereas Wasson learned only by reaction from Thoreau, he was propelled toward some of his most fundamental beliefs, as witness his essay of 1862, by conversations with Alcott.

But if Concord thus possessed its congenial aspect for Wasson, why did he leave it in 1860 to spend a year as seer and prophet in residence at the home of George L. Stearns in Medford, Massachusetts? It may have been fulfillment of a promise that sometime he would make an extended visit to Medford; some years earlier Stearns had attempted to promote Wasson's candidacy as minister of the First Medford Parish and his interest had persisted. There may also be truth in F.P. Stearns's observation that Wasson found the social atmosphere of Concord unfavorable.[36] But Wasson had doubtless been living in Concord on funds provided largely by his father and, it seems likely, his father-in-law as well, and the invitation from Stearns may have looked to him like the equivalent in modern terms of a grant from a respected foundation making possible his continuance as a writer.

But Stearns does not seem quite the person to champion a young man who, it will be recalled, had in 1854 "cast aside democracy and every one of its fundamental axioms." Stearns had not only been, like Higginson, a member of John Brown's Secret Six, but also he had been, in modern parlance, Brown's "angel," exceeded only by Gerrit Smith as a provider of funds. And he had gone further: as president of the Massachusetts Kansas Committee, Stearns had turned over to Brown the Sharp's carbines which wound up at Harper's Ferry. At about the time Wasson became his house guest, Stearns for his suspected, and quite properly suspected, complicity had been summoned to Washington to testify before the Senate committee investigating Brown's raid.[37]

Wasson was, if we can trust his sonnet "G.L.S.," somewhat baffled by his relationship with Stearns. He began confidently, "By all the purest love I bear my kind," but along toward the middle of the poem he wrote:

> I near thy spirit as Missouri bears
> His waters to his brother stream, not through
> Fondness, as wooed of thee, or thee to woo . . . .[38]

and then he limped, rather than flowed on, to the end. Frank Preston Stearns writes that his father liked Wasson's good talk, which was practically inexhaustible, and also valued his freedom from the eccentricities in thought and program found in "Alcott's vegetable diet, in Emerson's naturalism, or in Thoreau's idea of turning human beings back into oak trees." [39] But F.P. Stearns also notes that his father could not "adapt himself to Mr. Wasson's breadth," that is, his intellectual breadth. It was his breadth of another sort which disturbed Mrs. Stearns: "A certain Boston lady who came occasionally to see Mr. Wasson gave Mrs. Stearns great annoyance; but it was impossible to prevent this, for her father was one of Wasson's most helpful friends. What made the matter worse, she was a noted flirt." [40]

And where, we are led to inquire, were Mrs. Wasson and their five-year-old son, George Savary Wasson? The visits of the Boston flirt suggest that they were absent. The Stearns fellowship in creative prophecy was apparently limited to Wasson alone. Neither F.P. Stearns nor Frothingham refers to Mrs. Wasson's presence at Medford, and I think we must suppose that she spent the year with her child at the home of her parents. The more we look at it, the more anomalous the whole year appears even if we grant that in view of his writing and his poor health Wasson needed rest and quiet.

It seems clear in any case that Wasson's move to Medford is

not to be defined as a further swing toward radicalism. With the rampant, restless participation in reform which George Stearns illustrated, Wasson had no real sympathy at all. Apparently believing that prophecy begins at home, he wrote, while Stearns's house guest, an essay, "Rest and Motion," which was a protest against the "persistent excess of outward performance," the "haste and intemperance" which were "the Satans that beset virtuous Americans." [41] As he viewed the times he commented, "The incitement to thought is ever greater; but the possibility of thinking, especially of thinking in a deep, simple, central way, is ever less," and it was obviously his ambition to think as best he could precisely in the neglected fashion.[42]

To make one's life a constantly soaring flame, he argued, was not simply personal error but violation of cosmic law. Neither action nor thought can have wholeness or depth without some point of rest, some resource in repose: "Awake, we think, feel, act; sleeping, we *become*. Day feeds our consciousness; night, out of those stores which action has accumulated, nourishes the vital unconsciousness, the pure unit of the man. . . . Only that which comes from a divine depth can attain to a divine height. . . . The power of acting greatly includes that of greatly abstaining from action." [43]

In 1861 Wasson bought with funds from some unspecified source an old house in Worcester, and here, during the war years, he wrote a series of essays ("Individuality" was one of them) in which he established himself, with some relapses, as a Transcendentalist with a marked divergence from Emerson and Thoreau. In "Originality" and "Ease in Work" Wasson, admittedly, is restating in his own terms the organic theory of art developed earlier by Emerson, Thoreau, and Whitman. What the writer should aspire to, Wasson maintains, is vitality, a human product born like flower and fruit from "the ceaseless re-origination" of nature, a new life in the shoots and buds, the "truth of life and the heart, the world-old imaginations, the root-thoughts of human consciousness." [44] And Wasson anticipates no serious problem in such production: "The grand ideas, the master-imaginations and moving faiths of men, run in the blood of the race; and a given degree of pure human heat infallibly brings them out. Not more surely does the rose appear on the rose-bush, or the apple, pear, or peach upon the trees of the orchard, than these fruits of the soul upon nations of powerful and thrifty spirit." [45]

In reading the great writers, Wasson detected ripe fruit that had fallen by itself. This was something other than the fall of the worm-eaten apples of artifice and fabrication. The glib work was done easily because it was so successfully separated from the inward life; "the pure original thought" was born without effort because it was "the sincere, seasonable, and, as it were, inevitable flowering into expression of one's inward life," with "a genesis equally ancient, earnest, vital with any product in Nature. . . ." [46]

Wasson undoubtedly believed what he wrote, but "Originality" and "Ease in Work" are only grace notes in his thought. He struck his own distinctive chord in "Hindrance," published in the *Atlantic Monthly* in 1862. There he argued "that every definite action is conditioned upon a definite resistance, and is impossible without it." [47] The resistance of water is needed to keep the ship afloat; the tympanum of the ear must resist the sound waves to transmit their suggestion to the ear; objects must resist, that is reflect, the sun's rays to become visible; the marble, basalt, bronze must resist the sculptor to receive the impress of his thought. Inwardly and outwardly man needs resistance to evoke his insight, his wisdom, his art; the philosophers and saints were premature in lamenting the fact that body hampered spirit, for it was the very collision between them which struck out the spark of thought and kindled the sense of law.

Wasson's essay "The Law of Costs," appearing the following year, marks another divergence in his Transcendentalism. In "Compensation" Emerson had developed through a series of brilliant aphorisms and images the doctrine that there is a balance in everything—a grain of folly for every grain of wit, consolation for every deprivation, a tax for every benefit, tit for tat throughout the range of human life, with one lofty exception: "There is no penalty to virtue; no penalty to wisdom; they are

proper additions of being." [48] Writing in the midst of the Civil
War, Wasson came to an opposite conclusion. He thought it
self-evident that the nation was paying not only for its vice in
sustaining slavery but for its virtue in being committed to freedom and justice; and what was true of the nation was true of the
individual. In this world man pays for every refinement of spirit
and sensibility. Socrates paid with his life for "divine sincerity
and penetration"; John Brown paid with his life for the privilege
of being a true man; Raleigh lost his head for the privilege of
being Raleigh; and finally, the artist pays anything within reason
for excellence in his art. These are the true exhibitions of the law
of costs. [49]

In other essays belonging to the war years, "Mr. Buckle as a
Thinker" and "A Letter to Thomas Carlyle," Wasson is even
more vigorously at odds with his contemporaries. But this new
manner, we should note, was not entirely an innovation. Largely
it was a resumption of Wasson's practice in his first truly characteristic essay, "Dr. Isaac Barrow," published in the *New Englander* in 1851. There he protested against Macaulay and the
"smart" style and thought in contemporary English and American literature and argued for the more manly virtues of seventeenth-century prose. To Wasson, Barrow was a lesser figure than
Bacon, Milton, Hooker, and, as we can see in admiring references
elsewhere, Sir Thomas Browne. But Barrow had the virtues of his
time and place. He was copious in vital words and thoughts; he
was free from any attempt at "prettiness"; and he illustrated
the supreme virtue of courage. Wasson obviously hoped to embody these qualities in his own writing, particularly the virtue
of "rhetorical courage; a pouring of native force and sturdiness
into expression; a freedom and boldness in the ordering of
phrases and the use of words, tropes and metaphors. . . ." In
fact, Wasson's whole future opposition to the sentimentalities
and superficialities of nineteenth-century literature is fore-
shadowed in his statement in the Barrow essay that if an author
"turns pale at the imagination of standing alone, the world fronting him; if he has not that sustaining faith in the power of Truth
to work her own way, which alone qualifies one to be the minister

of Truth; better he should never assume the pen. For the author who is worthy of his vocation must make up his mind to utter some things, which not the largest half of the world will thank him for saying. . . ." [50]

All of this sounds a good deal like Thoreau in *A Week on the Concord and Merrimack Rivers,* which had appeared in 1849 and which Thoreau's admirer, T.W. Higginson, might well have called to Wasson's attention. But if we compare the passages in *A Week* where Thoreau celebrates seventeenth-century prose with the pertinent paragraphs in the Barrow essay, we find no real justification for suspecting influence. Wasson would seem to be one more instance of that almost innate predilection for the seventeenth century which characterizes such diverse nineteenth-century American writers as Hawthorne and Emerson, Thoreau and Melville, Bronson Alcott and Emily Dickinson. Furthermore, when Wasson wrote the phrase "standing alone, the world fronting him," which seems to look back to "Civil Disobedience" and to look ahead to *Walden,* it was probably Theodore Parker rather than Thoreau whom he had in mind if he was in fact thinking of any of his contemporaries. Parker was an inevitable hero, even model, for a young minister like Wasson who in 1851 was giving such a violent stir to the religious cauldron in Groveland, Massachusetts, and it is therefore not surprising that by 1856 Wasson had become one of Parker's chief protégés.[51]

Parker undoubtedly did much to help stiffen Wasson's thought and style of expression as well as to forewarn and forearm him against the aesthetic anarchism of Emerson and Thoreau, so different from his own feverish engagement with the institutions of church and state. Parker's influence would seem to have lapsed during Wasson's years in Concord but it by no means came to an end with Parker's death in 1860. Wasson came once more into Parker's electrifying presence in 1864 as he made an exhaustive appraisal of the figure revealed in the two huge volumes of *Life and Correspondence of Theodore Parker,* edited by John Weiss.

Wasson's verdict in his essay, "Character and Historical Position of Theodore Parker," published the same year in the *Christian Examiner,* is almost entirely favorable. Against the background of the Civil War boiling to its awful climax, Wasson now finds Parker right and himself wrong in regard to John Brown. Parker had seen that the struggle must come and he had taken the wise course as one of Brown's Secret Six in promoting the Harper's Ferry raid before the North was depleted of the moral and material means of victory. Wasson also finds a thoroughly exhilarating spectacle in Parker's simplicity of spirit, his moral irascibility, the Yankee humor which permeated his whole performance, his love of homeliness, his choice of Saxon words far in excess of Webster and Sumner, his mass, energy, and steadiness, his unwavering, uncritical commitment to the divine spirit as cognate with his own. But it is important to note that Wasson does not entirely approve of Parker, for even as he found limitations in Emerson and Thoreau, so he found limitations in the Transcendentalist he most admired.

In his appraisal Wasson found that Parker excelled in quantity, in a rugged bounteousness of nature, rather than in quality, in fineness of intellect and sensibility. Parker was wrong in attributing to himself "philosophical intellect." He lacked the capital quality of intellect, "imaginative intelligence"; his universe was a straight line; he could make little of Alcott, nothing of Thoreau; Weiss's *Life* furnished no evidence that Parker ever read a great poem as a poem; characteristically he went to history with a "moral yardstick" rather than imagination.[52] These charges, all I believe justified, warn us away from regarding Wasson as a re-issue in post-Civil-War America of one of its great pre-Civil-War prophets. Wasson is Parker but more subtle in sensibility and imagination; he adds to Parker's downright manner ranges of aesthetic awareness not only beyond Parker but doubtless beyond his probable appreciation.

Wasson's similarities to Parker explain easily why he was installed in 1865 as minister of the Twenty-Eighth Congregational Society, Boston, which Parker had organized and over which he had presided, sending his prophetic thunderbolts rumbling throughout the nation until they reached even Lincoln in Illinois. Wasson probably managed occasional thunderclaps reminiscent of his predecessor, but fresh from his own appraisal of

Parker's limitations, he would seem to have tried too hard to avoid them. O.B. Frothingham reports: "The installation took place in May, 1865. In 1867 the ministry ceased, in great measure from ill health. Besides, it must be confessed his preaching was too intellectual, too subtle, too close for the multitude. There was no topic of popular excitement, as in former days [Frothingham is referring to the slavery crisis], and his treatment of religious themes was not calculated to please a miscellaneous audience, who desired something more demonstrative, not to say more electrifying." [53]

Wasson now settled in a plain wooden house at West Medford, Massachusetts, and wrote two of his most profound and intricate essays, "Modern Speculative Radicalism" and "Epic Philosophy." But no one could support himself by writings of this kind. In May, 1868, Wasson sought the help of James T. Fields, the editor of the *Atlantic Monthly*, in appointment as storekeeper on Fiskes Wharf at the Boston Custom House, with this result, as he wrote in an unpublished letter to Higginson: "I am much occupied,—away from home, & without any quiet leisure, ten hours a day. Fifty nine cargoes or parts of cargoes— very considerable parts—have come to my charge since the first of January. I have to keep an eye upon deliveries as well as receipts & to make daily returns. Besides, I try to keep on a very little with my own proper studies & labors. So my head is full most of the time & it is only for special reasons that I attempt to do any book-noticing." [54] Inevitably we think of Hawthorne weighed down by similar drudgery thirty years earlier at the Boston Custom House. But Wasson's creativity was not stifled by contact with cargoes and parts of cargoes. He did keep on with his "proper studies & labors." Soon after his appointment he read an impressive essay, "Authority," to the Boston Radical Club, and by the close of his ordeal in 1873 he had managed a good deal of writing toward a book on modern politics.

The years at the Custom House, were, however, clearly an interruption in the important role Wasson began to play in May, 1867, at the meeting in Boston inaugurating the Free Religious Association. In his speech on this occasion Emerson blandly bestowed his blessing on religious liberalism, but only Lucretia Mott rivaled Wasson in fiery declaration of principle. Doubtless Wasson felt that history had dismally repeated itself in the recent attempt of the National Conference of Unitarian Churches to repress the radicals and to make "the Lordship of Jesus" rather than free inquiry the basis of fellowship.[55] Here, Wasson might well have supposed, was recapitulation of the attempt in the 1830's and 1840's to discredit Emerson and to silence Parker; and it would have been natural for Wasson to recall his own deeply unpleasant experience with the Congregational Church and Society at Groveland. In any case he was inevitably committed by ministerial descent from Parker to the essential aims of the Free Religious Association.

But to hear Wasson speak, the National Council of Unitarian Churches concerned him little. The point of his address at the Boston meeting was not vindication of free religion and free churches but denunciation of one of the young radicals, Francis Ellingwood Abbot, who in his speech proclaimed that the word for the new hour must be science. Science, said Abbot, was the natural and absolutely essential ally of religion. Science alone could tell us what we ought to think; religion alone could tell us what we ought to be; science, born from the head, and religion, born from the heart, must be one and harmonious if human nature was to be one and harmonious. Radicalism meant "a mighty affirmative faith in man"; we must go home having formed a fellowship for the diffusion of religion without superstition; we proclaim here and now the natural union of science and religion.[56]

In his address Wasson disagreed unequivocally. Religion, he stated, possessed its own logic, its own vindication; it could not be "substantiated and its import sustained otherwise than by itself." [57] The scientific and philosophical attempt to "compose a god inferentially" was simply one more example of "the modern fashion of Babel-building." [58] What, for example, were we to make of "the argument of design" as we perceived it in the cobra? How about "that nice little sac of excellent venom"? It demonstrated "a matchless artificer," but what kind of god? So far as Wasson was concerned, the argument of design obliged us to "creep and coil with snakes, raven with wild beasts and make friends with all the ferocities of nature, all the horror and uncleanness of the world. . . ." [59] There was only one proper definition of religion: "The absolute affirmation of Spirit made in and by the soul of man." We should place no trust whatsoever in the "self-defeating methods" of science. If we set out from "the self-enunciation of Spirit in the soul," we might come sweeping down on the world with eyes to see and tongue to tell what science could never discover or clarify. The voice and the speaker, "the everlasting Word," which was in every soul, "here breathed in the mild accents of meditative wisdom; there hymned sweet, flute-like, infinitely melodious, from the lips of enchanted saints; again, blown across the passionate turmoil of time in the trumpet-blasts of indignant prophets; but ever the same Word, ever the voice of Spirit, saying, I AM." [60]

Wasson's sarcastic and indignant comments on "the argument of design" suggest Brownson or Parker, but the passage I have just quoted is a set piece in Transcendental falsetto; we might be reading Emerson's "Divinity School Address" or his essay, "The Over-Soul," and in large terms that is precisely what we are doing. Wasson is not making the thoroughly modern comment on Abbot which we find in his essay of 1870, "Mr. Abbot's Religion," published in the *Radical*. Rather, in denouncing Abbot's proposition that science alone can tell us what to think, Wasson is refighting in old armor and with old weapons the war of 1838–1842. In those years—with an opening volley from Emerson—Orestes Brownson and George Ripley had assailed Andrews Norton of Harvard for promulgating similar doctrines to those Abbot preached, specifically the view, derived from John Locke, that we come into the world so many blank sheets of paper and can know God and his word only from the instruction of a learned ministry qualified to tell us what we should think.

In the following speeches, neither T.W. Higginson nor Emerson exhibited anything of Wasson's fervor regarding the proposed alliance of science and religion. In fact, the other speakers, including O.B. Frothingham, who was to become president of the Free Religious Association, were apparently willing to go along with Abbot at least part way.

Was Wasson, then, "the only Kangaroo among the Beauty" in sustaining the Transcendental position in its pristine purity? [61] I think not. Another Bowdoin man, Cyrus A. Bartol, probably agreed with everything, or almost everything, Wasson said in his speech. Bartol is best described as Emerson in slow motion. It had taken Emerson three years to exhaust the possibilities for himself at the Second Church, Boston, and only about fifteen to pass into and out of Transcendentalism. Bartol had been ordained minister of the West Church, Boston, in 1837, and remained until his retirement in 1889. In the 1830's he had been a member of the Transcendental or Hedge Club, but this we should never guess from his early sermons. [62] It was not until 1855 with his *Pictures from Europe*, which can be described as an international version of Thoreau's *A Week on the Concord and Merrimack Rivers*, that Bartol openly became a Transcendentalist; and his full Transcendental florescence did not occur until the 1870's, when he published those brightly aphoristic and poetic books, *Radical Problems*, *The Rising Faith*, and *Principles and Portraits*.

Bartol approved Swedenborg's statement that the oldest angels are the youngest, and he himself demonstrated the proposition, growing increasingly spontaneous, poetic, and mystical with the years. In 1867, when proposals for the Free Religious Association were being discussed by the young radicals, Bartol had reached the state of spiritual awareness and ecstasy that Emerson had attained in 1838. Indeed, Bartol may well have conceived of himself as Emerson's successor, who might, through leadership of the Free Religious Association, once again inspire liberal Unitarians to a Transcendental course. This would be accomplished by preaching life passed through the fire of thought, announcing the god within themselves, and thereby rousing the deity in others. Certainly something like this role is suggested by the fact that it was at Bartol's home in Boston that Wasson, Frothingham, John Weiss, Abbot, and other radicals had gathered in anticipation of the meeting which would publicly inaugurate the Free Religious Association. But in their discussions Bartol soon learned that he was not the man of the hour and that the F.R.A., as the movement came to be abbreviated, would in all likelihood be rationalistic and scientific rather than truly Transcendental. Consequently, Bartol, like Wasson, did not join the F.R.A. and it seems highly probable that he inspired Wasson or even conspired with him in the speech denouncing Abbot.[63] In any case, Bartol clearly would have fortified Wasson in his dissent from Abbot.

I think we may also name Amos Bronson Alcott as a figure sympathetic to Wasson's views in the second cycle of American Transcendentalism. In his *Journal* for August, 1867, Alcott reports: "At Emerson's, and meet Weiss and Wasson. We consider the aspects of religion and its instrumentalities. 'Tis thought much may be done by private clubs and conversations for inspiring a nobler divinity into the students, thus complementing the defects of the teaching at the schools. This, we hope, is the first of future meetings here at Emerson's or at my house." [64] Alcott had given his blessing to the F.R.A., and indeed he would remain one of its champions, but his phrase "inspiring a nobler divinity into the students," instructs us as to how we should understand his involvement. Alcott was no polemicist, but his activities and his writings all harmonize with this phrase, manifesting a denial even more profound than Wasson's of Abbot's proposition that science alone can tell us what to think. Alcott's masters were not Locke, Mill, Bentham, nor Charles Darwin, but rather, as he made clear in his contributions to the *Radical*, Coleridge, Berkeley, Boehme, Plato, Plotinus, the Greek mystics, and Plutarch.

Alcott's development, furthermore, bore a striking resemblance to Bartol's. He had, unlike Bartol, been a full-fledged Transcendentalist from the start; in fact he was the original American Transcendentalist anticipating Emerson, and we need no other evidence than the "Orphic Sayings" in the *Dial* and the disaster at the idealistic Fruitlands Community to be certain of his pristine Transcendental purity. Like Bartol, however, his florescence was a post-Civil-War phenomenon. His principal works are *Tablets* (1868), *Concord Days* (1872), *Table-Talk* (1877), and *Sonnets and Canzonets* (1882); his most notable public accomplishment was the establishment and leadership of the Concord School of Philosophy, which opened in 1879. In his conversation, "Woman," reported in the *Radical* in 1869, Alcott said, "It looks as if the problem of life was to remain young, nor know too much. . . .[65] We are interposed between; and if the Godhead flow through us freely, we shall fill and spill with beauty and delight. Whoever has not that overflow has not lived. But one must fill freely, not spill too fast. The spilling is the ecstasy, the pure delight." [66]

In the funeral address he delivered at Alcott's deathbed request, Bartol recalled the elder Henry James's report to him that Alcott had once declared, "I can say with Jesus, *I and my father are one,*" to which James had replied, "Did you ever get anybody to believe you?" [67] Had Wasson heard this quip, we can be sure he would have shared Bartol's amusement. Alcott's spiritual naïveté went considerably beyond Wasson's belief in the indwelling deity, and it is hard to imagine Wasson having anything more than intermittent sympathy with Alcott's doctrines of genesis, lapse, and ascent as propounded in his "Philosophemes" published over a period of years in the *Journal of Speculative Philosophy*. But the "Philosophemes," the eighteen items contributed by Alcott to the *Radical,* and the books in which these items, revised and abbreviated, were collected, would all, nevertheless, have been significant to Wasson. Like the phenomenon of Bartol's youth in age and like the meetings of the Boston Radical Club, where Emerson, Alcott, Bartol, Hedge, the elder Henry James, W.H. Channing, Phillips, Higginson, Weiss, and Frothingham assembled for heady conversations, they would have convinced Wasson that he stood in a second Transcendental flowering of New England.

This conviction largely explains Wasson's intransigence in his speeches before the F.R.A. and in his letters to the *Index* setting Abbot straight. Abbot emerges as an admirable man and editor in the pages of the *Index*. Clearly, he was permeated by a spirit of live and let live and was ready to regard Transcendentalism

as one more view, competing in the market place of ideas. He
repeatedly puffed the *Radical;* he reprinted Wasson's speeches
and gave him full opportunity to set forth his views in letters. But
to Wasson all truth was on his side. Unlike Bartol, who in his
letters to the *Index* tried to be generous and almost succeeded,
Wasson attacked Abbot bluntly, often seeking to win by sarcasm
rather than by a reasoned confrontation of Abbot's position. In
the context of his liberal, science-oriented discourse in the *Index,*
Wasson appears, consequently, not only arrogant but anachro-
nistic, a seer and prophet from another age relying on the absolute pronouncements of intuition which modern discussion has
long since ruled out of order.

Abbot ultimately pointed out that "a certain real but hitherto
unrecognized dogmatism" lurked in Transcendentalism. Did
not the Transcendentalists actually show contempt for those
unblessed like themselves with intuitions and insights? Abbot
summed up the Transcendentalist credo thus: "The intuition of
Infinite Spirit is a purely subjective and self-authenticated revelation of God in the soul,—not a truth learned by experience or
derived in any way from the outer universe, but an inward self-
revelation of God to man in the depths of his own spiritual
consciousness." [68]

A good many Transcendentalists would have embraced this
definition without modification, but Wasson is a Transcendentalist with a difference. If he had, in his speech inaugurating the
Free Religious Association and in some of his subsequent
speeches at its meetings, refought, as I have suggested, Emerson's
war on eighteenth-century sensationalism, he was in basic principles much closer to Orestes Brownson. In his criticism of "The
Divinity School Address" in the *Boston Quarterly Review* in
1838, Brownson had written: "We have one witness within us,
an important witness, too seldom examined; but as important as
he is, he is not alone sufficient. We must back up his individual
testimony with that of the race." [69] This passage would serve
nicely as an epigraph for Wasson, but it is necessary to make
distinctions.

At the meeting of the Boston Radical Club in 1880 when

Oliver Wendell Holmes did his best to demolish Jonathan Edwards once and for all, Wasson, as Mrs. Sargent reported, was "the most emphatic of all the opponents of the Edwards philosophy." [70] Indeed, Wasson argued that Edwards was not a good man; no good man could realize as Edwards vividly had done "the terrible import of eternal punishment and total depravity," roll those doctrines as a sweet morsel under his tongue, and then become a father; such a man was "a scoundrel." [71] Wasson offers a significant contrast with Wendell Phillips, who argued that we should trace to Edwards the energetic, self-respectful, independent, free-thought aura of New England in post-Civil-War America.

In another conversation, Wasson marked himself off from Phillips in a yet more significant way. Phillips was willing to accept W.H. Channing's proposal that modern radicals and reformers call themselves Christians because of their overwhelming indebtedness to Jesus. Wasson, however, lined himself up with Higginson and Weiss in the party outside the Christian fold, and went further. He felt, he said, "very little interest in claiming, or making any reference to, the name Christian. He thought facts more important than names. In regard to Jesus, he had no sense of any personal relation to him. . . . Christianity has had immense influence on the Western world, but not through the person of Jesus. . . . Christianity never has by itself transformed the world. Where it entered into the inheritance of Greek and Roman civilizations it succeeded; elsewhere it failed. . . . There was no reason, Mr. Wasson thought, to choose Christianity for *our* system, either at present or in the future." [72]

Brownson, who had become a Roman Catholic in 1844, would have found these remarks anathema, but they do not point, as one might suppose without other evidence, to Wasson's unmitigated reliance on his own intuition. If he did not insist, as did Brownson, on Christianity as the supreme testimony of God and the human race, he still maintained the absolute necessity for a testimony outside the individual, and like Brownson he found a major witness in history.

Wasson's observations on Christianity at the Radical Club

suggest that he would have little sympathy with medieval Christian culture, but nearly the reverse is the case. In his essay of 1864, "Character and Historical Position of Theodore Parker," Wasson wrote that "The old Catholic world was whole; crude indeed, narrow, ignorant, half-civilized indeed,—nevertheless whole." Its essential idea was "the absolute supremacy of institutions over man" and it made those institutions "representative of the loftiest spiritual imaginations known to the human race" with the result that, as it must, religion for a thousand years "stood at the centre and included the circumference of the social world," a superior parent in every family, a third party in the "rapturous plight of man and maid," the higher conscience in the heart of the individual.[73]

For Wasson the modern disaster began when the Church recognized the new worlds of classical literature and physical science as "profane truth" lying beyond its system. The intention had been to arrange a compromise between reason and revelation; the condition of the compromise had been that no inferences were to be carried back on the old faith. But this attempted compromise, like all compromises, had inevitably failed; not only had profane inferences been carried back on the old faith; profane truth had gained the upper hand; science had become the measure of truth in the modern world; revelation had been found preposterous.[74]

In the decline of Western civilization toward this situation, Wasson, in other essays again calling Brownson to mind, gave emphasis to eighteenth-century France and to Rousseau and Voltaire. Supposing spontaneous experience "a fanfaronade of fear, fraud and delusion," Rousseau stripped man of any sense of kindred with the Infinite and any impulse to fellowship, placing him in an imaginary state of nature, where in his "nude self," an utter individual and egotist, he concocted society in mere self-will and self-interest. Voltaire similarly found religion a delusion, the fruit of "the human spirit abandoned to itself," and did not dream of the reality of an "interior guidance," "of any divine structural idea involved in this spirit to be evolved by it." [75] Wasson believed we might read in the French Revolution

the results of this philosophy. The fundamental conditions
making it possible were the subversion and destruction of the
organic structure of a national society and Rousseauistic individualism as "the peculiar and enthusiastically cherished gospel
of France." [76]

Wasson is particularly interesting in what he has to say about
individualism. In direct opposition to his liberal American contemporaries, who regarded it as fundamental to strong personal
character, Wasson declared individualism "the egotism of liberty
and equality," fatal to personal development. This he believed
was demonstrated by a comparison of the Greek and Roman Re-
publics with France in the 1790's. In Athens and Rome we had,
as the scholars agreed, the individual absorbed in the state, but
the complementary fact was that Plutarch found powerful and
noble personalities in the leaders of classical civilization. On the
other hand, nothing was more noticeable about the French Revolution than "the littleness of the men it put forward," and that
littleness Wasson believed could be traced to the stripped "natural man," the "nude self" held up as a model by Rousseau. In the
crater of revolution the natural man, blind to his own spiritual
resources, became the mass man, losing form and melting away:
"The social demon spoke. Never was it the voice of independent
personal conviction. Men were persuaded, they themselves knew
not how, nor were enough themselves to inquire how. A demon,
whose name was legion, but its nature one,—a demon that must
inhabit a mass of men, to exist at all,—possessed them, substituted its inspirations for thought in their heads, gave itself tongue
by their mouths; and in France, one might almost say, there was
a people, but never a person; a human mass, and yet no man." [77]

There had been reactions (Wasson had special praise for
Goethe and the early Carlyle) to this collapse of personality and
society. There had not been, however, in his view, any cessation
in the eroding of the medieval Catholic world-view. As of 1867,
Wasson asserted in "Modern Speculative Radicalism," published
in the Radical, that Western civilization had reached a point
beyond which no previous civilization had been able to continue.
To maintain its vitality every civilization in the past had been

obliged to submit to its religious and social duties as simply, as unreflectingly, as uncritically as it submitted to gravitation, accepting as facts, like night and day, the symbolical forms in which its principles were embodied. Once men began to separate principle from symbol, once they reached the stage of theorizing about their beliefs, once they stood free from traditional, unconscious bondage to their gods and seemed about to enter upon a larger life of the spirit, at that moment previous cultures had proven themselves exhausted. The greater minds might go on, indeed typically did go on for a time to develop lofty speculations, but the greater number of minds either lingered with the past, trying to squeeze one drop more from the empty bottle of the old faith, or they fell away into "sophisms, egoisms, brutalities." [78]

Wasson found Greece and Rome, at their highest intellectual development, supports for his thesis: Socrates and Plato established moral truth on an eternal basis while the mass of the people gave themselves to pleasure; Cicero in *De Officiis* made "something in the nature of universal statement" concerning ethical law while Rome sank in rottenness, its only heaven a debased theater. For Wasson Western civilization had once again reached the same paradoxical development. In modern culture it had been the accepted practice for two hundred years that political obligation must be vindicated on the plane of principle; moral obligation, too, had become a matter for theorizing; and no one any longer identified religion, but rather associated it, with the original symbols of faith. And what were the concomitant phenomena? We had in London, Paris, New York, and Boston "the luxury of decadent Rome, the passion for pleasure of death-smitten Athens, theories which resolve duty into self-interest, authority into self-will, and religion into rhetoric. . . . A metaphysic which seeks to extinguish intellectual ideas by showing them as mere nominalisms, mere fictions borrowed from sensations, renders aid and comfort, often unwillingly to the practical egoism which negates all moral ideas." [79]

In fundamental analysis, Wasson differed little from Brownson and others who sought relief in a return to the Catholic

Church. This is seen rather clearly in his references to the "psychological unity" in the form of "habitual solicitude" which is infused in all men by the commercial spirit, and in his candid and very modern appraisal of the corruption and cheapening of our national life through destructive competition centering in the new corporations.[80] Wasson expressed sympathy and understanding toward those who turned to the Church: "I do not wonder, still less do I mock, at the instinct of self-preservation which leads many to recoil, and seek a renewal of the primitive forms of faith." [81] But every time men had tried to fend off inevitable developments in religious opinion they had failed; Athens had put the hemlock to Socrates' lips but it had not given itself new life. Having arrived at the juncture of history where radical theorizing had dissolved the old symbolical faith, we had no alternative but to attempt to sustain and inspirit Western civilization with universal principles. "Had the matter," Wasson wrote, "been in my power, as it could be in that of no man, I should not perhaps have dared to bring about this state of things. But there is One who has taken the responsibility; and now we *must* do our duty in the premises." [82]

Wasson was not sure that we should be successful in this unprecedented undertaking. In "The New Epoch in Belief," published in 1866, one year before the essay quoted above, he had, to be sure, found an image for the age in the form of a pine forest in June, where seemingly all was dead, but where actually there was a double movement, death and life struggling together, and where we could be confident that in time a new life would replace the dying one. But this image, suggesting ease and inevitability, like the similar use of the growing plant in his literary theory, does not express his essential vision. Wasson was actually quite as disenchanted with the Gilded Age, and almost as hopeless about it, as Orestes Brownson.

In fact Wasson, in his swing from orthodoxy through radicalism back to an approximation of orthodoxy, finally landed in the 1870's in a position differing in essentials from Brownson's only in that it was not buttressed by Roman Catholicism. Wasson's lecture "Social Ideals," delivered as one of the F.R.A.

lectures in Horticulture Hall, Boston, in 1872, follows in general conception Brownson's major clarification in *The American Republic,* published in 1866. Wasson, too, was a modern Federalist rather than a Jeffersonian democrat, finding that in the circumstances of his age, "everything admonishes us to return and resume the sober, constructive spirit of Washington, Adams, Jay, Hamilton, Ames, Osgood." [83] And it is clear that the Puritanism of which Wasson later disapproved in the theology of Jonathan Edwards now occupied in his thought a position roughly equivalent in authority to that occupied by Roman Catholicism in Brownson's reflections.

We hear a good deal in "Social Ideals" concerning the Puritans, and though Wasson does not name John Winthrop, Winthrop's famous speech on liberty to the General Court in 1645 seems certainly to have conditioned his thought. Winthrop described "natural liberty," the liberty of "man, as he stands in relation to man simply," to do as he wishes, as one "common to man with beasts and other creatures." Wasson observes that the ideal of liberty in the preamble to the "Declaration of Independence" (to which he believed Jefferson had been led by Rousseau) "would be quite as suitable to rats as human beings. Your rat is quite as much attached as a human creature can be to life, liberty and the pursuit of happiness—would be nothing less than absolute owner of himself, would make his private inclination his supreme law. . . ." The other kind of liberty, "civil liberty," Winthrop had defined as "liberty to that only which is good, just, and honest. This liberty you are to stand for, with the hazard (not only of your goods, but) of your lives, if need be." Wasson similarly proclaims, "Every man *has* a right to do what *is* right, and no other." [84]

The parallels do not cease here. Wasson also agrees with Winthrop concerning equality. He does not believe that all members of society are entitled to equal functions in the state; he advocates limiting the suffrage to the nineteenth-century equivalent of the "elect," that is to men whose education, character, and record of responsibility warrant intrusting the social destiny to their hands. He finds de Tocqueville right in his prediction that

the "ardent, insatiable, incessant, invincible" passion for equality
in democratic societies would result in a preference for "equality
in slavery" over liberty.[85] The insistence on equality, Wasson
declares, has developed into the fiercely levelling doctrines of
the International Association of French Communists, and these
doctrines mean death not only to the "spurious liberty" of Rousseau and Jefferson but to "the liberty of the good citizen to choose
his own occupation, own and bequeath property, and the like." [86]

Wasson couples these denunciations of the generally accepted
ideas of liberty and equality with an initial principle in "sound
doctrine." The supreme function of man is to create civilization
and its institutions; the term we should cherish is "interdependence," not "independence." [87] Some of Wasson's liberal listeners
must have wondered if he did not secretly aspire to restoration of
the whole Massachusetts Bay theocracy. But Wasson stops considerably short of any such ambition. As he would make clear in
1875 in "State and Church in America," he believed that our
whole development since the seventeenth century argued the
case for religious freedom and that, given our circumstances, any
other system would be fatal to our collective life.[88]

It is, furthermore, part of his conviction in "Social Ideals"
(and here we have the Transcendentalist reasserting himself)
that "spontaneity is precious. Spiritual, like physical, productivity is inseparable from it; room must be made for this, ample
room." [89] His central point is actually this: "No exclusive jurisdiction, then, of the social body, and none of the individual.
Either of them practically asserted as exclusive would make
human nature barren and prohibit civilization. What then? The
jurisdiction must be composite, partly social, partly individual.
With respect to our broadest and strictly necessary relations of
interdependence, it should be conceded to the corporate community; while with respect to all others, where the interdependence is less strict, and to which invariable rules could not well
apply, it should be assigned to the individual." [90]

Wasson makes this sound a good deal easier than it can in fact
be, and this he realized as he continued his speculation. He perceived that "just in proportion as social powers are yielded to

mindlessness and barbarism, this liberality becomes unsafe; there must be more governing in quantity to make up for the defect of quality; the functions of government are at once over-done and insufficient; and a fluctuating, confused, desultory mass-despotism sprawls over the whole field of human action, covering all, and usefully occupying no part of it." [91]

Had Brownson been present, he would have found himself largely and even enthusiastically in agreement with Wasson. The following year, in 1873, Brownson published in his *Quarterly Review* his essay "The Democratic Principle," in which he came to conclusions very similar to those Wasson had reached in "Social Ideals": "It is the spirit and opinions of the American people, or of the majority of them, that I want changed, and so changed as to interpret the constitution of American political society by the principles of law and justice, not by the democratic principle, which asserts the sovereignty of the arbitrary will of the people, or, practically, the unrestricted rule of the majority for the time: which is tyranny and repugnant to the very essence of liberty, which is will ruled by right, or power controlled by justice. . . . Now, as the modern statesmen exclude the moral order, and make no account of the divine element in society, and rely on the human element alone, they are unable to clothe power with right, or give it any stability." [92]

With financial assistance from unnamed friends, Wasson in 1873 gave up his job as storekeeper at the Custom House and went off for a three-year stay in Stuttgart where his son, George Savary Wasson, could prepare for a career as a marine painter and where Wasson, himself, was able to settle down in quiet to organize "Social Ideals" and other pieces into a work tentatively named *The Modern Epoch in Politics*.[93] O.B. Frothingham informs us in his "Memoir" that Wasson worked simultaneously on two books on social and political matters and that neither was completed because the author was dissatisfied with his work, "though chapters were published as essays, from time to time." [94]

I see no reason to disagree with Frothingham; he doubtless wrote from intimate knowledge, but what he apparently over-looked completely is the fact that by 1879 Wasson had in hand, if not a completed work, at least a substantial first version of a book on man in society. In a letter to Abbot, published in the *Index* in 1879, he defended at length his chapter on "Rights" and went on to report that he contemplated "the concrete fact, Man in Society" in all stages of its development, following the archeologists and historians, studying it particularly in America, without neglecting it elsewhere.

"It is slow work," he observed, "and I am a slow worker, and expect only a partial success at the best; but something may at least be done toward correcting that shallow or vicious opinion which mischievously meddles with the course of vital development and tends to pervert it." [95] Wasson did not, however, inform Abbot of the opportunity he had been afforded to correct shallow opinion at Concord, Massachusetts, where some of it had originated. Wasson had been appointed one of the "regular professors," together with Alcott, Higginson, William T. Harris, F.B. Sanborn, and others, to lecture at the first session of the Concord School of Philosophy, and in six months he would deliver ten lectures on "Political Philosophy." [96]

It is a strange oversight on Frothingham's part to make no mention whatsoever of these lectures in his "Memoir." Quite clearly the two most notable items he collected in *Essays: Religious, Social, Political* are "Social Texture" and "Conditions of Social Productiveness," and these were originally the lectures "Social Genesis and Texture" and "The Nation." This we see clearly in reading the summary of Wasson's lectures in the *Modern Argo* of Quincy, Illinois. There the anonymous reporter not only recapitulates Wasson's arguments in these essays, but dwells at length on the zoöphyte, discovered by Darwin, which Wasson employs as the initial and controlling image in the essay "Social Texture." [97]

Wasson's old friend Bronson Alcott, Dean of the Concord School of Philosophy, was properly appreciative. In his *Journal* he noted that in one of his lectures Wasson "treats of the prime elements in the individual and society as constituting a community. Individuals alone do not form society. It is the reciprocity between these, and becomes personal only as this takes place. The distinction between Individualism and Personality is discussed by several persons. This distinction is radical and runs through all true thinking. It discriminates the philosopher from the man of the senses, the Personal from the phenomenal." [98]

Alcott himself had been thinking recently in the same direction, as we see if we turn to the final section of *Table-Talk,* published in 1877, two years earlier. "Personality," Alcott wrote, "and Individuality differ as do man and brute. As animal and no more, man is individual; as Personal he is spiritual. His individuality distinguishes him from other individuals of his kind, his Personality unites and identifies him with all Persons." [99] In 1882, possibly fortified by Wasson's lectures, Alcott would emphasize this distinction even more strongly in a lecture, "Individualism," delivered before the Concord School of Philosophy: "Individuality is egotism. The individual sees only himself, like Narcissus looking in the pool. We cannot cut ourselves off from all human interests and live alone. . . . Our individuality must not be confounded with our differentiation—that which distinguishes us from other persons. . . . Individualism brings men into opposition with the divine will, and only as it is broken down is there harmony." [100]

In the 1870's Wasson and Alcott were not alone in recognizing the dangerous aspects of individualism. Further thought and the enormous social involvement necessitated by the Civil War had brought many American thinkers to the realization that the individual can fulfill himself only in a meaningful relation to society. Sometimes, admittedly, as in Emerson's *Society and Solitude,* this recognition seems a concession rather than a full-fledged conviction, but we find true social awareness, certainly, in Whitman's *Democratic Vistas* and in that ultimate clarification of long-held beliefs, the elder Henry James's *Society: The Redeemed Form of Man.* Only Brownson among Wasson's American contemporaries states, however, perennial truths with equal sight and insight, and for an obvious reason: only Brownson has an equivalent sense of history. Brownson and Wasson in many

instances obviously went to school to the same thinkers, but
there is an important exception. Brownson regarded Hegel as an
intellectual eccentric, whereas Wasson, it is clear from internal
evidence, found his most influential teacher in Hegel, whom he
probably first encountered in J. Sibree's translation of *Lectures
on the Philosophy of History,* published in 1857.

Wasson's response to this book offers a striking contrast to
Alcott's. In his *Journal* in 1861 Alcott writes: "I look into Hegel's
Philosophy of History, Sibree's translation, published by Bohn,
1857. I find the book much too dry and crabbed for my taste, as
I have found nearly all books claiming the merits of system; but
it contains valuable information and repays perusal. Hegel has
the advantage of writing later than his masters, and of drawing
largely from them all, borrowing oftentimes from the best, and
I think without due acknowledgement. I do not find anything
better than Plato or Behman have for me, and read best at first
hand what I wish to find, being sure of falling upon it in the
pages of these masters." [101]

Apparently Wasson had as little interest in Hegel's system as
Alcott, but he found much more than borrowings from Plato and
Boehme in the *Philosophy of History.* It was there that he learned
that a vital society was infinitely preferable to an actual or imaginary state of nature; there that he discovered that society, the
objective existence, was the reciprocal opposite of the subjective
existence, the personality of a people willing and conceiving it.
Hegel's influence on Wasson's interpretation of history can be
repeatedly detected, and nowhere more obviously, perhaps, than
in "Modern Speculative Radicalism," where he asserts that at
the spiritual heights of Greece and Rome men accepted their
religious and political beliefs without reflection or criticism, and
that the subsequent decline of these societies came about self-
consciously through the separation of principle from the symbol
in which it was originally embodied.

To Frothingham, these views of man and society made Wasson
an intellectual alien in post-Civil-War America: "Solitary, unknown, without fame, holding many unpopular opinions, in

sympathy neither with orthodox nor liberal, seeing his pet ideas
rejected by the generation he loved, out of bearing with the
democratic spirit of the age, he waited and watched, having unwavering belief in the ideas themselves." [102] Such an interpretation not only ignores Wasson's similarities to Alcott, the elder
Henry James, Brownson, and Whitman; it completely neglects
the phenomenon of the St. Louis Hegelians. What Frothingham
failed to perceive was that the world of thought and opinion was
catching up with Wasson rather than leaving him behind. Of
this we have amusing evidence in Denton J. Snider's lecture on
Shakespeare before the Concord School of Philosophy in 1880;
the whole incident is in a sense a comic reenactment of Wasson's
battle in the 1860's with Transcendental individualism.

Snider's offense was to observe that Concord's famous men in
flight from the social order had "lived through a great comedy
of the Shakespearean model." The remark had brought F.B.
Sanborn to his feet in defense of Thoreau; William T. Harris
had entered the fray to defend Snider, and peace had been restored only by Alcott, the chairman, who admitted his own flights
from society and declared himself still young enough to play
"the Shakespearean Comedy of flight and return." Wasson, who
was giving two lectures on "Philosophy of History" in the same
series, could justifiably have felt that his younger contemporaries
were beginning to rally to the banner he had raised twenty years
earlier.[103]

Snider, it seems clear from his autobiographical writings,
would have found highly congenial Wasson's dictum: "Individual character without the spiritual bond of unity, degenerates,
becomes a mere blurt of egotism and lawlessness; social cohesion
without reverence for individual character degenerates, becomes
scaly and reptile, a boa constrictor conservatism." [104] Unlike
their European counterparts, American Hegelians did not sub-
merge the individual in society and history; Snider and Harris
insisted on recognition of the individual, as well as society, much
as did Wasson. But this recognition in Wasson is under greater
pressure and explodes into more striking insights. There is an

urgency, an intellectual excitement, in his performance as "the corrective and antidote" to his predecessors and contemporaries which one seeks in vain in the St. Louis Hegelians.[105]

III

I have left to the last a detailed discussion of the central principle in Wasson's thought: his insistence on open relations with opposites. In this doctrine Wasson calls to mind Emerson as described by Stephen E. Whicher: "his thought was controlled by a shifting, complex dialectic of opposites" and "survives precisely because he refused to violate its living multiplicity with an imposed unity." [106] This is not entirely wrong but it is, I fear, too generous. Characteristically, Emerson is not engaged in what we can truly term dialectic: he is merely shifting in intellectual and emotional discomfort from one extreme to another, taking one step forward and two steps backward in a process which leaves us puzzled as to where he really stands at any particular time on many intellectual and spiritual fronts.

Wasson's insistence on open relations with opposites is another matter. He did not fall into it as a matter of behavior and then seek a theory to justify himself; he came to the theory first and then made it a norm for intellectual performance. His idea doubtless had a variety of sources—Plato and Hegel certainly, and Goethe also, as Wasson makes evident in an essay on *Wilhelm Meister's Apprenticeship*. But it is less a conception derived from the thinking of others than it is Wasson's own thought freshly discovered in indignation over the superficiality of other nineteenth-century thinkers.

Wasson's debt to the historian Henry Thomas Buckle was obviously deep, but not in a fashion Buckle would have appreciated. As Wasson viewed the matter in "Mr. Buckle as a Thinker" in 1863, Buckle, despite his brilliance as a writer and admirable qualities as a man, was a singular failure, "an adventurer in the kingdoms of thought," because his materialistic, mechanical, pseudo-scientific interpretation reduced man to a statistic.[107] Wasson found Buckle's insistence on circumstances of time and

place as determiners of individual action analogous to the conclusion that because there was a relation between the straightness
or want of straightness in railroad tracks and the speed of the
train, therefore, "the speed of the train 'instead of having any
connection' with the locomotive and the force of steam, is 'completely controlled' by the line of the road!" [108]

Buckle was representative. Typically the nineteenth-century
radical was "the partisan of a particular term as against its fraternal opposite," the champion of a specious and audacious
generalization in which he could fit out his readers or listeners
with a full philosophical suit in five minutes.[109] This was the
limitation of the later Carlyle, as Wasson would make clear in his
brilliantly indignant, arrogant open letter of 1864. To Wasson
no man could be an able thinker if he lacked the power "to comprehend that law of reciprocal opposites, on which the world is
built. . . . Infinite and Finite, Same and Diverse, Eternal and
Temporary, Universal and Special,—here they are, purest opposites, yet mutual, reciprocal, necessary to each other; and he is a
narrow man who cannot stand in open relations with both terms,
reconciling in the depths of his life, though he can never explain,
the mystery of their friendship. . . . From these opposites we
never escape; Destiny and Freedom, Rest and Motion, Individual
and Society, Origination and Memory, Intuition and Observation, Soul and Body,—you meet them everywhere; and everywhere they are, without losing their character of opposites, nay,
in very virtue of their opposition, playing into and supporting
each other." [110]

Among the mutual, reciprocal opposites Wasson lists, the key
ones in his own development of Transcendentalism are "the
Individual and Society, Origination and Memory, Intuition and
Observation," and it is to the last cluster that we must now address ourselves to reach the heart of his insight. It was only, Wasson wrote in "Modern Speculative Radicalism," as a sense of the
past, as memory and observation, played into and supported
origination and intuition, that radicalism could be mature. Its
aspiration must be "to discover the unity of man's visible experience with his living intelligence, the unity of Spirit embodied

with Spirit thinking and feeling." [111] Agassiz and Thoreau had demonstrated that regard for the embodied facts of nature might suggest the Ineffable, the Unnameable; the world must learn to bestow a similar reverence on the higher embodied facts of man's spiritual history, for "We recover our own consciousness by the study of a more primitive experience." [112]

In a sense, Wasson walked a well-worn path in New England intellectual history. As early as 1839 Convers Francis had proposed to Theodore Parker a "World Bible" to include "Confucius, Zoroaster, Pythagoras, Socrates, Plato, Moses, Jesus, Paul, Mohammed, Thomas à Kempis, Luther, Fénélon, Henry More, the German thinkers, etc. . . ." [113] In the 1840's the *Present,* the *Spirit of the Age,* and the *Dial* had all printed selections from the ancient "ethnical," that is, non-Christian, scriptures. Thoreau himself had furnished selections for the *Dial* from "The Laws of Menu," Confucius, and the Buddha. In *A Week on the Concord and Merrimack Rivers,* Thoreau had quoted the Bhagavad-Gita and in *Walden* he had quoted even more extensively from the Oriental scriptures, imagined meeting the servant of a Brahmin priest coming for Walden water, and conceived of himself as the artist of Kouroo, Oriental sage and artist in one person. We need only recall Emerson's famous poem "Brahma" to recognize that he, too, apparently demonstrated a reverence for the higher embodied facts of man's spiritual history.

If we examine carefully, however, these acknowledgments of of the past, we discover that they are highly selective to say the least. A case in point is Thoreau's collection of sayings from "The Laws of Menu" in the *Dial.* According to Wasson's friend Samuel Johnson in his authoritative work on *India* (1872), "The Laws of Manu" is a "discipline of entire self-renunciation," with no "slightest loop-hole" left "for the self-assertion of private reason or will." Furthermore it provides "the penalty of dreadful transmigrations for ages" for the minutest infraction of its precepts, and the Yogi, the product of its teachings, is "a creature of penances, purifications, and ascetic feats. . . ." [114] We need sharp eyes, indeed, to discover in Thoreau's selections this fierce asceticism; what we find, rather, is a collection of sentences

adumbrating the kind of forest sage Thoreau himself would become in two years with his move to Walden Pond.[115] In the light
of the reality of "The Laws of Manu," it is simply perverse for
Thoreau in *A Week* to promote "Manu" and downgrade the
New Testament because it "is too constantly moral and personal,
to alone content me, who am not interested solely in man's religious or moral nature, or in man even." [116]

Thoreau's practice is typical of Wasson's Transcendental predecessors and contemporaries. From Emerson to Moncure Conway in the *Sacred Anthology* (1874), the Transcendentalist
characteristically quarried rather than confronted the past. In
the past as a reality he had little interest; primarily he anthologized it for its modern, its universal elements as confirmation of
present insights. Wasson's approach was fundamentally different.
He sought the past not only as a witness but as an experience
which might instruct him and deepen his understanding, as a
reciprocal opposite to the immediate, spontaneous response of
intuition.

As I have indicated, his appraisal of classical Greece and Rome,
the medieval Catholic world, and the French Revolution all involved some contradiction of Transcendental liberalism, and in
"Modern Speculative Radicalism" he added the contradiction of
Calvinism. "As matter of opinion," he wrote, he "could accuse"
Calvinism but, on the other hand, it "is much more than a mere
opinion, to be tried in an opinion scale, found wanting, and flung
aside as a cheat. It is a vast out-birth from the heart of Nature,
with profound, infinite thoughts in it, wherein, however crudely
stated, are the thoughts of eternal Spirit itself. . . . Without
Calvinism what were America, Great Britain, Western Europe
indeed, now? Causes are worthy of their effects, in history as elsewhere." [117]

In some of his essays and lectures—I have in mind particularly
his addresses in 1867 and 1874 at meetings of the Free Religious
Association—Wasson supports the standard Transcendental pro-
nouncement that spontaneous insight and impulse can in themselves give us all the light we need. Wasson's more important
accomplishment is his advocacy of intuitive awareness of past

and present as parts of a reciprocal whole. In so doing he recognizes that it is no easy matter to reconcile origination and memory, intuition and observation; that it must be in the depths of life, if at all, that we reconcile, though we cannot explain, the mystery of friendship between opposites.

In holding himself back from the premature Transcendental plunge and immersion into a usually overspiritualized, rhapsodical unity, Wasson calls to mind Keats's doctrine of "negative capability." In a letter to his brothers, Keats wrote: "I mean *Negative Capability,* that is, when a man is capable of being in uncertainties, mysteries, doubts, without any irritable reaching after fact and reason—Coleridge, for instance, would let go by a fine isolated verisimilitude caught from the Penetralium of mystery, from being incapable of remaining content with half-knowledge." [118] At his best Wasson clearly was free from any "irritable reaching after fact and reason." He began his essay "Doubt" in 1868 with the admission: "I remark it in myself that doubt, or somewhat closely akin to it, though apparently a poison to so many, is to me, a salt upon my food, and necessary to my health. Fixed and rigid opinion, upon matters of infinite scope, gives me an indigestion. . . . My most endeared persuasion nourishes and comforts me, only while accompanied by a certain inward reserve, a reticence as of the soul itself, which keeps it always flowing and undefined, an air to breathe, rather than a block to handle." [119]

Nor was this all. Unlike Emerson and Thoreau and other Transcendentalists of the first cycle, Wasson understood that doubt, some inward reserve, was an important ingredient in the aesthetic perception of reality. "Ever," he wrote, "it is by some gentle union of opposites, or at least of diversities, that all finest effect is reached." [120] Thus the sky was blue by the presence of foreign elements in the air; the diamond and ruby gleamed because they were imperfectly transparent; and he supposed it might be their appreciation of shadow which gave the greatest poets, "one and all," their taste for tragedy: "They love to cast the beams of their genius on that which chiefly clouds the wish of man's heart; so, like the sun at morning and evening, to make out of cloud itself a new glory." [121]

In this Wasson anticipated his essay "Epic Philosophy," published in the *North American Review* in 1868; there he would deal with one of those greatest poets, Homer in the *Iliad*. But "Epic Philosophy" is much more than literary criticism; it is the culmination of Wasson's effort "to comprehend that law of opposites, on which the world is built" and to reconcile in the depths of his life origination and memory, intuition and observation. It is more: it is the major demonstration of what he meant when he insisted that mature radicalism must discover "the unity of Spirit embodied with Spirit thinking and feeling."

To Wasson the *Iliad* is a true symbol of the human condition because Homer represented "the soul pulled overboard by the fish it was drawing in,—the soul caught in the mesh of its own mechanism, ground in its own mill," that is destroying itself in the name and cause of good, freeing the Special Self which is "demon all and only," liberating devils in building up its own "architecture." [122] And this situation, in which the crime of a coxcomb had driven two nations to mutual destruction because of their loftiest sentiment, national honor, was one which Wasson found paralleled in all the institutions of civilized society. In its aspiration for the better culture and discipline of mankind, the human soul establishes private property and then is lured into cupidity and consumed with a rage of appetite which sometimes destroys entire civilizations. To incarnate the spirit of community the soul builds the state and finds itself involved in horrible struggles for dominion. To "house a thought higher still" the soul builds churches "and again it makes fire; and this time may make the very fire of hell, bigotry, conscientious hatred, holy cruelty, lying for God, tyranny that not only oppresses, but makes in its victims a hunger to be oppressed." [123]

Wasson states that the opposition of good and evil is never to be explained away, that we face "forced" conclusions both in the Emersonian assumption that evil is illusory, mere good in the making, and in the Calvinistic reference to a supernatural Satan.

He now reasserts more vigorously than ever his doctrine of opposites. The world is perpetual contradiction, "antithesis expressed in ten thousand shapes, and pushed with such inexorable energy and excess that we wonder how the bands of eternity do not burst, and suffer the world to welter in immitigable craze. Oppositions and emulations arise, multiply, rage, gain appetite by what they feed on . . . existence sprouts all over in horns, fangs, tusks, claws, while from its horrid alembic venoms, hates, envies distill, and drip, drip upon its own blistering heart . . . strife is around man, and strife is within him; the lightning thrusts its blazing scymitar through his roof, the thief creeps in at his door, and remorse at his heart." [124]

We must, Wasson states, shun the "huddled thinking" that attempts to reconcile these realities to the soul. Poetic truth calls not for denial of duality, of contradiction, but as in the *Iliad* for "the expression of comprehending spiritual unity by means of that which opposes and apparently denies it." [125] In the height of his own consciousness, as in Homer's and Shakespeare's tragic vision, man possesses "a unity of comprehension and embrace, which, though it contains contradiction, yet does indeed *contain* it, and therefore remains itself unbroken." [126] By his true substantive being, man both walks in nature and soars above it; in his breast is "the exceeding great mystery,—the infinite separation of Nature from Spirit, the perfect poetic comprehension of Nature by Spirit." [127]

Wasson here anticipates A.C. Bradley's *Shakespearean Tragedy* by almost forty years, and he is well beyond 1868 in yet other significant ways. While making no mention of Hawthorne and Melville, he would seem to have arrived at a mid-twentieth-century perspective from which to view the clash of opposites in *The Scarlet Letter, Moby-Dick,* and *Billy Budd.* "Epic Philosophy" is, of course, in broad terms Hegelian, but Wasson is more his own man than we might at first suppose. To Hegel the *Iliad* was a primitive, a naïve production; [128] Wasson is more modern in his appreciation. I find, in fact, the closest approximation to Wasson's interpretation of the *Iliad* in the most anti-Hegelian of his younger contemporaries, William James.

In "The Religion of Healthy-Mindedness" (1901), James made this crucial distinction between the earlier Greeks (particularly Homer) and Walt Whitman: "Instinctive good they did not reckon sin; nor had they any such desire to save the credit of the universe as to make them insist, as so many of *us* insist, that what immediately appears as evil must be 'good in the making,' or something equally ingenious. Good was good, and bad just bad, for the earlier Greeks. They neither denied the ills of nature,— Walt Whitman's verse, 'What is called good is perfect and what is called bad is just as perfect,' would have been mere silliness to them,—nor did they, in order to escape from those ills, invent 'another and a better world' of the imagination, in which, along with the ills, the innocent goods of sense would also find no place. This integrity of the instinctive reactions, this freedom from all moral sophistry and strain, gives a pathetic dignity to ancient pagan feeling. And this quality Whitman's outpourings have not got." [129]

James here exemplifies the radical empiricist, "the tough-minded" thinker, whose qualities he would describe six years later in the opening lecture in *Pragmatism,* and when we notice the similarities between Wasson and James's "tough-minded" intellectual we begin to see that in a number of interesting ways Wasson anticipates James. There are, for example, close parallels between Wasson's insistence on open relations with opposites in his essay on Buckle in 1863 and James's assertion in 1876 that "philosophic study means the habit of always seeing an alternative, of not taking the usual for granted, of making conventionalities fluid again, of imagining foreign states of mind." [130] James and Wasson are particularly interesting in their common use of the word "open" and its cognates. Alice James thought her brother perfectly expressed himself and his environment when he described his house at Chocorua, "Oh, it's the most delightful house you ever saw; it has fourteen doors, all opening outwards." [131] Even more to the point, perhaps, is James's dedication of *Pragmatism* "To the Memory of John Stuart Mill, from Whom I First Learned the Pragmatic Openness of Mind. . . ." [132]

In view of this similarity in temperament and approach in

Wasson and James, it is not very surprising, therefore, to learn from F.P. Stearns that when "Professor James of Harvard" was asked a few days after Wasson's death in 1887 what he thought of him, he replied, "I look upon him as one of the great instructors of mankind." [133] We naturally wonder, of course, in view of such a remark, whether James was not in Wasson's debt, but neither Ralph Barton Perry in *The Thought and Character of William James* nor F.O. Matthiessen in *The James Family* makes even so much as a single reference to Wasson, and it would seem that we deal only in possibility if we suppose influence.

Furthermore, there is a whole series of lessons which James might have learned from Wasson which obviously he did not.[134] James protested against our imperialism in the Spanish American War, but as Matthiessen points out, "For a long time WJ hardly thought in terms of a social context at all." [135] Nor is there in James a sign that he was aware of the limitations in Emerson and Thoreau to which a full immersion in Wasson would certainly have directed him. In fact, as James himself made clear, he was inspired to make his own report on the universe by rereading all of Emerson in preparation for his address at Concord on the centenary of Emerson's birth.

But James, nevertheless, saw to the heart of the matter. Mildred Wasson, the Maine novelist and widow of Wasson's grandson, recalls that in a letter now lost or sold James once wrote, "The trouble with you, Wasson, is that you are thinking about fifty years ahead of your time." [136] Precisely so. Although he was almost twenty years older than James, Wasson as a post-Emersonian actually belongs to a later generation. His opposition to nineteenth-century liberalism and his responsiveness to tradition make him a contemporary of Paul Elmer More; and when we recall Wasson's strictures on Rousseau and Voltaire, he seems to anticipate even more clearly another New Humanist. I am thinking, of course, of Babbitt in *Rousseau and Romanticism*. But just as Wasson belongs in quality of mind and concern somewhat further on in the intellectual procession than William James, so in important respects is he actually more modern than Irving Babbitt. In fact, in his essay on Theodore Parker in 1864, Wasson anticipated the limitations of a mind like Babbitt's when he wrote that Parker lacked the capital quality of intellect, "imaginative intelligence," that his universe was a straight line, that he never read a great poem as a poem, and that charactcristically he went to history with a "moral yardstick" rather than imagination.

Indeed, once we discount his style and some of his sentiments, Wasson confronts us with the startling and paradoxical spectacle of a nineteenth-century American thinker who seems to have absorbed Babbitt's antiromanticism, learned important lessons from Allen Tate's *Reactionary Essays on Poetry and Ideas* (1936) and T.S. Eliot's *Notes toward the Definition of Culture* (1949), and then to have moved on to the latest phase of the New Criticism brilliantly developed by Joseph Frank in *The Widening Gyre* (1963). I do not mean to suggest that Wasson anticipates Mr. Frank's major insight into the crucial dilemma in modern culture, "the dilemma of a culture whose creations more and more tend to deny or negate some essential aspect of the human agency at their source and to escape from its control." [137] Rather, I have in mind Mr. Frank's subtle awareness of the central place of religion in civilization and his pervasive concern with dialectic, which he illuminates as a crucial quality in André Malraux, Robert Penn Warren, Thomas Mann, and other notable figures in twentieth-century literature. Clearly, Mr. Frank, like Wasson, has been a long and careful student of Hegel, to whom he repeatedly refers, and the lessons he has learned lead to some extraordinarily interesting statements. We read, for example, in the chapter, "R.P. Blackmur: The Later Phase," the following: "the dialectic between unity and chaos, or order and disorder, or orthodoxy and heresy, controls the framework of Mr. Blackmur's reflections. . . . The symbolic imagination [Blackmur's concept] . . . embodies and actualizes the same sense of life as a dialectical opposition whose extremes do not exclude but interact with and complement each other." [138] This, I submit, sounds very much like Wasson's doctrine of reciprocal opposites in his essay on Buckle published precisely a century earlier.

Obviously, F.P. Stearns made a perceptive observation when he suggested in 1895 that Americans of the next century might find Wasson's work "more congenial to their modes of thought than do those of the present era." [139] But Wasson is much more than a mere anticipator of certain twentieth-century ideas and attitudes; he is a critic of precisely those nineteenth-century convictions, rooted in exaggerated individualism and now ripening into decay, which constitute "modernity" in its most self-destructive aspects. His relevance has increased rather than diminished with the years. His copiousness, or perhaps we should say bluntly his prolixity, will undoubtedly count fatally against him with some readers, but if his pages are overcrowded, they are overcrowded not simply with words but with sight and insight and profound good sense. Now that his most pertinent uncollected writings are at last gathered into a book, he will, I believe, increasingly make his presence felt as a counterforce to Emerson and Thoreau and to much that has passed for thought in our own day. I dare to predict that with time Wasson's work will prove one more illustration of the truth of T.S. Eliot's insight: "The existing monuments form an ideal order among themselves, which is modified by introduction of the new (the really new) work of art among them. The existing order is complete before the new work arrives; for order to persist after the supervention of novelty, the *whole* existing order must be, if ever so slightly, altered; and so the relations, proportions, values of each work of art toward the whole are readjusted; and this is conformity between the old and the new." [140]

NOTES

1. For Alcott's judgments of Wasson see Odell Shepard, ed., *The Journals of Bronson Alcott* (Boston, 1938), particularly pp. 349, 420, 503. William James described Wasson as "one of the great instructors of mankind," according to F.P. Stearns in *Sketches from Concord and Appledore* (New York and London, 1895), p. 173. Writing to Charles Sumner in 1864 to promote Wasson's candidacy as a United States consul, Emerson recommended him in these high terms: "He is known to me as a man of superior understanding, and of a broad comprehensive genius, an excellent writer, and, as a preacher, the first choice of the 'Fraternity' people after Parker. Of serious papers, he is perhaps the best contributor to the 'Atlantic

Monthly.' He is a social man of agreeable manners. . . . He is one of those who ought to be gratified, as it is the saving & maturing of a great man." Ralph L. Rusk, ed., *The Letters of Ralph Waldo Emerson* (New York, 1939), V, 391.

2. Ednah D. Cheney, ed., Preface to *Poems by David Atwood Wasson* (Boston, 1888), pp. 1–2.

3. Emerson anthologized Wasson's "Love against Love" and "Royalty" in *Parnassus* (Boston, 1875), pp. 83, 198.

4. *Journals of Bronson Alcott*, p. 420.

5. In his *Transcendentalism in New England: A History* (New York, 1876), p. 350, Frothingham wrote, "A volume of Mr. Wasson's prose essays and poems would be a valuable contribution to the literature of Transcendentalism; for he is, on the whole, the most capable critic on its side." Here, obviously, Frothingham anticipates the collection of essays and lectures he published in 1889, but the startling omissions and odd inclusions in *Essays: Religious, Social, Political* lead me to suppose that Frothingham made no systematic review of Wasson's published writings when he worked on his anthology.

6. These pieces were published in 1863, 1867, and 1868.

7. F.P. Stearns's essay "David Wasson" in *Sketches*, pp. 134–179, is the most insightful comment on Wasson which I have discovered. There is no article on Wasson in the *Dictionary of American Biography*; Van Wyck Brooks, who describes a host of little-known figures in *New England: Indian Summer* (1940) and devotes a chapter to the Boston Radical Club, mentions Wasson's name only in a footnote quotation from Emerson; Perry Miller merely lists Wasson's *Essays: Religious, Social, Political* in the bibliography accompanying *The Transcendentalists: An Anthology* (1950). The brief essay by Robert Spence, "D.A. Wasson, Forgotten Transcendentalist," *American Literature*, 27 (March, 1955), 31–41, runs almost completely counter to my own interpretation and seems to me misleading. The only twentieth-century scholar in American literature who seems aware of Wasson's quality is Frank Luther Mott in *A History of American Magazines* (1930–1938). Mott describes Wasson, III, 230, as "that acute and brilliant essayist" and, II, 18, calls attention to the verdict of John Burroughs in 1862: "With the exception of Emerson (whom he excells in finish if not in calm dignity) I know of no writer, so original, so profound."

8. For details of Brownson's intellectual history I have relied on Alvan S. Ryan's authoritative introduction to *The Brownson Reader* (New York, 1955).

9. Stearns, *Sketches*, p. 138.

10. Ibid., p. 138.

11. Frothingham, ed., *Essays*, "Memoir," p. 41.

12. Wasson, "A Letter to Thomas Carlyle," *Atlantic Monthly*, XII (Oct. 1864), 497.

13. Frothingham, ed., *Essays,* "Memoir," p. 13.

14. Emerson, *Journals* (Boston and New York, 1909——), IX, 407–408.

15. Charles Lane, "Interior or Hidden Life," *Dial,* IV (Jan. 1844), 373–378.

16. Wasson, "Autobiography," *Frothingham,* ed., *Essays,* p. 35.

17. Ibid., p. 50.

18. Stearns, *Sketches,* p. 162.

19. Ibid., pp. 143–144.

20. Ibid., pp. 144–145. Stearns also informs us that "Years afterward M.D. Conway told Carlyle of walking in the woods at Groveland with Wasson, and how his face became radiant with internal light when he spoke of 'Sartor Resartus' " (p. 144).

21. Ibid., pp. 146–148.

22. *Confession of Faith of David A. Wasson, as Given in to the Council at His Ordination at Groveland, September 4th, 1851,* an unnumbered three-page pamphlet preserved in the files of the American Antiquarian Society at Worcester, Massachusetts.

23. In his "Memoir," *Essays,* p. 55, Frothingham writes that beginning in the autumn of 1855, Wasson substituted at Higginson's Free Church for six months. This leaves a strange gap of a half year in Higginson's pulpit, since he did not return from Fayal until June, 1856. It would seem safer to suppose that Wasson served at the Worcester Free Church during the entire absence, as Mary Thatcher Higginson reports in *Thomas Wentworth Higginson: The Story of His Life* (Boston and New York, 1914), p. 163.

24. *Letters of Lydia Maria Child* (Boston, 1883), with a biographical introduction by John G. Whittier and an appendix by Wendell Phillips, p. 91.

25. For T.W. Higginson's attempt to rescue Anthony Burns, see his own account in *Cheerful Yesterdays* (Boston and New York, 1898), pp. 147–166. In *Heralds of a Liberal Faith* (Boston, 1910), ed. Samuel A. Eliot, III, 375, Abby A. Wasson recalled how Wasson had "chafed under the disabilities which hindered his taking part in the rescue of Anthony Burns. . . ." Higginson's report of the last resolution at the State Disunion Convention at Worcester in 1857 may be found in W.P. Garrison and F.J. Garrison, *William Lloyd Garrison: The Story of His Life Told by His Children* (New York, 1899), III, 457. The quoted phrase is from a letter of Theodore Parker to Higginson reprinted in John Weiss, *Life and Correspondence of Theodore Parker* (New York, 1864), II, 193.

26. Fannie Hardy Eckstorm, "George Savary Wasson, Artist and Writer, 1855–1932," *Essex Institute Historical Collections,* LXXIX (Jan. 1943), 50. In *Sketches,* p. 137, F.P. Stearns writes that Wasson "went to Concord in 1859 intending to make it his permanent abode, but the offer of a philanthropic gentleman who wished to take him into his own house for a year . . .

induced him to emigrate again." This seems not so probable an account as the "year and a half in Concord where he saw a good deal of Emerson and Thoreau," noted by Frothingham, "Memoir," p. 58. Once we locate Wasson as Higginson's colleague in 1856–57 and accept Frothingham's report that in the spring (apparently of 1857) Wasson sailed to Smyrna and back and then settled in Concord, 1857 rather than 1859 seems the more likely date when Wasson established residence. The end of that residence is clearly marked as 1860, when Wasson became the guest of George Luther Stearns, as F.P. Stearns reported in the life of his father, *The Life and Public Service of George Luther Stearns*, p. 220.

After a diligent search in my behalf, Mrs. Marcia E. Moss, reference librarian at the Concord Free Public Library, was unable to find any document making certain the years of Wasson's Concord residency.

27. Wasson, "The New World and the New Man," *Atlantic Monthly*, II (Sept. 1858), 522, 528.

28. Robert Frost, "Build Soil—A Political Pastoral," *Complete Poems of Robert Frost* (New York, 1949), p. 429.

29. Wasson, "Individuality," *Atlantic Monthly*, IX (Apr. 1862), 428.

30. Wasson, "Wilhelm Meister's Apprenticeship," *Atlantic Monthly*, XVI (Oct. 1865), 449. Wasson does not specify the person to whom Thoreau made the remark about marriage. F.P. Stearns writes of Thoreau, however, that "Once while walking across a field with David A. Wasson he kicked a skunk-cabbage and said, "There, marriage is like that." F.P. Stearns, "Concord Thirty Years Ago," in *Sketches*, p. 26.

31. Wasson, "Modern Speculative Radicalism," *Radical*, II (July, 1867), 645.

32. Wasson, "Ice and Esquimaux," *Atlantic Monthly*, XIV (Dec. 1864), 728.

33. "Ktaadn," *The Maine Woods* in *The Writings of Henry David Thoreau* (Boston and New York, 1906), III, 71.

34. Thoreau, letter to Harrison Blake, ibid., III, 71.

35. *Journals of Bronson Alcott*, p. 306.

36. Stearns, *Life of George Luther Stearns*, p. 220.

37. For information on G.L. Stearns and John Brown, I have drawn on various passages in Oswald Garrison Villard, *John Brown: A Biography Fifty Years After* (Boston and New York, 1911). Villard also discusses at length the activities of the men I have called John Brown's Secret Six, that is, (in addition to G.L. Stearns) F.B. Sanborn, Theodore Parker, T.W. Higginson, Gerrit Smith, and Samuel G. Howe. Wasson was acquainted with the first four of these men and may, though I find no evidence, have also known Gerrit Smith and Dr. Howe.

38. *Poems by David Atwood Wasson*, p. 79.

39. Stearns, *Life of George Luther Stearns*, p. 222.

40. Ibid., p. 222.

41. Wasson, "Rest and Motion," *Atlantic Monthly,* VII (May 1861), 534–535.

42. Ibid., 531.

43. Ibid., 532–533.

44. Wasson, "Originality," *Atlantic Monthly,* X (July 1862), 67.

45. Ibid., 65.

46. Wasson, "Ease in Work," *Atlantic Monthly,* IX (Feb. 1862), 242–243.

47. Wasson, "Hindrance," *Atlantic Monthly,* IX (May, 1862), 607.

48. *Complete Works of Ralph Waldo Emerson* (Boston and New York, 1918), II, 122.

49. Wasson, "The Law of Costs," *Atlantic Monthly,* XI (Feb. 1863), 243.

50. Wasson, "Dr. Isaac Barrow," *New Englander,* IX (Nov. 1851), 508 and 506.

51. It is also clear that Parker tried to mold Wasson into a masculine prophet of his own kind. In a letter, June 30, 1856, he advised Wasson to go as minister to Columbus, Ohio, rather than to Medford, Massachusetts, where G. L. Stearns hoped he might settle: "At Columbus I suppose you will find things much in the rough; earnest, hearty, vigorous men and women, progressive also, but a little coarse, irregular, not cultivated. . . . You will work hard, fare hard, and grow to great stature. You will not have the nice culture so easily acquired at Medford, so graceful, so beautiful, so desirable. But strength of manhood, nobleness of life, you will have, it seems to me. I know you better than you think I do, and let me say there is no minister in New England from whom I expect so much." Weiss, *Life of Theodore Parker,* I, 335.

52. Wasson, "Character and Historical Position of Theodore Parker," *Christian Examiner,* LXXVII (Jan. 1864), 23–24.

53. Frothingham, "Memoir," *Essays,* p. 60.

54. Letter to "Mr. Fields" (James T. Fields), headed "West Medford, May 5, 1868," and letter to "Higginson" (Thomas Wentworth Higginson), headed "Custom House, Boston, June 23, 1869," in the manuscript collections at the Houghton Library, Harvard University. I quote from the letter to Higginson by permission of the Harvard College Library. In the "Memoir," *Essays,* p. 61, Frothingham describes a visit to Wasson at the Custom House and the intellectual vigor and high spirits in which he found him.

55. Stow Persons, *Free Religion: An American Faith* (New Haven, 1947), p. 15.

56. *Free Religion: Report of Addresses at a Meeting Held in Boston, May 30, 1867, to consider the Conditions, Wants and Prospects of Free Religion in America Together with the Constitution of the Free Religious Association there Organized* (Boston, 1867), pp. 37–40.

57. Ibid., p. 41.

58. Ibid., p. 44.

59. Ibid., pp. 45–46.

60. Ibid., p. 47.

61. Emily Dickinson in a letter to T.W. Higginson, July, 1862, Thomas H. Johnson and Theodora Ward, eds., *The Letters of Emily Dickinson* (Cambridge, 1958), II, 412.

62. George Willis Cooke, *An Historical and Biographical Introduction to the* Dial (Boston, 1902), I, 49–50. For Bartol's early sermons see, for example C.A. Bartol, *Discourses on the Christian Spirit and Life* (Boston, 1850), second edition, with an introduction.

63. See Persons, *Free Religion,* p. 25 and pp. 43–44, for Bartol's relations to the Free Religious Association.

For Bartol's responses pro and con to Transcendentalism and Emerson, see Ch. III, "Transcendentalism," in C.A. Bartol, *Radical Problems* (Boston, 1872) and Bartol's lecture in 1884 on "Emerson's Religion," reprinted in F.B. Sanborn, ed., *The Genius and Character of Emerson: Lectures at the Concord School of Philosophy* (Boston and New York, 1889), pp. 109–145.

64. *Journals of Bronson Alcott,* pp. 387–388.

65. "Woman: A Conversation by Bronson Alcott," reported by B.F. Yerrington for *Radical,* V (Feb. 1869), 95.

66. Ibid., 98.

67. Cyrus A. Bartol, *Amos Bronson Alcott: His Character* (Boston, 1888), p. 9.

68. F.E. Abbot, "Free Religion versus Transcendentalism," *Index,* VIII (Apr. 19, 1877), 186.

69. Orestes Brownson, "Mr. Emerson's Address," *Boston Quarterly Review, I* (Oct. 1838), 512.

70. Mrs. John T. Sargent, ed., *Sketches and Reminiscences of the Radical Club* (Boston, 1880), p. 370.

71. Ibid., pp. 370–371.

72. Ibid., p. 81.

73. Wasson, "Character and Historical Position of Theodore Parker," 26–28.

74. Ibid., 28–31.

75. Wasson, "Modern Speculative Radicalism," II, 653–655.

76. Wasson, "Social Texture," in *Essays: Religious, Social, Political,* p. 253.

77. Ibid., p. 250.

78. Wasson, "Modern Speculative Radicalism," 658.

79. Ibid., 660–661.

80. Wasson, "The New Type of Oppression," in *Essays: Religious, Social, Political,* pp. 326–356.

81. Wasson, "Modern Speculative Radicalism," 659.

82. Ibid., 660.

83. Wasson, "Social Ideals," *Index*, III (Feb. 10, 1872), 41.

84. The quotations from Winthrop's speech are drawn from Perry Miller and Thomas H. Johnson, eds., *The Puritans* (New York, Cincinnati, etc., 1938), pp. 206–207. The quotations from Wasson are drawn from "Social Ideals," 41–42.

85. Wasson, "Social Ideals," 42.

86. Ibid., 42–43.

87. Ibid., 42.

88. Wasson's "State and Church in America" was copied from the New York *Tribune* for May 12, 1872, in *Index*, VI (Dec. 16, 1872), 590–593.

89. Wasson, "Social Ideals," 42.

90. Ibid., 42.

91. Ibid., 42.

92. Orestes A. Brownson, "The Democratic Principle," reprinted in Russell Kirk, ed., *Orestes Brownson: Selected Essays* (New York, Chicago, Los Angeles, 1955), pp. 199–200 and p. 206.

93. "Notes," *Radical*, IX (August, 1871), 80.

94. Frothingham, ed., "Memoirs," *Essays*," p. 1.

95. "A Letter from Mr. Wasson," *Index*, X (Jan. 16, 1879), p. 31.

96. The complete roster of the "regular professors" is furnished in the prospectus, "The Concord Summer School of Philosophy and Literature," in the files of the Concord Free Public Library, Concord, Massachusetts. This prospectus also indicates that Wasson's subject was "Political Philosophy."
The titles of Wasson's lectures in 1879 are given in Raymond L. Bridgman, ed., *Concord Lectures on Philosophy* (Cambridge, 1883), p. 10, and are as follows: "1. Social Genesis and Textures. 2. The Nation. 3. Individualism as a Political Principle. 4. Public Obligation. 5. Sovereignty. 6. Absolutism Crowned and Uncrowned. 7. Representation. 8. Rights. 9. The Making of Freedom. 10. The Political Spirit of '76."

97. "Summer School of Philosophy. A Brief Resume of Mr. Wasson's Lectures," *Modern Argo*, Quincy, Ill., August 30, 1879, in the files of the Concord Free Public Library, Concord, Massachusetts.

98. *Journals of Bronson Alcott,* p. 503, entry for July 30, 1879.

99. Amos Bronson Alcott, *Table-Talk* (Boston, 1877), p. 156.

100. Bridgman, *Concord Lectures,* p. 130.

101. *Journals of Bronson Alcott,* p. 340.

102. Frothingham, ed., "Memoir," *Essays*, p. 64.

103. Denton J. Snider, *The St. Louis Movement in Philosophy, Literature, Education, Psychology with Chapters of Autobiography* (St. Louis, 1920), pp. 271–277. Snider's dates are 1841–1925; he was thus eighteen years Wasson's junior. For Wasson's lectures in 1880, see Bridgman, *Concord Lectures,* p. 11.

104. Wasson, "Conditions of Social Productiveness" in *Essays: Religious, Social, Political,* p. 291.

105. Stearns, *Sketches,* p. 134. I have found Stearns's phrase very illuminating in my study of Wasson, but his list is disappointing. He names Wasson together with James Russell Lowell as a "corrective and antidote" to Bryant, Longfellow, Emerson, Hawthorne, and Whittier.

106. Stephen E. Whicher, Introduction to *Selections from Ralph Waldo Emerson* (Boston, 1957), p. xiv.

107. Wasson, "Mr. Buckle as a Thinker," *Atlantic Monthly,* XI (Jan. 1863), 39.

108. Ibid., 39.

109. Ibid., 40–41.

110. Ibid., 41.

111. Wasson, "Modern Speculative Radicalism," 652.

112. Ibid., 651.

113. Quoted by Clarence L.F. Gohdes in *The Periodicals of American Transcendentalism* (Durham, 1931), p. 190, from the MSS in the library of the Massachusetts Historical Society.

114. Samuel Johnson, *Oriental Religions and Their Relation to Universal Religion: India* (Boston, 1873), pp. 175–177.

115. H.D. Thoreau, ed., "The Laws of Menu," *Dial,* III (Jan. 1843), 331–340.

116. Thoreau, *A Week on the Concord and Merrimack Rivers,* in *The Writings of Henry David Thoreau,* I, 74.

117. Wasson, "Modern Speculative Radicalism," 646.

118. Letter to George and Thomas Keats, December 21, 1817, Maurice Buxton Forman, ed., *The Letters of John Keats* (New York, 1935), p. 72.

119. Wasson, "Doubt," *Radical,* III (Jan. 1868), 293.

120. Ibid., 298.

121. Ibid., 299.

122. Wasson, "Epic Philosophy," *North American Review,* CVII (Oct. 1868), 530–531.

123. Ibid., 530.

124. Ibid., 504.

125. Ibid., 509.

126. Ibid., 535.

127. Ibid., 533.

128. G.W.F. Hegel in *The Phenomenology of the Mind,* trans. by J.B. Baillie, reprinted in Anne and Henry Paolucci, eds., *Hegel on Tragedy* (Garden City, N.Y., 1962), pp. 288–91 and pp. 732–49.

129. William James, "The Religion of Healthy-Mindedness," in F.O. Matthiessen, ed., *The James Family Including Selections from the Writings*

of Henry James, Senior, William, Henry & Alice James (New York, 1948), pp. 496–497.

130. William James, "The Teaching of Philosophy in Our Colleges," *Nation*, Sept. 21, 1876, quoted in *The James Family*, p. 222.

131. Alice James, quoted in *The James Family*, p. 226.

132. Matthiessen calls attention to the dedication to Mill, *The James Family*, p. 211.

133. Stearns, *Sketches*, p. 173.

134. Matthiessen notes, for example, that for William James the "hottest side" of Emerson was "his nonconformist conviction of the unsurpassable value of the individual." *The James Family*, p. 431.

135. Ibid., p. 623.

136. Letter to Charles H. Foster from Mildred Wasson (Mrs. David A. Wasson), Bray House, Kittery Point, Maine, Oct. 8, 1964. Quotation used with Mrs. Wasson's permission.

137. Joseph Frank, *The Widening Gyre: Crisis and Mastery in Modern Literature* (New Brunswick, N.J., 1963), pp. xi–xii.

138. Ibid., pp. 238–239.

139. Stearns, *Sketches*, p. 179.

140. T. S. Eliot, "Tradition and the Individual Talent," *Selected Essays 1917–1932* (New York, 1932), p. 5.

PART *II*

Selected Writings of
David Atwood Wasson

A NOTE ON THE TEXT

Wasson's essays are here reproduced verbatim except for correction of obvious typographical errors. Had Wasson himself collected these pieces he would, of course, have regularized punctuation, capitalization, hyphenation, etc., but I have not thought it appropriate to tamper with his writings as he and his editors once approved them.

DR. ISAAC BARROW

≈≤≈≤≈≤≈≤≈≤≈≤≈≤≈≤≈≤≈≤≈≤≈≤

The Works of Isaac Barrow, D.D.: To which are prefixed, a Life of the Author, by Abraham Hill, and a Memoir, by James Hamilton, with the Notes and References carefully revised, and Indexes prepared expressly for this Edition. In three volumes. New York: John C. Riker, 129 Fulton Street. 1845.

It has been often remarked, in substance, that the great wealth of English thought may be compacted into a comparatively small space; a shelf of no great length will contain it nearly all. It is true, the scholar needs many books; rather, however, as tools and material, by and upon which to shape his thought, than as aliment to the thought itself; but the works which afford leading ideas, and abound in those productive hints that become the sources of thought in others, are not many. And yet it is upon this fruitful and fruit-making few, that the great labor of any one, who aspires to become a thinker, should be expended. Probably one great defect in the courses of reading and study usually pursued by American students is, that we neglect the masters, and apply ourselves to popular, and of course diluted expositions of thought.

One quality, worth almost all others, which is possessed by the greatest writers, and seldom to any considerable degree by those of an inferior order, is that of suggestiveness; the power of scattering intimations of deep truths along the path of their discussions. The object more directly aimed at, may be local and temporary; but the argument constantly alludes to far underlying principles, and the writer, like a great military tactician, brings the whole art of war and the utmost stretch of reason to bear upon a skirmish of hundreds, hardly less than he would upon a battle between hemispheres. Of this, Milton's Areopagitica will always remain an eminent instance. Respectable thinkers bring you good thoughts, well coined, and enough for your present use, if not for your wealth; but the Great Few show you into the mine, into the thought-world itself.

Now it cannot be claimed for Barrow that he belongs emphatically to this high class of elect thinkers. He is not the peer of Bacon, of Milton (considered simply as a prose writer), no, nor, in our estimation, of Hooker either. It would be enough to shut him out from these, that he does not possess the property of suggestiveness in any eminent degree. He gives, it has been often said, an exhaustive treatment to every subject; and this is high praise; but it is the characteristic of great thinkers to make every subject inexhaustible, by overpassing the limits that ordinarily inclose it, and showing us to what an infinite distance its relations and congruities extend.

Barrow seems to us to display the very bloom, vigor, and, as it were, eloquence of common sense. He is a man of capacious, rather than creative mind; he has many thoughts, weighty, sound and good; but has not that subtle, penetrative faculty, which constitutes one pre-eminently a thinker. As a writer, however, or deliberative rhetorician, he exhibits rare excellences; for he is what so few can be, at once amazingly copious and truly forceful throughout; he possesses the singular power of compressing the sense while he spreads out the expression. No man gives you either better words, or more of them; and his words are good because they have a solid meaning in them, and do most effectually bring it out. The thought itself, though always of right genuine and unmistakable worth, has, however, no surpassing richness dwelling in it, like that of some few that might be named in English literature; but the language, as in all truly vigorous and masculine writing, has often a noble picturesqueness, a wholesome flavor, which makes it relish wonderfully to a healthy and manly taste. But, perhaps, we shall easiest come to a nearer and more specific consideration of him, if we begin by enumerating some of the classes who will not readily make him a favorite. We name:

1. Those who are of a strongly dialectic turn of mind. There are minds which have a natural and insuperable fondness for subtle, we do not say useless, distinctions; which like always to see the lines of difference sharply drawn and defined. Such, by eminence, was the native bent of Baxter's genius. Now though this tendency indulged to a great extreme runs out into scholasticism and vain hair-splittings; yet such minds have their proper work to do, and it is often a work most needful to be done. But it is easy to see that such men will be apt to read Barrow with a degree of dissatisfaction, perhaps of displeasure, and sometimes with a disposition to think him an over-estimated writer. For he ever takes things in their broad scope and bearing; his strokes are all large and weighty, looking towards the general effect upon human conduct. Every subject represents itself to his eye in a certain general and common consistence, and is represented by him in like manner; so that, without any clear-cut precision in the arrangement of the parts, he seems always, even under different heads, to be dealing with it somewhat as a whole; but all this, be it understood, without any confusion; his thought is large and unprecise, but not confused. So in the composition of his sentences there are no nice balancings of opposites, no precise exactitude of meanings mathematically set over against each other in sharp antithesis; but the members branch out like the limbs of a tree, abundant, irregular, waving.

2. We name also those of the very opposite tendency; those who love above all things to discover subtle and interior resemblances; these may not readily take to Barrow. We do not speak of men of wit, unless the word be used in a very large and now unusual sense; for though wit is said to consist in the perception of unlooked-for resemblances, yet the resemblance there intended is one opposed to congruity; and it is in this opposition that the wittiness consists. The persons whom we here mean are

those who possess a superior faculty of discerning hidden affinities, and who, by consequence, are always delighted when they have discovered an interior oneness where is the greatest outward dissemblance. It is a noble faculty; and when existing in large measure, and combined as it may be with a good degree of its opposite, constitutes an intellect right excellently endowed. This is one of those great gifts, which Bacon possessed beyond almost all others; as will appear to any one who, having read the "Advancement of Learning," remembers what is said upon the "Philosophia Prima"; indeed will appear to one who has closely observed his style of thought anywhere in his writings. And, whoever has a faculty like in kind to his, however it may fall short in degree, will always find a delight in reading Bacon. But Barrow exhibits no eminence in this kind, more than in the former. He stands in the broad middle ground between the two; takes about the same view of things as is taken by sound-minded men at large, only sees more of it, apprehends its interior relations better, and gives it a more energetic expression.

3. Those who are possessed with admiration of the modern smart style cannot be expected to relish Barrow.

These care not so much what sort of Pegasus a writer mounts, or whither he journeys, to Heaven or to Hades; provided only that when he does mount he puts the creature into a clattering gallop, and tears along with an immense demonstration of speed. This is the taking style of writing at present; perhaps was measurably so in old times; only it happened then (as it does now) that there were some who had the good sense not to fall into it, and also happened (as it will again) that those who did fall into it were a little while cried up, and then vanished out of the world, works and all, perhaps with no loss to the world; leaving the truly great and sober writers to come down to our time. This style of writing we say is much in vogue now; and many of our young men, whose native tastes would have taught them better, are misled by the rage for it, and the applause that awards success in it. We consider it the especial bane of American literature. There are among us a number of writers, who mounted their steed too early, rode him too hard, and broke his wind before he was fairly grown; and now, though they do not cease to urge him on, the miserable animal cannot accomplish a sorry canter without hoarse pantings and agonizing sobs. The school of smart writers, indeed, embraces many varieties; of which the French generally are the most vicious; indeed so utterly vicious that, in our estimation, there are few of them who are less than contemptible, and even that few are no favorites with us. The author of "A Discourse of Matters pertaining to Religion" exhibits the smart rhetoric in a somewhat forcible and effective phase. But it is in Macaulay that this style has reached its perfection; freed from all the faults that are not inseparable from it, united to the utmost of such beauties as it admits, and grounded upon the genuine British sturdiness and sense. Macaulay *is* what all such writers are forever trying to be; and no man looks down with more contempt upon the unfortunates who are jerking their limbs out of joint in the endeavor to do as he does, and to gain the applauses that are lavished upon him. He is a master in his way; his sentences come off with a crack like a coach whip. It is this, in our judgment, which gives him two-thirds of his popularity; and it is this which insures his writing against ever becoming classic English. His thought, too, is no less smart than his style; indeed must in the nature of the case be so, else it could never accommodate itself to such a style; and this after all is the great objection to that manner of writing. Johnson's "rolling and sonorous diction" has been sufficiently censured, in part justly; and yet that has considerable scope and sweep; but this short, sharp, pert style is utterly unfit to bear the burden of a large and generous thought.

Now persons who are greatly carried away with admiration of this modern smartness, coming to Barrow will certainly find him a very heavy, cumbersome and unpleasing writer; they will not fail to be offended with the slow sweeping movement of his sentences, each spanning over wide spaces, like the sweep of very long oars; they will miss the fierce twang, with which in their favorite authors the thoughts are wont to be shot off; and the conclusion from all this, (for what reader was ever known to take the blame to himself?) the conclusion will be highly unfavorable to Dr. Barrow. So (would they tell truly) it would in a like case be to Milton. But Barrow must be peculiarly uninteresting to such; for while no writer is more truly nervous and masculine, none is less smart than he. Those sharp affirmations, each constituting a period, following each other in quick but distinct succession, which in Macaulay's prose smite upon the ear with a smart percussion, like the sound of strokes with a hammer, are all wanting here; and instead we have the long-drawn notes of a great organ, or better, the sound of the sea-swell falling on the shore. Not that Barrow is a truly rhythmical writer; he has not, he is far from having, the grand native, yet artistic, rhythm of Milton, or the sober cadences of Hooker; but he has what is next best, a true depth of tone, and that variety, sometimes rugged, but always welcome, which is to the ear what the native woods and pastures are to the eye.

Not to push any further this enumeration, we may consider positively some things which distinguish Dr. Barrow as a writer. And,

1. His great copiousness usually furnishes to his critics a topic of remark. It must be acknowledged that he pushes this to the verge of redundancy; into which, however, he never passes; for it will be difficult to point out anywhere in him that word, which has not a good and solid meaning in the place where it stands; and redundancy consists not in the copious amplification of one's meaning, but in the use of words which, where they stand, mean nothing, everything which they could express having been said before. This copiousness we might at first be disposed to attribute, in good part, to that wonderful and vast wealth of words,—solid, significant words, too, worth a man's having,—which he possessed almost beyond any other writer in the language, unless Milton be the exception; but upon a closer examination we shall see that it proceeds still more from the power he has to specify and draw out all the lesser contributory meanings which go to make up a general one; of which his definition of wit is a notable instance. And all this without any appearance of nicety, without ever losing the air of largeness in his thought. He is like an oak, which is commonly a tree of wide-spreading top and very many

branches; but withal has a tough and sturdy trunk to hold them up. Were he a man of less sinewy and compacted sense, we might think him redundant and top-heavy: as it is, one likes to see him spread out his boughs; they become him well; there is vigorous wood in the least of all his branchlets, and it would take a hard gale (of criticism) to break one of them off.

2. We may also note, as a matter of more consequence than might at first appear, the absence in Barrow of everything like prettiness; a property arising from an attempt at beauty, or rather at the conscious *beautifying* of one's style. No writer can be farther remote from this. Even those fine quirks of speech, which so great a writer as Coleridge does not always disdain, could by no possibility creep into the style of Barrow, he remaining Barrow. He makes no more attempt at beauty than a pine tree does; and yet reaches a genuine, though not indeed artistic beauty, even as pines do, by being himself a part of nature. There is, indeed, a beauty which is a truly spiritual idea, and there is a genuinely artistic style of writing, against which we have nothing to urge; only we think it extremely dangerous for a young man to fancy himself one of those few who are qualified to write in that way; neither indeed do we think it desirable that many should write so, even supposing many could. But in this case the beauty resides in the thought, sprang into being with it, and constitutes an inseparable essence in it, without which it would no longer be the same thought. And aside from this, there is a bold, picturesque expression, a leafing out into words that have the life and hues of nature; which will almost always take place where a writer has the real sap of meaning in him in any abundance. If one has living, working roots running down into nature, that is, into the soil of thought, be sure there will be nature and trope in his words. But as this comes to pass because he vigorously means something, and has by right of sound, earnest and fearless thinking a privilege to mean it; so prettiness comes by one's being scant of meaning, while at the same time he has a foolish eagerness to write finely, and get praise thereby. Now the ground idea of prettiness is not beauty, but ornament; a very different thing. And as a woman may sometimes be seen to hang

flaring ribbons about an insipid and meaningless countenance; as a dandy may, by use of the curling tongs, come to wear the locks of Apollo, (if Apollo's had been oiled,) upon a skull which hath not much good sense within it; so the pretty writer tags his artificial fineries to that which has extremely little significance in itself. But even good writers may be, by evil influences, or some unhappy weakness, betrayed into expression, which is not precisely finical indeed, but is yet a *little* too curiously nice to be quite manly; we have intimated that, in our opinion, Coleridge sometimes is. It is a dangerous thing to seek after the "curiosa felicitas" in expression; it is a dangerous thing to *indulge* in too far, even where it does not have to be sought. We allow, indeed, that true art is not to be despised; we are aware that Nature herself has her flowers of exquisite finish; and if one has the real beauty in him, if by spontaneous creation, nay, if by careful culture, he can produce thoughts that have a native grace and words that are true blossoms; we will call his a most rare gift, and honor him accordingly. But the pretty writer gives you, not roses on the native stalk, but French flowers, made of cloth, hung upon thoughts, (we must, perhaps, call them thoughts,) which have no better similitude in nature than those dry stubs sometimes seen in our forests, in which the sap has long ago done circulating. Now, Barrow is alive and not dead, and therefore not pretty; he has, again, no touch of the artist in his composition; but we know not where one could go to get a *feeling* of what nervous, manly writing is, better than to him. And one who has much read him,—or indeed read any of his peers,—in the true love of him, will, as we conceive, be in small danger of ever becoming one of your pretty, finical sort of writers.

The truth is, however, that the disease of prettiness is deeper-seated than in mere style; unless you consider style as a revelation of the whole man, a manifestation of what he really is. We have already said that it proceeds from a poverty of meaning, to which is unfortunately added an itching for literary distinction; that is, it proceeds from a total misapprehension of what the right end of all writing is, and also from a lack of all that which qualifies and privileges any man to write. The function of Writer is a true office, into which one should not be inaugurated without the possession of a certain excellent peculiarity, grounded in what he is a man, which favorably distinguishes, and, as it were, secludes him from the mass of men, and constitutes in him a fitness for right worthy things. Good writing is not a trick, to be caught by any cunning handicraftsman; pretty writing, fair writing perhaps is; but not good. He who is fit to be a writer at all will be rendered incapable of prettiness by that very thing which constitutes his fitness. The true author is a master, not of arts perhaps, but of thought, of truth; he is one who has within him deeper meanings and richer significances than dwell in the most; else how is he fitted to authorize anything? And it is the inevitable workings and seekings of this inward fountain which should make it pierce the crust, and flow forth into a rill or river, of written speech. In fine, one should write because there is that in his mind which he, in sad duty, and not in frivolous plaudit-seeking, veritably *needs* to utter, and which the world as truly needs to hear. And if a man, with any genuine sense of what he is about, assumes office as one of the priesthood of thought, be sure he will find something better to do than to be always tagging ornaments to his robes.

It will corroborate this view to observe that all the great prose works in our language were written soberly and sincerely in answer to what was felt by the writer as an imperative call for them. We instance Bacon's great treatises, Milton's 'Reformation' and 'Areopagitica,' Hooker's 'Ecclesiastical Polity,' and we think one may refer with not less appositeness to most of Barrow's sermons. This fact is significant, and will instruct us what works in our own time may be expected to abide; for those which were written not in answer to any great need, but with mere ambitious aims, cannot help being ephemeral. Now, this need is commonly not conspicuous, not apparent to all, sometimes not apparent to any but that one, or those few, in whose souls lie the deep meanings that constitute the elements of a fit response; they apprehend it, and know that, however for peace sake they might wish to be still, they cannot choose but speak.

Barrow answers to, and illustrates all the conditions we have

mentioned. He wrote because there was something which ought
to be said, and which he felt it in himself to say. He wrote because
he well apprehended the deepest moral wants of his time; wrote
sincerely and courageously, with an inward fullness and force of
meaning which made his words, like the leaves of trees, green,
odorous and wholesome; and in consequence of all this, what he
has written is apposite to the moral wants of many times.

3. Lastly, as a quality of the man, which had much to do with
his worth and eminence as a writer, we name his courage. We
give this the last place by way of emphasis; not for its distinguish-
ing Barrow beyond several others, that might be named in English literature, but because, while he exhibits it in such eminence
and modesty, both as makes him a safe model and illustration; it
is in itself, if we mistake not greatly, a matter most worthy of
consideration. And as we might not otherwise be able to set
forth its application to Barrow in the light that it appears to us,
it may not be out of place to enter upon a slight discussion of the
abstract subject. But we have an interest in it beyond any special
applications of it. Indeed, if there be one thing, which more than
aught else in the present article, we would be glad at once to call
the attention of others to, and ourselves to consider, balance and
pronounce upon justly and wisely, it is the relation of courage
to excellence in thinking and writing. For there is a legitimate,
and also a bastard courage; the former is a vital property in all
living thought and all worthy speech; the latter is one of the
most foolish and detestable of human qualities.

But, assuredly, without courage nothing great was ever accomplished in any province of human affairs. And the writer, so
far from being able to dispense with it, needs it more than any—
more than even the soldier. For, he who solves the problems and
writes to the deepest wants of his time, must *dare* beyond the
measure of facing physical danger. That is, indeed, a well-
upborne and valorous mind, which can preserve the prompt and
just working of its thought amid the shock of armies and the
thunderous din of martial strife; but there are influences vastly
more disturbing than those of battle; things apter to make the
eyes blink than the near flashing of a sword; and many a man, to

whom the roar of cannon and the clash of steel was a bracing
music, has sunk down in helpless and blank dismay when he
heard the low, under-ground rumbling of enraged public opinion. Now, if one can be altogether frightened from the propriety
of his thought at the sound, or in anticipation, of these hoarse,
elemental growlings; if he turns pale at the imagination of standing alone, the world fronting him; if he has not that sustaining
faith in the power of Truth to work her own way, which alone
qualifies one to be the minister of Truth; better he should never
assume the pen. For the author who is worthy of his vocation
must make up his mind to utter some things, which not the
largest half of the world will presently thank him for saying;
which possibly, he must wait for even his own, and the truth's,
best friends to accept. Otherwise, if he will say nothing till he can
find that it has been humanly authorized before, nay, till he can
be sure that it is already generally received, especially by those
whom he is to address; then in a vain and pusillanimous attempt
to please everybody, he sinks into moral, as well as literary,
nothingness. Intellectual and moral timidity is synonymous with
intellectual and moral weakness. The over-timorous intellect
sees a bugbear in every fresh thought that would fain come and
enrich it; it dares not push out and push down its roots into the
soil, and draw up the virgin strength of it, but seeks about on the
surface for some old hole made by a former root, into which its
stiff and sun-dried fibers may creep. Then, too, it must have, not
only thoughts, but phrases also, made to its hand; and so all sinks
into a mean mimicry; and in the end such a mind either becomes
a retailer of goods bought and sold with profits for its own
pockets, or, supplied with a goodly heap of authorities, and
shrunken to unimaginable minuteness, disappears finally in the
paths of a petty and dastardly criticism, lost in the lumber it
meant to use against all who were not as commonplace and servile
as itself.

On the other hand, there is a headlong and intemperate boldness, which violates the modesty of truth, and which, though
often rewarded with the huzzas of the multitude, truly deserves
nothing so much as to be whipped into a meeker behavior. This

presumptuous and over-officious bravery, however, has certain invariable tokens, by which an observant eye may detect it. And first, it is thoroughly immodest, treating with irreverent slight and contempt beliefs, which have received the not hasty nor ill-considered assent of almost all the wise and good, and fancying that the mere whims, raw notions and rank steams of its own brain are worth more than the deep-studied and slow-grown thought of all the ages. Secondly, it is obtrusive, thrusting itself forward without occasion, and seeking opportunity for the display of its bravery and wit. Now, those persons who in momentous times have stood foremost, and done service for which mankind will not let them be forgotten, were never forward persons; they waited sometimes without even knowing they were waiting, until occasion came, drew them forth and unequivocally pointed out to them a place. Finally, this bravery dares for the sake of daring, or for the reputation of boldness, not for truth's sake. It is more solicitous to say things new and startling than true things; and if truth will not afford it an opportunity to indulge its vein, it will by no means on that account forego the indulgence. Its great object is to use expressions that no one else would use, to say things that others are afraid, commonly nobly afraid, to say; and to astonish the multitude thereby; a profane, and not a 'holy boldness.'

True courage we may consider in its relation, first to thought, and secondly to speech; as a help to the acquisition of ideas and principles, or as a furtherance to expression. Intellectual courage, or courage in its relation to thought, enables the mind to assert its standing and uprightness against the invisible tide of prevalent opinion; enables it in its retirement to meet and confront notions that visit it with the lordly air of authority without due show of reason; and teaches it to venture out in remote excursions, following trains of thought variously suggested, and pursuing them on to their distant results and out to their distant affinities. The man intellectually timid is shy of all such radical meditations. He wills to abide in the safe atmosphere of authorized notions. Now it undoubtedly is the duty of any one to think long and severely before definitely making up his mind to depart from the received opinion of his time, or even of his locality; it as undoubtedly is the duty of each thinker to test such opinions impartially and courageously in his thought, in order that, though he may not be led to differ, he may, by compliance with the laws of reason, receive into his mind *intellectually* what the most must receive in part traditionally, and in part from a moral satisfaction in it. Doubtless also he should not upon the first affirmation of reason conclude the common opinion wrong; but he should be withheld from instant decision only by reverence for truth, and for that opinion as the exponent of truth, not from fear to allow free scope to his understanding, and to abide by its last and sincere judgments. So that intellectual courage, so far from favoring rash decisions, is every way favorable to the most candid and careful investigation, and the most prudent suspense of judgment, so long as suspense is truly prudent. While without it, the individual reason dares not assert any rights of its own, nor to lift its voice at all otherwise than in reiteration of what, some nobler reason having had the courage to utter, and so far authorize it first, has now become the common converse of men; it ventures not to betake itself to any untried element, but only swims imitatively upon a table; and so, like a subdued and spiritless people, sinks into a tame and emasculate dependency, in the end seeking only, like a good dog, to obtain the approval of its master (the public), by barking always according to his bidding.

Courage in respect to speech is two-fold, moral and rhetorical; courage in matter and courage in manner; the first leading one upon due occasion to put forth and publicly assert his convictions of truth, the second to follow his own genius in expression, without regard to the authorized artificialities and rhetorical fashions of the day. The moralist, preacher, or thinker, who is possessed of any great power of thought, will often need to encounter the current of public opinion or public affection in his time, at more or less risk of injury to himself; and in proportion to the depth of his thought and his faithfulness in uttering, also to the violence of popular attachment to the current sins, errors, or prejudices, this encounter will be rude and jostling; so that if one be bold in thinking, but morally timid,—as Erasmus, for instance,—he is sure to be speedily alarmed, and perhaps silenced. Hence comes a perpetual "staggering between conscience and the pope," with bad results to himself, and possibly no good ones to the world.

Again, rhetorical courage; a pouring of native force and sturdiness into expression; a freedom and boldness in the ordering of phrases and the use of words, tropes, and metaphors; is indispensable to vigorous and effective writing. It is necessary, to be sure, that this quality should be under the control of good taste; but the taste itself, however chaste, however cultivated, must be courageous and one's own. This sort of courage is, indeed, that which most easily recommends itself and becomes popular. It has ever characterized, and ever must, all distinguished writers. Macaulay has it in high degree; Carlyle still more; Johnson, Burke, Milton, all possessed it eminently.

We come now to consider Barrow more especially as an illustration of this quality. And if of the first named species of courage, that is, of intellectual, he seems not to exhibit an extraordinary share; it is because his genius did not require him to make this conspicuous. He is not a man of speculative mind; he attempts not, as Hooker, the solution of any great problem, not, indeed, from lack of heart to grapple with such, but because his thoughts were otherwise employed, and did not tend that way; by the natural current of his meditations he is borne towards the more common moralities and average duties of our daily life. But here he exhibits a courageous rectitude of thought, a deliberate and resolute thoroughness in the discussion of his subjects, which is not very noticeable, to be sure, because never speculatively startling, yet not the less worthy of praise.

Of the other species of courage, in both departments of it, he is a notable instance. A devoted adherent of the court, there was the strongest temptation for him to blink over the vices to which that court was especially given, and which its example had made prevalent, and to expend his strength, as South did, in brazen and servile denunciation of the defeated and disgraced Puritans. Yet to Barrow we owe the most impartial discussion and the weightiest condemnation of several of those vices, which has come down to our time. And it is an eminent instance of the manner in which Providence, through the instrumentality of faithful and courageous men, is wont to compel great evils to yield a harvest of good, that the levity, impiety, and profane license of the court of Charles Second gave occasion to those sermons of Barrow, beginning with the thirteenth, and constituting a series of some twenty numbers, in which the morality of speech is so boldly and thoroughly discussed. Of rhetorical courage Barrow is even a still better illustration. It exhibits itself in his manfulness and freedom; in the fact that he made a style for himself, in which he yet stands alone; in his being able, while admiring Aristotle so greatly, even excessively, yet to depart from him so utterly in manner of speech. It does not indeed prompt him, as Burke, to flame out in flashing, startling oratory and metaphor, simply because he is not an imaginative man; but it is the upbraced and valiant habit of his soul that puts him upon the use of those sinewy terms, which crowd and enrich his pages. And if one will know how great a wealth of right manly and muscular speech our language contains, and will learn what a wholesome and invigorating rhetoric these plain words may be wrought into, when employed by a writer who manfully means somewhat; let him study the sermons of Barrow.

To all students, theological or otherwise, we say, read him; not exclusively indeed, by no means; there are others as worthy, some few worthier of attention; yet read him thoroughly; it will do you good; you will find it, like conversing with the woods and breathing the open air, a cure for many sentimentalities and affectations, which come upon us from dwelling too much in the hot and close atmosphere of modern literature. You will also, if you have not before, thereby gain a feeling of how it is that a man writes, and so will not be content yourselves to write in other than a manly way. And this will lead to serious thoughts; you will come to see that it is not by trick, not by ambitious striving, but by preparation of the soul, by becoming rich in the inner man, that one is fitted to address his age in words that have an abiding significance, and therefore will not be suffered to die.

A LETTER TO
WILLIAM LLOYD GARRISON

꣓꣓꣓꣓꣓꣓꣓꣓꣓꣓꣓꣓꣓꣓꣓꣓꣓꣓

Worcester, Dec. 13th, 1860

Dear Mr. Garrison:—It seems to me of importance to keep it constantly in view, that the anti-slavery cause has its root and its strength in the simple principle of justice, and that it is weakened by every remove from this ground. Our inexpugnable claim is, that the Africans are human beings, and, therefore, that all the rights of human beings are theirs, and must not be withholden from them. The moment our cause begins to be urged upon the ground of admiration for the African race, of private taste and liking, or of any special estimate of its abilities, that moment we begin to admit it as a necessary implication that, were they not admirable to us, or not congenial to our tastes, or not of a certain order of ability, the obligation to accord them their freedom would be annulled, or, at least, would be diminished. To me, therefore, it appears extremely desirable that we should discern what are our *real* premises, and should establish our practical conclusions steadily upon these, and not on others.

To set forth the admirable qualities which appertain to this race—to celebrate and commemorate its heroes—is certainly a legitimate labor. Done heartily, ingenuously, reasonably, as Wendell Phillips does it, for example,—it always refreshes me; and I reckon such testimonies valuable auxiliaries to the main argument. But if substituted for the main argument, even these

The Liberator, Dec. 31, 1860.

noble services would prove disserviceable. Any removal of our cause from its grounds in justice, to grounds in special admiration, makes its logic no longer unanswerable. Now, this removal will never be made directly, at least not by those whom I should care to address upon the subject; but, by possibility, it may be effected, inadvertently, in a negative and indirect way. If we deny to anyone anti-slavery fellowship, simply because he confesses a distaste to this race, or because he forms too low an estimate (as we deem) of its capacities, are we not drawing the roots of our cause from their proper soil? Is he not a colaborer, and to be welcomed to all the sympathy which accompanies co-operation, who stands steadfastly with us on our main ground, namely, that negroes are men, and who joins with us in the consequent oath, that being such, they shall, so help us God, enjoy their lawful heritage of human rights?

For my part, I would have Africans treated precisely as other men. If I go to Turkey, and don't like the Turks, or Greeks, or Armenians, or the missionaries to Turks, Greeks and Armenians —I say so without hesitation; and no one infers my inhumanity in consequence. I am permitted, without censure, to like or dislike Spaniards and Moors; to take a hopeful or an unhopeful view of the capacities of Tartars, Japanese, Sandwich Islanders, &c. Why should we not be equally free to consider the capabilities, and pronounce upon the aspects, of Africans, expressing toward them satisfaction or censure, as we honestly can?

It were well, indeed, to bear in mind that the position of the negro in America is peculiar, and demands, in some degree, a peculiar treatment. It must not be forgotten what a prejudice is popularly indulged against him—a prejudice which, in its unreasoning and unmitigated extreme, becomes base, barbarous, and almost diabolical. It must not be forgotten that thousands are eager for any pretext to deny him his rights as one of the human family. We should, therefore, not permit in ourselves any uncandor, not concede less or affirm more than scientific truth respecting him; we should speak considerately; and even by our censures of him, should such be necessary, indicate our recognition of him as belonging to the brotherhood of humanity.

And yet we must not so far yield to these pretexts as to admit their pertinence, even were they true. We shall lose infinitely more by allowing the logic of these adversaries, than by any, however able and convincing, controversy of their alleged facts. As an opponent of slavery, as a servant of freedom, I have nothing whatever to do with the question of the relative rank of races, African or other. I might admit everything that can be alleged against the negro, and yet safely let my case go to the court upon a demurrer. I obey the law of a sympathy which runs not alone upon a level, but reaches up to the sunlit height, and down into the sunless chasm, joining in one vast marriage bond the loftiest and the lowliest—him who knows beyond computation the secrets of Nature, and him who knows not how to number his ten fingers; and omitting from the fellowship it makes, only the irredeemably selfish and bad. Natural or involuntary defect, it matters not how great, can exclude no one from that bond of brotherhood, which makes of many men of many nations and diverse races, one humanity. No gift is for private use—all are for communication. The eyes of the seeing are due to the blind, the strength of the strong to him that is weak; and, therefore, no want of gifts can shut out anyone rightly from the flowing uses of life, and the great communities of right and benefit. Let us preserve this broad basis of our movement, nor even, in the noble desire to repel detraction from the African, be led to forsake it. Still less, let us drive from us, upon account of side issues, those who are with us in our binding argument.

Again, it should be remembered that there is a kind of aspersion in excess of tenderness. If I offer a man crutches, I imply that he is a cripple. Attentions are suitable to the sick and unable, which, to the strong and healthy, it were a shame to receive. To shield the African too carefully from criticism, is indirectly to affirm the inferiority of that race, which it is necessary thus to patronize. His heart must indeed be stone, who does not pity the negro in America, the free only less than the enslaved; yet may we not so pity him that our *babying* commiseration shall detract more from his claim to manhood, than the disparagement of limited minds, who see no farther than to his epidermis, or the sneers of selfish and malignant minds, who see no farther than to their own passions and interests?

I say this more freely, because I neither possess, nor can for a moment conjure up, any repugnance to the negro, as such. Beyond my will, I am destitute of any such feeling. To me he is simply a man, and to be judged as other men are. If a man of sense and refinement, he is personally agreeable to me; if gross and stupid, he is personally disagreeable. For his complexion, I care no more than for the color of his clothes; and a gentleman in black is no less acceptable than one in white. And I would that all Africans might insist upon being treated simply as men— might insist upon their freedom to be liked or disliked, valued or under-valued, reckoned equal or reckoned inferior, without prejudice to their claim to a man's share in the common rights of man. And let us all bear in mind that ours is no question of taste or distaste, of beauty or ugliness, of wit or dulness, but simply a question of justice and humanity.

REST AND MOTION

Motion and Rest are the two feet upon which existence goes. All action and all definite power result from the intimacy and consent of these opposite principles. If, therefore, one would construct any serviceable mechanism, he must incorporate into it, and commonly in a manifold way, a somewhat passive, a somewhat contrary, and, as it were, inimical to action, though action be the sole aim and use of his contrivance. Thus, the human body is penetrated by the passive and powerless skeleton, which is a mere weight upon the muscles, a part of the burden that, nevertheless, it enables them to bear. The lever of Archimedes would push the planet aside, provided only it were supplied with its indispensable complement, a fulcrum, or fixity: without this it will not push a pin. The block of the pulley must have its permanent attachment; the wheel of the locomotive engine requires beneath it the fixed rail; the foot of the pedestrian, solid earth; the wing of the bird rests upon the relatively stable air to support his body, and upon his body to gain power over the air. Nor is it alone of operations mechanical that the law holds good: it is universal; and its application to pure mental action may be shown without difficulty. A single act of the mind is represented by the formation of a simple sentence. The process consists, first, in the mind's *fixing upon and resting in* an object, which thereby becomes the subject of the sentence; and, secondly, in predica-

Atlantic Monthly, May, 1861.

tion, which is movement, represented by the verb. The reader will easily supply himself with instances and illustrations of this, and need not, therefore, be detained.

In the economy of animal and vegetable existence, as in all that Nature makes, we observe the same inevitable association. Here is perpetual fixity of form, perpetual flux of constituent,—the ideas of Nature never changing, the material realization of them never ceasing to change. A horse is a horse through all the ages; yet the horse of to-day is changed from the horse of yesterday.

If one of these principles seem to get the start, and to separate itself, the other quickly follows. No sooner, for example, does any person perform an initial deed, proceeding purely (let us suppose) from free will, than Nature in him begins to repose therein, and consequently inclines to its repetition for the mere reason that it has been once done. This is Habit, which makes action passive, and is the greatest of labor-saving inventions. Custom is the habit of society, holding the same relation to progressive genius. It is the sleeping partner in the great social firm; it is thought and force laid up and become fixed capital. Annihilate this,—as in the French Revolution was attempted,—and society is at once reduced to its bare immediate force, and must scratch the soil with its fingers.

Sometimes these principles seem to be strictly hostile to each other and in no respect reciprocal, as where habit in the individual and custom in society oppose themselves bitterly to free will and advancing thought: yet even here the special warfare is but the material of a broader and more subtile alliance. An obstinate fixity in one's bosom often serves as a rock on which to break the shell of some hard inclosed faculty. Upon steppingstones of our *slain* selves we mount to new altitudes. So do the antagonisms of these principles in the broader field of society equally conceal a fundamental reciprocation. By the opposition to his thought of inert and defiant custom, the thinker is compelled to interrogate his consciousness more deeply and sacredly; and being cut off from that sympathy which has its foundation in similarity of temperaments and traditions, he must fall back with simpler abandonment upon the pure idea, and must seek responses from that absolute nature of man which the men of his time are not human enough to afford him. This absolute nature, this divine identity in man, underrunning times, temperaments, individualities, is that which poet and prophet must address: yet to speak *to* it, they must speak *from* it; to be heard by the universal heart, they must use a universal language. But this marvellous vernacular can be known to him alone whose heart is universal, in whom even self-love is no longer selfish, but is a pure respect to his own being as it is Being. Well it is, therefore, that here and there one man should be so denied all petty and provincial claim to attention, that only by speaking to Man as Man, and in the sincerest vernacular of the human soul, he can find audience; for thus it shall become his need, for the sake of joy no less than of duty, to know himself purely as man, and to yield himself wholly to his immortal humanity. Thus does fixed custom force back the most moving souls, until they touch the springs of inspiration, and are indued with power: then, at once potent and pure, they gush into history, to be influences, to make epochs, and to prevail over that through whose agency they first obtained strength.

Thus, everywhere, through all realms, do the opposite principles of Rest and Motion depend upon and reciprocally empower each other. In every act, mechanical, mental, social, must both take part and consent together; and upon the perfection of this consent depends the quality of the action. Every progress is conditioned on a permanence; every permanence *lives* but in and through progress. Where all, and with equal and simultaneous impulse, strives to move, nothing can move, but chaos is come; where all refuses to move, and therefore stagnates, decay supervenes, which is motion, though a motion downward.

Having made this general statement, we proceed to say that there are two chief ways in which these universal opposites enter into reciprocation. The first and more obvious is the method of alternation, or of rest *from* motion; the other, that of continuous equality, which may be called a rest *in* motion. These two methods, however, are not mutually exclusive, but may at once occupy the same ground, and apply to the same objects,—as oxygen and nitrogen severally fill the same space, to the full capacity of each, as though the other were absent.

Instances of the alternation, either total or approximative, of these principles are many and familiar. They may be seen in the systole and diastole of the heart; in the alternate activity and passivity of the lungs; in the feet of the pedestrian, one pausing while the other proceeds; in the waving wings of birds; in the undulation of the sea; in the creation and propagation of sound, and the propagation, at least, of light; in the alternate acceleration and retardation of the earth's motion in its orbit, and in the waving of its poles. In all vibrations and undulations there is a going and returning, between which must exist minute periods of repose; but in many instances the return is simply a relaxation or a subsidence, and belongs, therefore, to the department of rest. Discourse itself, it will be observed, has its pauses, seasons of repose thickly interspersed in the action of speech; and besides these has its accented and unaccented syllables, emphatic and unemphatic words,—illustrating thus in itself the law which it here affirms. History is full of the same thing; the tides of faith and feeling now ascend and now subside, through all the ages, in the soul of humanity; each new affirmation prepares the way for new doubt, each honest doubt in the end furthers and enlarges belief; the pendulum of destiny swings to and fro forever, and earth's minutest life and heaven's remotest star swing with it, rising but to fall, and falling that they may rise again. So does rhythm go to the very bottom of the world: the heart of Nature pulses, and the echoing shore and all music and the throbbing heart and swaying destinies of man but follow and proclaim the law of her inward life.

The universality and mutual relationship of these primal principles have, perhaps, been sufficiently set forth; and this may be the place to emphasize the second chief point,—that the perfection of this mutuality measures the degree of excellence in all objects and actions. It will everywhere appear, that, the more regular and symmetrical their relationship, the more beautiful and acceptable are its results. For example, sounds proceeding from vibrations wherein the strokes and pauses are in invariable relation are such sounds as we denominate *musical*. Accordingly all sounds are musical at a sufficient distance, since the most irregular undulations are, in a long journey through the air, wrought to an equality, and made subject to exact law,—as in this universe all irregularities are sure to be in the end. Thus, the thunder, which near at hand is a wild crash, or nearer yet a crazy crackle, is by distance deepened and refined into that marvellous bass which we all know. And doubtless the jars, the discords, and moral contradictions of time, however harsh and crazy at the outset, flow into exact undulation along the ether of eternity, and only as a pure proclamation of law attain to the ear of Heaven. Nay, whoso among men is able to plant his ear high enough above this rude clangor may, in like manner, so hear it, that it shall be to him melody, solace, fruition, a perpetual harvest of the heart's dearest wishes, a perpetual corroboration of that which faith affirms.

We may therefore easily understand why musical sounds *are* musical, why they are acceptable and moving, while those affront the sense in which the minute reposes are capricious, and, as it were, upon ill terms with the movements. The former appeal to what is most universal and cosmical within us,—to the pure Law, the deep Nature in our breasts; they fall in with the immortal rhythm of life itself, which the others encounter and impugn.

It will be seen also that verse differs from prose as musical sounds from ordinary tones; and having so deep a ground in Nature, rhythmical speech will be sure to continue, in spite of objection and protest, were it, if possible, many times more energetic than that of Mr. Carlyle. But always the best prose has a certain rhythmic emphasis and cadence: in Milton's grander passages there is a symphony of organs, the bellows of the mighty North (one might say) filling their pipes; Goldsmith's flute still breathes through his essays; and in the ampler prose of Bacon there is the swell of a summer ocean, and you can half fancy you hear the long soft surge falling on the shore. Also in all good writing, as in good reading, the pauses suffer no slight; they are treated handsomely; and each sentence rounds gratefully and clearly into rest. Sometimes, indeed, an attempt is made to reach in an illegitimate way this force of firm pauses, as in exaggerated French style, wherein the writer seems never to stride or to run, but always to jump like a frog.

Again, as reciprocal opposites, our two principles should be of equal dignity and value. To concede, however, the equality of rest with motion must, for an American, be not easy; and it is therefore in point to assert and illustrate this in particular. What better method of doing so than that of taking some one large instance in Nature, if such can be found, and allowing this, after fair inspection, to stand for all others? And, as it happens, just what we require is quite at hand;—the alternation of Day and Night, of sleep and waking, is so broad, obvious, and familiar, and so mingled with our human interests, that its two terms are easily subjected to extended and clear comparison; while also it deserves discussion upon its own account, apart from its relation to the general subject.

Sleep is now popularly known to be coextensive with Life,—inseparable from vital existence of whatever grade. The rotation of the earth is accordingly implied, as was happily suggested by Paley, in the constitution of every animal and every plant. It is quite evident, therefore, that this necessity was not laid upon man through some inadvertence of Nature; on the contrary, this arrangement must be such as to her seemed altogether suitable, and, if suitable, economical. Eager men, however, avaricious of performance, do not always regard it with entire complacency. Especially have the saints been apt to set up a controversy with Nature in this particular, submitting with infinite unwillingness to the law by which they deem themselves, as it were, defrauded of life and activity in so large measure. In form, to be sure, their accusation lies solely against themselves; they reproach themselves with sleeping beyond need, sleeping for the mere luxury and delight of it; but the venial self-deception is quite obvious,—nothing plainer than that it is their necessity itself which is repugnant to them, and that their wills are blamed for not sufficiently withstanding and thwarting it. Pious William Law, for example, is unable to disparage sleep enough for his content.

"The poorest, dullest refreshment of the body," he calls it, . . . "such a dull, stupid state of existence, that even among animals we despise them most which are most drowsy." You should therefore, so he urges, "begin the day in the spirit of renouncing sleep." Baxter, also,—at that moment a walking catalogue and epitome of all diseases,—thought himself guilty for all sleep he enjoyed beyond three hours a day. More's Utopians were to rise at very early hours, and attend scientific lectures before breakfast.

Ambition and cupidity, which, in their way, are no whit less earnest and self-sacrificing than sanctity, equally look upon sleep as a wasteful concession to bodily wants, and equally incline to limit such concession to its mere minimum. Commonplaces accordingly are perpetually circulating in the newspapers, especially in such as pretend to a didactic tone, wherein all persons are exhorted to early rising, to resolute abridgment of the hours of sleep, and the like. That Sir Walter Raleigh slept but five hours in twenty-four; that John Hunter, Frederick the Great, and Alexander von Humboldt slept but four; that the Duke of Wellington made it an invariable rule to "turn out" whenever he felt inclined to turn over, and John Wesley to arise upon his first awaking: instances such as these appear on parade with the regularity of militia troops at muster; and the precept duly follows,—"Whoso would not be insignificant, let him go and do likewise." "All great men have been early risers," says my newspaper.

Of late, indeed, a better knowledge of the laws of health, or perhaps only a keener sense of its value and its instability, begins to supersede these rash inculcations; and paragraphs due to some discreet Dr. Hall make the rounds of the press, in which we are reminded that early rising, in order to prove a benefit, rather than a source of mischief, must be duly matched with early going to bed. The one, we are told, will by no means answer without the other. As yet, however, this is urged upon hygienic grounds alone; it is a mere concession to the body, a bald necessity that we hampered mortals lie under; which necessity we are quite at liberty to regret and accuse, though we cannot with safety resist it. Sleep is still admitted to be a waste of time, though one with

which Nature alone is chargeable. And I own, not without re-
luctance, that the great authority of Plato can be pleaded for this
low view of its functions. In the "Laws" he enjoins a due measure
thereof, but for the sake of health alone, and adds, that the sleeper
is, for the time, of no more value than the dead. Clearly, mankind
would sustain some loss of good sense, were all the dullards and
fat-wits taken away; and Sancho Panza, with his hearty, "Bless-
ings on the man that invented sleep!" here ekes out the scant
wisdom of sages. The talking world, however, of our day takes
part with the Athenian against the Manehegan philosopher, and,
while admitting the present necessity of sleep, does not rejoice
in its original invention. If, accordingly, in a computation of the
length of man's life, the hours passed in slumber are carefully
deducted, and considered as forming no part of available time,
not even the medical men dispute the justice of such procedure.
They have but this to say:—"The stream of life is not strong
enough to keep the mill of action always going; we must therefore periodically shut down the gate and allow the waters to
accumulate; and he ever loses more than he gains who attempts
any avoidance of this natural necessity."

As medical men, they are not required, perhaps, to say more;
and we will be grateful to them for faithfully urging this,—especially when we consider, that, under the sage arrangements now
existing, all that the physician does for the general promotion
of health is done in defiance of his own interests. We, however,
have further questions to ask. Why is not the life-stream more
affluent? Sleep is needful,—but *wherefore?* The physician vin-
dicates the sleeper; but the philosopher must vindicate Nature.

It is surely one step toward an elucidation of this matter to
observe that the necessity here accused is not one arbitrarily laid
upon us *by* Nature, but one existing *in* Nature herself, and
appertaining to the very conception of existence. The elucidation, however, need not pause at this point. The assumption that
sleep is a piece of waste, as being a mere restorative for the body,
and not a service or furtherance to the mind,—this must be
called in question and examined closely; for it is precisely in this
assumption, as I deem, that the popular judgment goes astray. *Is*

sleep any such arrest and detention of the mind? That it is a shutting of those outward gates by which impressions flow in upon
the soul is sufficiently obvious; but who can assure us that it is
equally a closing of those inward and skyward gates through
which come the reinforcements of faculty, the strength that
masters and uses impression? I persuade myself, on the contrary,
that it is what Homer called it, *divine,*—able, indeed, to bring
the blessing of a god; and that hours lawfully passed under the
pressure of its heavenly palms are fruitful, not merely negatively,
but positively, not only as recruiting exhausted powers, and enabling us to be awake again, but by direct contribution to the
resources of the soul and the uses of life; that, in fine, one awakes
farther on in *life,* as well as farther on in *time,* than he was at
falling asleep. This deeper function of the night, what is it?

Sleep is, first of all, a filter, or sieve. It strains off the impressions that engross, but not enrich us,—that superfluous *material*
of experience which, either from glutting excess, or from sheer
insignificance, cannot be spiritualized, made human, transmuted
into experience itself. Every man in our day, according to the
measure of his sensibility, and with some respect also to his position, is *mobbed* by impressions, and must fight as for his life, if he
escape being taken utterly captive by them. It is our perpetual
peril that our lives shall become so sentient as no longer to be reflective or artistic,—so beset and infested by the immediate as to
lose all amplitude, all perspective, and to become mere puppets
of the present, mere Chinese pictures, a huddle of foreground
without horizon, or heaven, or even earthly depth and reach. It is
easy to illustrate this miserable possibility. A man, for example,
in the act of submitting to the extraction of a tooth, is, while the
process lasts, one of the poorest poor creatures with whose existence the world might be taunted. His existence is but skin-
deep, and contracted to a mere point at that: no vision and
faculty divine, no thoughts that wander through eternity, now:
a tooth, a jaw, and the iron of the dentist,— these constitute, for
the time being, his universe. Only when this monopolizing, enslaving, sensualizing impression has gone by, may what had been
a point of pained and quivering animality expand once more to

the dimensions of a human soul. Kant, it is said, could withdraw his attention from the pain of gout by pure mental engagement, but found the effort dangerous to his brain, and accordingly was fain to submit, and be no more than a toe-joint, since evil fate would have it so. These extreme cases exemplify a process of impoverishment from which we all daily suffer. The external, the immediate, the idiots of the moment, telling tales that signify nothing, yet that so overcry the suggestion of our deeper life as by the sad and weary to be mistaken for the discourse of life itself,— these obtrude themselves upon us, and multiply and brag and brawl about us, until we have neither room for better guests, nor spirits for their entertainment. We are like schoolboys with eyes out at the windows, drawn by some rattle of drum and squeak of fife, who would study, were they but deaf. Reproach sleep as a waste, forsooth! It is this tyrannical attraction to the surface, that indeed robs us of time, and defrauds us of the uses of life. We cannot hear the gods for the buzzing of flies. We are driven to an idle industry,—the idlest of all things.

And to this description of loss men are nowadays peculiarly exposed. The modern world is all battle-field; the smoke, the dust, the din fill every eye and ear; and the hill-top of Lucretius, where is it? The indispensable, terrible newspaper, with its late allies, the Titans and sprites of steam and electricity,—bringing to each retired nook, and thrusting in upon each otherwise peaceful household, the crimes, follies, fears, solicitudes, doubts, problems of all kingdoms and peoples,—exasperates the former Scotch mist of impressions into a flooding rain, and almost threatens to swamp the brain of mankind. The incitement to thought is ever greater; but the possibility of thinking, especially of thinking in a deep, simple, central way, is ever less. Problems multiply, but how to attend to them is ever a still greater problem. Guests of the intellect and imagination accumulate until the master of the house is pushed out of doors, and hospitality ceases from the mere excess of its occasion. That must be a greater than Homer who should now do Homer's work. He, there in his sweet, deep-skied Ionia, privileged with an experience so simple and yet so salient and powerful, might well hope to act upon this

victoriously by his spirit, might hope to transmute it, as indeed
he did, into melodious and enduring human suggestion. Would
it have been all the same, had he lived in our type-setting modern
world, with its multitudinous knowledges, its aroused conscience,
its spurred and yet thwarted sympathies, its new incitements to
egotism also, and new tools and appliances for egotism to use,—
placed, as it were, in the focus of a vast whispering-gallery, where
all the sounds of heaven and earth came crowding, contending,
incessant upon his ear? One sees at a glance how the serious
thought and poetry of Greece cling to a few master facts, not
being compelled to fight always with the many-headed monster of
detail; and this suggests to me that our literature may fall short
of Grecian amplitude, depth and simplicity, not wholly from inferiority of power, but from complications appertaining to our
position.

The problem of our time is, How to digest and assimilate the
Newspaper? To complain of it, to desire its abolition, is an
anachronism of the will; it is to complain that time proceeds, and
that events follow each other in due sequence. It is hardly too
bold to say that the newspaper *is* the modern world, as distinct
from the antique and the mediaeval. It represents, by its advent,
that epoch in human history wherein each man must begin, in
proportion to his capability of sympathy and consideration, to
collate his private thoughts, fortunes, interests with those of the
human race at large. We are now in the crude openings of this
epoch, fevered by its incidents and demands; and one of its
tokens is a general exhaustion of the nervous system and failure
of health, both here and in Europe,—those of most sensitive
spirit, and least retired and sheltered from the impressions of the
time, suffering most. All this will end, *must* end, victoriously. In
the mean time can we not somewhat adjust ourselves to this new
condition?

One thing we can and must not fail to do: we can learn to
understand and appreciate Rest. In particular, we should build
up and reinforce the powers of the night to offset this new intensity of the day. Such, indeed, as the day now is has it ever been,
though in a less degree: always it has cast upon men impressions

significant, insignificant, and of an ill significance, promiscuously and in excess; and always sleep has been the filter of memory, the purifier of experience, providing a season that follows closely upon the impressions of the day, ere yet they are too deeply imbedded, in which our deeper life may pluck away the adhering burrs from its garments, and arise disburdened, clean, and free. I make no doubt that Death also performs, though in an ampler and more thorough way, the same functions. It opposes the tyranny of memory. For were our experience to go on forever accumulating, unwinnowed, undiminished, every man would sooner or later break down beneath it; every man would be crushed by his own traditions, becoming a grave to himself, and drawing the clods over his own head. To relieve us of these accidental accretions, to give us back to ourselves, is the use, in part, of that sleep which rounds each day, and of that other sleep— brief, but how deep!—which rounds each human life.

Accordingly, he who sleeps well need not die so soon,—even as in the order of Nature he will not. He has that other and rarer half of a good memory, namely, a good forgetting. For none remembers so ill as he that remembers all. "A great German scholar affirmed that he knew not what it was to forget." Better have been born an idiot! An unwashed memory,—faugh! To us moderns and Americans, therefore, who need above all things to forget well,—our one imperative want being a simplification of experience,—to us, more than to all other men, is requisite, in large measure of benefit, the winnowing-fan of sleep, sleep with its choices and exclusions, if we would not need the offices of death too soon.

But a function of yet greater depth and moment remains to be indicated. Sleep enables the soul not only to shed away that which is foreign, but to adopt and assimilate whatever is properly its own. Dr. Edward Johnson, a man of considerable penetration, though not, perhaps, of a balanced judgment, has a dictum to the effect that the formation of blood goes on during our waking hours, but the composition of tissue during those of sleep. I know not upon what grounds of evidence this statement is made; but one persuades himself that it must be approximately true of the body, since it is undoubtedly so of the soul. Under the eye of the sun the fluid elements of character are supplied; but the final edification takes place beneath the stars. Awake, we think, feel, act; sleeping, we *become*. Day feeds our consciousness; night, out of those stores which action has accumulated, nourishes the vital unconsciousness, the pure unit of the man. During sleep, the valid and serviceable experience of the day is drawn inward, wrought upon by spiritual catalysis, transmuted into conviction, sentiment, character, life, and made part of that which is to attract and assimilate all subsequent experience. Who, accordingly, has not awaked to find some problem already solved with which he had vainly grappled on the preceding day? It is not merely that in the morning our invigorated powers work more efficiently, and enable us to reach this solution immediately *after* awaking. Often, indeed, this occurs; but there are also numerous instances —and such alone are in point—wherein the work is complete *before* one's awakening: not unfrequently it is by the energy itself of the new perception that the soft bonds of slumber are first broken; the soul hails its new dawn with so lusty a cheer, that its clarion reaches even to the ear of the body, and we are unconsciously murmuring the echoes of that joyous salute while yet the iris-hued fragments of our dreams linger about us. The poet in the morning, if true divine slumber have been vouchsafed him, finds his mind enriched with sweeter imaginations, the thinker with profounder principles and wider categories: neither begins the new day where he left the old, but each during his rest has silently, wondrously, advanced to fresh positions, commanding the world now from nobler summits, and beholding around him an horizon beyond that over which yesterday's sun rose and set. Milton gives us testimony very much in point:—

> "My celestial patroness, who deigns
> Her nightly visitation unimplored,
> And dictates to me slumb'ring."

Thus, in one important sense, is day the servant of night, action the minister of rest. I fancy, accordingly, that Marcus Antoninus may give Heraclitus credit for less than his full meaning in saying that "men asleep are then also laboring"; for he understands him to signify only that through such the universe is still accomplishing its ends. Perhaps he meant to indicate what has been here affirmed,—that in sleep one's personal destiny is still ripening, his true life proceeding.

But if, as the instance which has been under consideration suggests, these two principles are of equal dignity, it will follow that the ability to rest profoundly is of no less estimation than the ability to work powerfully. Indeed, is it not often the condition upon which great and sustained power of action depends? The medal must have two sides. "Danton," says Carlyle, "was a great nature that could rest." Were not the force and terror of his performance the obverse fact? I do not now mean, however true it would be, to say that without rest physical resources would fail, and action be enfeebled in consequence; I mean that the soul which wants the attitude of repose wants the condition of power. There is a petulant and meddlesome industry which proceeds from spiritual debility, and causes more; it is like the sleeplessness and tossing of exhausted nervous patients, which arises from weakness, and aggravates its occasion. As few things are equally wearisome, so few are equally wasteful, with a perpetual indistinct sputter of action, whereby nothing is done and nothing let alone. Half the world *breaks* out with action; its performance is cutaneous, of the nature of tetter. Hence is it that in the world, with such a noise of building, so few edifices are reared.

We require it as a pledge of the sanity of our condition, and consequent wholesomeness of our action, that we *can* withhold our hand, and leave the world in that of its Maker. No man is quite necessary to Omnipotence; grass grew before we were born, and doubtless will continue to grow when we are dead. If we act, let it be because our soul has somewhat to bring forth, and not because our fingers itch. We have in these days been emphatically instructed that all speech not rooted in silence, rooted, that is, in pure, vital, silent Nature, is poor and unworthy; but we should be aware that action equally requires this solemn and celestial perspective, this issue out of the never-trodden, noiseless realms of the soul. Only that which comes from a divine depth can attain to a divine height.

There is a courage of withholding and forbearing greater than any other courage; and before this Fate itself succumbs. Wellington won the Battle of Waterloo by heroically standing still; and every hour of that adventurous waiting was heaping up significance for the moment when at length he should cry, "Up, Guards, and at them!" What Cecil said of Raleigh, "He can toil terribly," has been styled "an electric touch"; but the "masterly inactivity" of Sir James Mackintosh, happily appropriated by Mr. Calhoun, carries an equal appeal to intuitive sense, and has already become proverbial. He is no sufficient hero who in the delays of Destiny, when his way is hedged up and his hope deferred, cannot reserve his strength and bide his time. The power of acting greatly includes that of greatly abstaining from action. The leader of an epoch in affairs should therefore be some Alfred, Bruce, Gustavus Vasa, Cromwell, Washington, Garibaldi, who can wait while the iron of opportunity heats at the forge of time; and then, in the moment of its white glow, can so smite as to shape it forever to the uses of mankind.

One should be able not only to wait, but to wait strenuously, sternly, immovably, rooted in his repose like a mountain oak in the soil; for it may easily happen that the necessity of refraining shall be most imperative precisely when the external pressure toward action is most vehement. Amid the violent urgency of events, therefore, one should learn the art of the mariner, who, in time of storm lies to, with sails mostly furled, until milder gales permit him again to spread sail and stretch away. With us, as with him, even a fair wind may blow so fiercely that one cannot safely run before it. There are movements with whose direction we sympathize, which are yet so ungoverned that we lose our freedom and the use of our reason in committing ourselves to them. So the seaman who runs too long before the increasing gale has thereafter no election; go on he must, for there is death in pausing, though it be also death to proceed. Learn, therefore, to wait. Is there not many a one who never arrives at fruit, for no better reason than that he persists in plucking his own blossoms?

Learn to wait. Take time, with the smith, to raise your arm, if you would deliver a telling blow.

Does it seem wasteful, this waiting? Let us, then, remind ourselves that excess and precipitation are more than wasteful,—they are directly destructive. The fire that blazes beyond bounds not warms the house, but burns it down, and only helps infinitesimally to warm the wide out-of-doors. Any live snail will outtravel a wrecked locomotive, and besides will leave no trail of slaughter on its track. Though despatch be the soul of business, yet he who outruns his own feet comes to the ground, and makes no despatch—unless it be of himself. Hurry is the spouse of Flurry, and the father of Confusion. Extremes meet, and overaction steadfastly returns to the effect of non-action,—bringing, however, the seven devils of disaster in its company. The ocean storm which heaps the waves so high may, by a sufficient increase, blow them down again; and in no calm is the sea so level as in the extremest hurricane.

Persistent excess of outward performance works mischief in one of two directions,—either upon the body or on the soul. If one will not accommodate himself to this unreasonable quantity by abatement of quality,—if he be resolute to put love, faith, and imagination into his labor, and to be alive to the very top of his brain,—then the body enters a protest, and dyspepsia, palsy, phthisis, insanity, or somewhat of the kind, ensues. Commonly, however, the tragedy is different from this, and deeper. Commonly, in these cases, action loses height as it gains lateral surface; the superior faculties starve, being robbed of sustenance by this avarice of performance, and consequently of supply, on the part of the lower,—they sit at second table, and eat of remaindercrumbs. The delicate and divine sprites, that should bear the behests of the soul to the will and to the houses of thought in the brain her intuitions, are crowded out from the streets of the cerebral cities by the mob and trample of messengers bound upon baser errands; and thus is the soul deprived of service, and the man of inspiration. The man becomes, accordingly, a great merchant who values a cent, but does not value a human sentiment; or a lawyer who can convince a jury that white is black, but cannot convince himself that white is white, God God, and the sustaining faiths of great souls more than moonshine. So if the apple-tree will make too much wood, it can bear no fruit; during summer it is full of haughty thrift, but the autumn, which brings grace to so many a dwarfed bush and low shrub, shows it naked and in shame.

How many mistake the crowing of the cock for the rising of the sun, albeit the cock often crows at midnight, or at the moon's rising, or only at the advent of a lantern and a tallow candle! And yet what a bloated, gluttonous devourer of hopes and labors is this same precipitation! All shores are strown with wrecks of barks that went too soon to sea. And if you launch even your well-build ship at half-tide, what will it do but strike bottom, and stick there? The perpetual tragedy of literary history, in especial, is this. What numbers of young men, gifted with great imitative quickness, who, having, by virtue of this, arrived at fine words and figures of speech, set off on their nimble rhetorical Pegasus, keep well out of the Muse's reach ever after! How many go conspicuously through life, snapping their smart percussion-caps upon empty barrels, because, forsooth, powder and ball do not come of themselves, and it takes time to load!

I know that there is a divine impatience, a rising of the waters of love and noble pain till they *must* overflow, with or without the hope of immediate apparent use, and no matter what swords and revenges impend. History records a few such defeats which are worth thousands of ordinary victories. Yet the rule is, that precipitation comes of levity. Eagerness is shallow. Haste is but half-earnest. If an apple is found to grow mellow and seemingly ripe much before its fellows on the same bough, you will probably discover, upon close inspection, that there is a worm in it.

To be sure, any time is too soon with those who dote upon Never. There are such as find Nature precipitate and God forward. They would have effect limp at untraversable distances behind cause; they would keep destiny carefully abed and feed it upon spoon-victual. They play duenna to the universe, and are perpetually on the *qui vive*, lest it escape, despite their care, into improprieties. The year is with them too fast by so much as it

removes itself from the old almanac. The reason is that *they* are
the old almanac. Or, more distinctly, they are at odds with universal law, and, knowing that to them it can come only as judgment and doom, they, not daring to denounce the law itself, fall
to the trick of denouncing its agents as visionaries, and its effects
as premature. The felon always finds the present an unseasonable
day on which to be hanged: the sheriff takes another view of the
matter.

But the error of these consists, not in realizing good purposes
too slowly and patiently, but in failing effectually to purpose
good at all. To those who truly *are* making it the business of their
lives to accomplish worthy aims, this counsel cannot come amiss,
—TAKE TIME. Take a year in which to thread a needle, rather
than go dabbing at the texture with the naked thread. And
observe, that there is an excellence and an efficacy of slowness, no
less than of quickness. The armadillo is equally secure of his prey
with the hawk or leopard; and Sir Charles Bell mentions a class
of thieves in India, who, having, through extreme patience and
command of nerve, acquired the power of motion imperceptibly
slow, are the most formidable of all peculators, and almost defy
precaution. And to leave these low instances, slowness produced
by profoundness of feeling and fineness of perception constitutes
that divine patience of genius without which genius does not
exist. Mind lingers where appetite hurries on; it is only the
Newtons who stay to meditate over the fall of an apple, too trivial
for the attention of the clown. It is by this noble slowness that
the highest minds faintly emulate that inconceivable deliberate-
ness and delicacy of gradation with which solar systems are built
and worlds habilitated.

Now haste and intemperance are the Satans that beset virtuous
Americans. And these mischiefs are furthered by those who
should guard others against them. The Rev. Dr. John Todd, in a
work not destitute of merit, entitled "The Student's Manual,"
urges those whom he addresses to study, while about it, with their
utmost might, crowding into an hour as much work as it can possibly be made to contain; so, he says, they will increase the power
of the brain. But this is advice not fit to be given to a horse, much

less to candidates for the graces of scholarly manhood. I read that race-horses, during the intervals between their public contests, are permitted only occasionally and rarely to be driven at their extreme speed, but are assiduously made to *walk* several hours each day. By this constancy of *moderate* exercise they preserve health and suppleness of limb, without exhaustion of strength. And it appears, that, were such an animal never to be taken from the stable but to be pushed to the top of his speed, he would be sure to make still greater speed toward ruin. Why not be as wise for men as for horses?

And here I desire to lay stress upon one point, which American students will do well to consider gravely,—*It is a* PURE, *not a strained and excited, attention which has signal prosperity.* Distractions, tempests, and head-winds in the brain, by-ends, the sidelong eyes of vanity, the overleaping eyes of ambition, the bleared eyes of conceit,—these are they which thwart study and bring it to nought. Nor these only, but all impatience, all violent eagerness, all passionate and perturbed feeling, fill the brain with thick and hot blood, suited to the service of desire, unfit for the uses of thought. Intellect can be served only by the finest properties of the blood; and if there be any indocility of soul, any impurity of purpose, any coldness or carelessness, any prurience or crude and intemperate heat, then base spirits are sent down from the seat of the soul to summon the sanguineous forces; and these gather a crew after their own kind. Purity of attention, then, is the magic that the scholar may use; and let him know, that, the purer it is, the more temperate, tranquil, reposeful. Truth is not to be run down with foxhounds; she is a divinity, and divinely must he draw nigh who will gain her presence. Go to, thou bluster-brain! Dost thou think to learn? Learn docility first, and the manners of the skies. And thou egotist, thinkest thou that these eyes of thine, smoky with the fires of diseased self-love, and thronged with deceiving wishes, shall perceive the essential and eternal? They shall see only silver and gold, houses and lands, reputes, supremacies, fames, and, as instrumental to these, the forms of logic and seemings of knowledge. If thou wilt discern the truth, desire IT, not its accidents and collateral effects. Rest in the pursuit of it, putting *simplicity of quest* in the place of either force or wile; and such quest cannot be unfruitful.

Let the student, then, shun an excited and spasmodic tension of brain, and he will gain more while expending less. It is not toil, it is morbid excitement, that kills; and morbid excitement in constant connection with high mental endeavor is, of all modes and associations of excitement, the most disastrous. Study as the grass grows, and your old age—and its laurels—shall be green.

Already, however, we are trenching upon that more intimate relationship of the great opposites under consideration which has been designated Rest *in* Motion. More intimate relationship, I say,—at any rate, more subtile, recondite, difficult of apprehension and exposition, and perhaps, by reason of this, more central and suggestive. An example of this in its physical aspect may be seen in the revolutions of the planets, and in all orbital or circular motion. For such, it will be at once perceived, is, in strictness of speech, *fixed and stationary* motion: it is, as Sir Isaac Newton demonstrated, an exact and equal obedience, in the same moment, to the law of fixity and the law of progression. Observe especially, that it is not, like merely retarded motion, a partial neutralization of each principle by the other, an imbecile Aristotelian compromise and half-way house between the two; but it is at once, and in virtue of the same fact, perfect Rest *and* perfect Motion. A revolving body is not hindered, but the same impulse which begot its movement causes this perpetually to return into itself.

Now the principles that are seen to govern the material universe are but a large-lettered display of those that rule in perfect humanity. Whatsoever makes distinguished order and admirableness in Nature makes the same in man; and never was there a fine deed that was not begot of the same impulse and ruled by the same laws to which solar systems are due. I desire, accordingly, here to take up and emphasize the statement previously made in a general way,—that the secret of perfection in all that appertains to man—in morals, manners, art, politics—must be sought in such a correspondence and reciprocation of these great opposites as the motions of the planets perfectly exemplify.

It must not, indeed, be overlooked or unacknowledged, that the planets do not move in exact circles, but diverge slightly into ellipses. The fact is by no means without significance, and that of an important kind. Pure circular motion is the type of perfection in the universe as a *whole,* but each part of the whole will inevitably express its partiality, will acknowledge its special character, and upon the frankness of this confession its comeliness will in no small degree depend; nevertheless, no sooner does the eccentricity, or individuality, become so great as to suggest disloyalty to the idea of the whole, than ugliness ensues. Thus, comets are portents, shaking the faith of nations, not supporting it, like the stars. So among men. Nature is at pains to secure divergence, magnetic variation, putting into every personality and every powerful action some element of irregularity and imperfection; and her reason for doing so is, that irregularity appertains to the state of growth, and is the avenue of access to higher planes and broader sympathies; still, as the planets, though not moving in perfect circles, yet come faithfully round to the same places, and accomplish *the ends* of circular motion, so in man, the divergence must be special, not total, no act being the mere arc of a circle, and yet *revolution* being maintained. And to the beauty of characters and deeds, it is requisite that they should never *seem* even to imperil fealty to the universal idea. Revolution perfectly exact expresses only necessity, not voluntary fidelity; but departure, *still deferential to the law of the whole,* in evincing freedom elevates its obedience into fealty and noble faithfulness: by this measure of eccentricity, *cen*tricity is not only emphasized, but immeasurably exalted.

But having made this full and willing concession to the element of individuality in persons and of special character in actions, we are at liberty to resume the general thesis,—that orbital rest of movement furnishes the type of perfect excellence, and suggests accordingly the proper targe of aspiration and culture.

In applying this law, we will take first a low instance, wherein the opposite principles stand apart, rather upon terms of outward covenant, or of mere mixture, than of mutual assimilation. *Man* is infinite; *men* are finite: the purest aspect of great laws never appears in collections and aggregations, yet the same laws rule here as in the soul, and such excellence as is possible issues from the same sources. As an instance, accordingly, of that ruder reciprocation which may obtain among multitudes, I name the Roman Legion.

It is said that the success of the armies of Rome is not fully accounted for, until one takes into account the constitution of this military body. It united, in an incomparable degree, the different advantages of fixity and fluency. Moderate in size, yet large enough to give the effect of mass, open in texture, yet compact in form, it afforded to every man room for individual prowess, while it left no man to his individual strength. Each soldier leaned and rested upon the Legion, a body of six thousand men; yet around each was a space in which his movements might be almost as free, rapid, and individual as though he had possessed the entire field to himself. The Macedonian Phalanx was a marvel of mass, but it was mass not penetrated with mobility; it could move, indeed could be said to have an existence, only as a whole; its decomposed parts were but *débris*. The Phalanx, therefore, was terrible, the constituent parts of it imbecile; and the Battle of Cynocephalæ finally demonstrated its inferiority, for the various possible exigencies of battle, to the conquering Legion. The brave rabble of Gauls and Goths, on the other hand, illustrated all that private valor, not reposing upon any vaster and more stable strength, has power to achieve; but these rushing torrents of prowess dashed themselves into vain spray upon the coördinated and reposing courage of Rome.

The same perpetual opposites must concur to produce the proper form and uses of the State,—though they here appear in a much more elevated form. Rest is here known as *Law*, motion as *Liberty*. In the true commonwealth, these, so far from being mutually destructive or antagonistic, incessantly beget and vivify each other; so that Law is the expression and guaranty of Freedom, while Freedom flows spontaneously into the forms of

Justice. Neither of these can exist, neither can be properly *conceived of*, apart from its correlative opposite. Nor will any condition of mere truce, or of mere mechanical equilibrium, suffice. Nothing suffices but a reciprocation so active and total that each is constantly resolving itself into the other.

The notion of Rousseau, which is countenanced by much of the phraseology, to say the least, of the present day, was, indeed, quite contrary to this. He assumed freedom to exist only where law is not, that is, in the savage state, and to be surrendered, piece for piece, with every acknowledgment of social obligation. Seldom was ever so plausible a doctrine equally false. Law is properly *the public definition of freedom and the affirmation of its sacredness and inviolability as so defined;* and only in the presence of it, either express or implicit, does man become free. Duty and privilege are one and the same, however men may set up a false antagonism between them; and accordingly social obligation can subtract nothing from the privilege and prerogative of liberty. Consequently, the freedom which is defined as the negation of social duty and obligation is not true regal freedom, but is that worst and basest of all tyrannies, the tyranny of pure egotism, masked in the semblance of its divine contrary. That, be it observed, is the freest society, in which the noblest and most delicate human powers find room and secure respect,—wherein the loftiest and costliest spiritualities are most invited abroad by sympathetic attraction. Now among savages little obtains appreciation, save physical force and its immediate allies: the divine fledglings of the human soul, instead of being sweetly drawn and tempted forth, are savagely menaced, rudely repelled; whatsoever is finest in the man, together with the entire nature of woman, lies, in that low temperature, enchained and repressed, like seeds in a frozen soil. The harsh, perpetual contest with want and lawless rivalry, to which all uncivilized nations are doomed, permits only a few low powers, and those much the same in all,—lichens, mosses, rude grasses, and other coarse cryptogamous growths,— to develop themselves; since these alone can endure the severities of season and treatment to which all that would clothe the fields of the soul must remain exposed. Meanwhile the utmost of that wicked and calamitous suppression of faculty, which constitutes the essence and makes the tragedy of human slavery, is equally effected by the inevitable isolation and wasteful trampling and consequent barrenness of savage life. Liberty without law is not liberty; and the converse may be asserted with like confidence.

Where, then, the fixed term, State, or Law, and the progressive term, Person, or Freewill, are in relations of reciprocal support and mutual reproduction, there alone is freedom, there alone public order. We were able to command this truth from the height of our general proposition, and closer inspection shows those anticipations to have been correct.

But man is greater than men; and for the finest aspect of high laws, we must look to individual souls, not to masses.

What is the secret of noble manners? Orbital action, always returning into and compensating itself. The gentleman, in offering his respect to others, offers an equal, or rather the same, respect to himself; and his courtesies may flow without stint or jealous reckoning, because they feed their source, being not an expenditure, but a circulation. Submitting to the inward law of honor and the free sense of what befits a man,—to a law perpetually made and spontaneously executed in his own bosom, the instant flowering of his own soul,—he commands his own obedience, and he obeys his own commanding. Though throned above all nations, a king of kings, yet the faithful humble vassal of his own heart; though he serve, yet regal, doing imperial service; he escapes outward constraint by inward anticipation; and all that could be rightly named as his duty to others, he has, ere demand, already discovered, and engaged in, as part of his duty to himself. Now it is the expression of royal freedom in loyal service, of sovereignty in obedience, courage in concession, and strength in forbearance, which makes manners noble. Low may he bow, not with loss, but with access of dignity, who bows with an elevated and ascending heart: there is nothing loftier, nothing less allied to abject behavior, than this grand lowliness. The worm, because it is low, cannot be lowly; but man, uplifted in token of supremacy, may kneel in adoration, bend in courtesy, and stoop in condescension. Only a great pride, that is, a great and reverential repose in one's own being, renders possible a noble humility, which is a great and reverential acknowledgment of the being of others; this humility in turn sustains a high self-reverence; this again resolves itself into a more majestic humility; and so run, in ever enhancing wave, the great circles of inward honor and outward grace. And without this self-sustaining return of the action into itself, each quality feeding itself from its correlative opposite, there can be no high behavior. This is the reason why qualities loftiest in kind and largest in measure are vulgarly mistaken, not for their friendly opposites, but for their mere contraries,—why a very profound sensibility, a sensibility, too, peculiarly of the spirit, not of nerve only, is sure to be named coldness, as Mr. Ruskin recently remarks,—why vast wealth of good pride, in its often meek acceptance of wrong, in its quiet ignoring of insult, in its silent superiority to provocation, passes with the superficial and petulant for poverty of pride and mere mean-spiritedness,—why a courage which is not partial, but *total*, coexisting, as it always does, with a noble peacefulness, with a noble inaptness for frivolous hazards, and a noble slowness to take offence, is, in its delays and forbearances, thought by the half-courageous to be no better than cowardice;—it is, as we have said, because great qualities revolve and repose in orbits of reciprocation with their opposites, which opposites are by coarse and ungentle eyes misdeemed to be contraries. Feeling transcendently deep and powerful is unimpassioned and far lower-voiced than indifference and unfeelingness, being wont to express itself, not by eloquent ebullition, but by extreme understatement, or even by total silence. Sir Walter Raleigh, when at length he found himself betrayed to death—and how basely betrayed!—by Sir Lewis Stukely, only said, "Sir Lewis, these actions will not turn to your credit." The New Testament tells us of a betrayal yet more quietly received. These are instances of noble manners.

What actions are absolutely moral is determined by application of the same law,—those only which repose wholly in themselves, being to themselves at once motive and reward. "Miserable is he," says the "Bhagavad Gita," "whose motive to action lies, not in the action itself, but in its reward." Duty purchased with covenant of special delights is not duty, but is the most pointed possible denial of it. The just man looks not beyond justice; the merciful reposes in acts of mercy; and he who would be bribed to equity and goodness is not only bad, but shameless. But of this no further words.

Rest is sacred, celestial, and the appreciation of it and longing for it are mingled with the religious sentiment of all nations. I cannot remember the time when there was not to me a certain ineffable suggestion in the apostolic words, "There remaineth, therefore, a rest for the people of God." But the repose of the godlike must, as that of God himself, be *infinitely* removed from mere sluggish inactivity; since the conception of action is the conception of existence itself,—that is, of Being in the act of self-manifestation. Celestial rest is found in action so universal, so purely identical with the great circulations of Nature, that, like the circulation of the blood and the act of breathing, it is not a subtraction from vital resource, but is, on the contrary, part of the very fact of life and all its felicities. This does not exclude rhythmic or recreative rest; but the need of such rest detracts nothing from pleasure or perfection. In heaven also, if such figure of speech be allowable, may be that toil which shall render grateful the cessation from toil, and give sweetness to sleep; but right weariness has its own peculiar delight, no less than right exercise; and as the glories of sunset equal those of dawn, so with equal, though diverse pleasure, should noble and temperate labor take off its sandals for evening repose, and put them on to go forth "beneath the opening eyelids of the morn." Yet, allowing a place for this rhythm in the detail and close inspection even of heavenly life, it still holds true on the broad scale, that pure beauty and beatitude are found there only where life and character sweep in orbits of that complete expression which is at once divine labor and divine repose.

Observe, now, that this rest-motion, as being without waste or loss, is a *manifested immortality,* since that which wastes not ends not; and therefore it puts into every motion the very character and suggestion of immortal life. Yea, one deed rightly done, and

the doer is in heaven,—is of the company of immortals. One deed
so done that in it is *no* mortality; and in that deed the meaning
of man's history,—the meaning, indeed, and the glory, of existence itself—are declared. Easy, therefore, it is to see how any
action may be invested with universal significance and the utmost
conceivable charm. The smaller the realm and the humbler the
act into which this amplitude and universality of spirit are carried, the more are they emphasized and set off; so that, without
opportunity of unusual occasion, or singular opulence of natural
power, a man's life may possess all that majesty which the imagination pictures in archangels and in gods. Indeed, it is but simple
statement of fact to say, that he who rests *utterly* in his action
shall belittle not only whatsoever history has recorded, but all
which that poet of poets, Mankind, has ever dreamed or fabled
of grace and greatness. He shall not peer about with curiosity to
spy approbation, or with zeal to defy censure; he shall not know
if there be a spectator in the world; his most public deed shall be
done in a divine privacy, on which no eye intrudes,—his most
private in the boundless publicities of Nature; his deed, when
done, falls away from him, like autumn apples from their boughs,
no longer his, but the world's and destiny's; neither the captive
of yesterday nor the propitiator of to-morrow, he abides simply,
majestically, like a god, in being and doing. Meanwhile, blame
and praise whirl but as unrecognized cloudlets of gloom or glitter
beneath his feet, enveloping and often blinding those who utter
them, but to him never attaining.

It is not easy at present to suggest the real measure and significance of such manhood, because this age has debased its imagination, by the double trick, first, of confounding man with his
body, and next, of considering the body, not as a symbol of truth,
but only as an agent in the domain of matter,—comparing its size
with the sum total of physical space, and its muscular power with
the sum total of physical forces. Yet

> "What know we greater than the soul?"

A man is no outlying province, nor does any province lie beyond
him. East, West, North, South, and height and depth are con-

tained in his bosom, the poles of his being reaching more widely, his zenith and nadir being more sublime and more profound. We are cheated by nearness and intimacy. Let us look at man with a telescope, and we shall find no star or constellation of sweep so grand, no nebulæ or star-dust so provoking and suggestive to fancy. In truth, there are no words to say how either large or small, how significant or insignificant, men may be. Though solar and stellar systems amaze by their grandeur of scale, yet is true manhood the maximum of Nature; though microscopic and sub-microscopic protophyta amaze by their inconceivable littleness, yet is mock manhood Nature's minimum. The latter is the only negative quantity known to Nature; the former the only revelation of her entire heart.

In concluding, need I say that only the pure can repose in his action,—only he obtain deliverance by his deed, and after deliverance from it? The egotism, the baseness, the partialities that are in our performance are hooks and barbs by which it wounds and wearies us in the passage, and clings to us being past. Law governs all; no favor is shown; the event is as it must be; only he who has no blinding partiality toward himself, who is whole and one with the whole, he who *is* Nature and Law and divine Necessity, can be blest with that blessedness which Nature is able to give only by her presence. There is a labor and a rest that are the same, one fact, one felicity; in this are power, beauty, immortality; by existence as a whole it is always perfectly exemplified; to man, as the eye of existence, it is also possible; but it is possible to him only as he is purely man,—only as he abandons himself to the divine principles of his life: in other words, this Sabbath remaineth in very deed to no other than the people of God.

INDIVIDUALITY

━━

At a certain depth, as has already been intimated in our literature, all bosoms communicate, all hearts are one. Hector and Ajax, in Homer's great picture, stand face to face, each with advanced foot, with levelled spear, and turgid sinew, eager to kill, while on either side ten thousand slaughterous wishes poise themselves in hot breasts, waiting to fly with the flying weapons; yet, though the combatants seem to surrender themselves wholly to this action, there is in each a profound element that is no party to these hostilities. It is the pure nature of man. Ajax is not all Greek, nor is Hector wholly Trojan: both are also men; and to the extent of their mutual participation in this pure and perpetual element of Manhood, they are more than friends, more than relatives,—they are of identical spirit. For there is an imperishable nature of Man, ever and everywhere the same, of which each particular man is a testimony and representation. As the solid earth underruns the "dissociating sea"—*Oceano dissociabili*—and joins in one all sundered lands, so does this nature dip beneath the dividing parts of our being, and make of all men one simple and inseparable humanity. In love, in friendship, in true conversation, in all happiness of communion between men, it is this unchangeable substratum or substance of man's being that is efficient and supreme: out of divers bosoms, Same calls, and replies to Same with a great joy of self-recognition. It is only in

Atlantic Monthly, April, 1862.

108

virtue of this nature that men understand, appreciate, admire, trust each other,—that books of the earliest times remain true in the latest,—that society is possible; and he in whom the virtue of it dwells divinely is admitted to the secret confidence of all bosoms, lives in all times, and converses with each soul and age in its own vernacular. Socrates looked beyond the gates of death for happy communion with Homer and all the great; but already we interchange words with these, whenever we are so sweetly prospered as to become, in some good degree, identical with the absolute nature of man.

Not only, moreover, is this immortal substance of man's being common and social, but it is so great and venerable that no one can match it with an equal report. All the epithets by which we would extol it are disgraced by it, as the most brilliant artificial lights become blackness when placed between the eye and the noonday sun. It is older, it is earlier in existence than the earliest star that shone in heaven; and it will outlive the fixed stars that now in heaven seem fixed forever. There is nothing in the created universe of which it was not the prophecy in its primal conception; there is nothing of which it is not the interpretation and ultimatum in its final form. The laws which rule the world as forces are, in it, thoughts and liberties. All the grand imaginations of men, all the glorified shapes, the Olympian gods, cherubic and seraphic forms, are but symbols and adumbrations of what it contains. As the sun, having set, still leaves its golden impress on the clouds, so does the absolute nature of man throw up and paint, as it were, on the sky testimonies of its power, remaining itself unseen. Only, therefore, is one a poet, as he can cause particular traits and events, without violation of their special character, or concealment of their peculiar interest, to bear the deep, sweet, and infinite suggestion of this. All princeliness and imperial worth, all that is regal, beautiful, pure in men, comes from this nature; and the words by which we express reverence, admiration, love, borrow from it their entire force: since reverence, admiration, love, and all other grand sentiments, are but modes or forms of *noble unification* between men, and are therefore shown to spring from that spiritual unity of which persons are exponents; while, on the other hand, all evil epithets suggest division and separation. Of this nature all titles of honor, all symbols that command homage and obedience on earth, are pensioners. How could the claims of kings survive successions of Stuarts and Georges, but for a royalty in each peasant's bosom that pleads for its poor image on the throne?

In the high sense, no man is great save he that is a large continent of this absolute humanity. The common nature of man it is; yet those are ever, and in the happiest sense, uncommon men, in whom it is liberally present.

But every man, besides the nature which constitutes him man, has, so to speak, another nature, which constitutes him a particular individual. He is not only like all others of his kind, but, at the same time, unlike all others. By physical and mental feature he is distinguished, insulated; he is endowed with a quality so purely in contrast with the common nature of man, that in virtue of it he can be singled out from hundreds of millions, from all the myriads of his race. So far, now, as one is representative of absolute humanity, he is a Person; so far as, by an element peculiar to himself, he is contrasted with absolute humanity, he is an Individual. And having duly chanted our *Credo* concerning man's pure and public nature, let us now inquire respecting this dividing element of Individuality—which, with all the force it has, strives to cut off communication, to destroy unity, and to make of humanity a chaos or dust of biped atoms.

Not for a moment must we make this surface nature of equal estimation with the other. It is secondary, *very* secondary, to the pure substance of man. The Person first in order of importance; the Individual next,—

> "Proximus huic, longo sed proximus intervallo,"—

"next with an exceeding wide remove." Take from Epaminondas or Luther all that makes him man, and the rest will not be worth selling to the Jews. Individuality is an accompaniment, an accessory, a red line on the map, a fence about the field, a copyright on the book. It is like the particular flavors of fruits,—of no account but in relation to their saccharine, acid, and other staple elements. It must therefore keep its place, or become an impertinence. If it grow forward, officious, and begin to push in between the pure nature and its divine ends, at once it is a meddling Peter, for whom there is no due greeting but "Get thee behind me, Satan." If the fruit have a special flavor of such ambitious pungency that the sweets and acids cannot appear through it, be sure that to come at this fruit no young Wilhelm Meister will purloin keys. If one be so much an Individual that he wellnigh ceases to be a Man, we shall not admire him. It is the same in mental as in physical feature. Let there, by all means, be slight divergence from the common type; but by all means let it be no more than a slight divergence. Too much is monstrous: even a very slight excess is what we call *ugliness*. Gladly I perceive in my neighbor's face, voice, gait, manner, a certain charm of peculiarity; but if in any the peculiarity be so great as to suggest a doubt whether he be not some other creature than man, may he not be neighbor of mine!

A little of this surface nature suffices; yet that little cannot be spared. Its first office is to guard frontiers. We must not lie quite open to the inspection or invasion of others: yet, were there no medium of unlikeness interposed between one and another, privacy would be impossible, and one's own bosom would not be sacred to himself. But Nature has secured us against these profanations; and as we have locks to our doors, curtains to our windows, and, upon occasion, a passport system on our borders, so has she cast around each spirit this veil to guard it from intruding eyes, this barrier to keep away the feet of strangers. Homer represents the divinities as coming invisibly to admonish their favored heroes; but Nature was beforehand with the poet, and every one of us is, in like manner, a celestial nature walking concealed. Who sees *you*, when you walk the street? Who would walk the street, did he not feel himself fortressed in a privacy that no foreign eyes can enter? But for this, no cities would be built. Society, therefore, would be impossible, save for this element, which seems to hinder society. Each of us, wrapt in his opaque individuality, like Apollo or Athene in a blue mist, remains hidden, if he will; and therefore do men dare to come together.

But this superficial element, while securing privacy to the pure nature, also aids it to expression. It emphasizes the outlines of Personality by gentle contrast. It is like the shadow in the landscape, without which all the sunbeams of heaven could not reveal with precision a single object. Assured lovers resort to happy banter and light oppositions, to give themselves a sweeter sense of unity of heart. The child, with a cunning which only Nature has taught, will sometimes put a little honey of refusal into its kisses before giving them; the maiden adds to her virgin blooms the further attraction of virgin coyness and reserve; the civilizing dinner-table would lose all its dignity in losing its delays; and so everywhere, delicate denial, withholding reserve have an inverse force, and add a charm of emphasis to gift, assent, attraction, and sympathy. How is the word Immortality emphasized to our hearts by the perpetual spectacle of death! The joy and suggestion of it could, indeed, never visit us, had not this momentary loud denial been uttered in our ears. Such, therefore, as have learned to interpret these oppositions in Nature, hear in the jarring note of Death only a jubilant proclamation of life eternal; while all are thus taught the longing for immortality, though only by their fear of the contrary. And so is the pure universal nature of man affirmed by these provocations of contrast and insulation on the surface. We feel the personality far more, and far more sweetly, for its being thus divided from our own. From behind this veil the pure nature comes to us with a kind of surprise as out of another heaven. The joy of truth and delight of beauty are born anew for us from each pair of chanting lips and beholding eyes; and each new soul that comes promises another gift of the universe. Whoever, in any time or under any sky, sees the worth and wonder of existence, sees it for me; whatever language he speak, whatever star he inhabit, we shall one day meet, and through the confession of his heart all my ancient possessions will become a new gain; he shall make for me a natal day of creation, showing the producing breath, as it goes forth from the lips of God, and spreads into the blue purity of sky, or rounds into the luminance of suns; the hills and their pines, the vales and their blooms, and heroic men and beauteous women, all that I have loved or reverenced, shall come again, appearing and trooping out of skies never visible before. Because of these dividing lines between souls, each new soul is to all the others a possible factor of heaven.

Such uses does individuality subserve. Yet it is capable of these ministries only as it does indeed *minister*. All its uses are lost with the loss of its humility and subordinance. It is the porter at the gate, furthering the access of lawful, and forbidding the intrusion of unlawful visitors to the mansion; who becomes worse than useless, if in surly excess of zeal he bar the gate against all, or if in the excess of self-importance he receive for himself what is meant for his master, and turn visitors aside into the porter's lodge. Beautiful is virgin reserve, and true it is that delicate half-denial reinforces attraction; yet the maiden who carries only *No* upon her tongue, and only refusal in her ways, shall never wake before dawn on the day of espousal, nor blush beneath her bridal veil, like Morning behind her clouds. This surface element, we must remember, is not income and resource, but an item of needful, and, so far as needful, graceful and economical expenditure. Excess of it is wasteful, by causing Life to pay for that which he does not need, by increase of social fiction, and by obstruction of social flow with the fructifications which this brings, not to be spared by any mortal. Nay, by extreme excess, it may so cut off and sequester a man, that no word or aspect of another soul can reach him; he shall see in mankind only himself, he shall hear in the voices of others only his own echoes. Many and many a man is there, so housed in his individuality, that it goes, like an impenetrable wall, over eye and ear; and even in the tramp of the centuries he can find hint of nothing save the sound of his own feet. It is a frequent tragedy,—but profound as frequent.

One great task, indeed *the* great task of good-breeding is, accordingly, to induce in this element a delicacy, a translucency, which, without robbing any action or sentiment of the hue it imparts, shall still allow the pure human quality perfectly and perpetually to shine through. The world has always been charmed with fine manners; and why should it not? For what are fine manners but this: to carry your soul on your lip, in your eye, in the palm of your hand, and yet to stand not naked, but clothed upon by your individual quality,—visible, yet inscrutable,—given to the hearts of others, yet contained in your own bosom,—nobly and humanly open, yet duly reticent and secured from invasion? *Polished* manners often disappoint us; *good* manners never. The former may be taken on by indigent souls: the latter imply a noble and opulent nature. And wait you not for death, according to the counsel of Solon, to be named happy, if you are permitted fellowship with a man of rich mind, whose individual savor you always finely perceive, and never more than finely,—who yields you the perpetual sense of community, and never of confusion, with your own spirit. The happiness is all the greater, if the fellowship be accorded by a mind eminently superior to one's own; for he, while yet more removed, comes yet nearer, seeming to be that which our own soul may become in some future life, and so yielding us the sense of our own being more deeply and powerfully than it is given by the consciousness in our own bosom. And going forward to the supreme point of this felicity, we may note that the worshipper, in the ecstasy of his adoration, feels the Highest to be also Nearest,—more remote than the borders of space and fringes of heaven,—more intimate with his own being than the air he breathes or the thought he thinks; and of his double sense is the rapture of his adoration, and the joy indeed of every angel, born.

Divineness appertains to the absolute nature of man; piquancy and charm to that which serves and modifies this. Infinitude and immortality are of the one; the strictest finiteness belongs to the other. In the first you can never be too deep and rich; in the second never too delicate and measured. Yet you will easily find a man in whom the latter so abounds as not only to shut him out from others, but to absorb all the vital resource generated in his own bosom, leaving to the pure personality nothing. The finite nature fares sumptuously every day; the other is a heavenly Lazarus sitting at the gate.

Of such individuals there are many classes; and the majority of eccentric men constitute one class. If a man have very peculiar ways, we readily attribute to him a certain depth and force, and think that the polished citizen wants character in comparison. Probably it is not so. Singularity may be as shallow as the shallowest conformity. There are numbers of such from whom if you deduct the eccentricity, it is like subtracting red from vermilion or six from half a dozen. They are grimaces of humanity,— no more. In particular, I make occasion to say, that those oddities, whose chief characteristic it is to slink away from the habitations of men, and claim companionship with musk-rats, are, despite Mr. Thoreau's pleasant patronage of them, no whit more manly or profound than the average citizen, who loves streets and parlors, and does not endure estrangement from the Post-Office. Mice lurk in holes and corners; could the cat speak, she would say that they have a genius *only* for lurking in holes. Bees and ants are, to say the least, quite as witty as beetles, proverbially blind; yet they build insect cities, and are as invincibly social and city-loving as Socrates himself.

Aside, however, from special eccentricity, there are men, like the Earl of Essex, Bacon's *soi-disant* friend, who possess a certain emphatic and imposing individuality, which, while commonly assumed to indicate character and force, is really but the *succedaneum* for these. They are like oysters, with extreme stress of shell, and only a blind, soft, acephalous body within. These are commonly great men so long as little men will serve; and are something less than little ever after. As an instance of this, I should select the late chief magistrate of this nation. His whole ability lay in putting a most imposing countenance upon commonplaces. He made a mere *air* seem solid as rock. Owing to this possibility of presenting all force on the outside, and so creating a false impression of resource, all great social emergencies are followed by a speedy breaking down of men to whom was generally attributed an able spirit; while others of less outward *mark,* and for this reason hitherto unnoticed, come forward, and prove to be indeed the large vessels of manhood accorded to that generation.

Our tendency to assume individual mark as the measure of personality is flattered by many of the books we read. It is, of course, easier to depict character, when it is accompanied by some striking individual hue; and therefore in romances and novels this is conferred upon all the forcible characters, merely to favor the author's hand: as microscopists feed minute creatures with colored food to make their circulations visible. It is only the great master who can represent a powerful personality in the purest state, that is, with the maximum of character and the minimum of individual distinction; while small artists, with a feeble hold upon character, habitually resort to extreme quaintnesses and singularities of circumstance, in order to confer upon their weak portraitures some vigor of outline. It takes a Giotto to draw readily a nearly perfect O; but a nearly perfect triangle any one can draw. Shakspeare is able to delineate a Gentleman,—one, that is, who, while nobly and profoundly a man, is so delicately individualized, that the impression of him, however vigorous and commanding, cannot be harsh: Shakspeare is equal to this task, but even so very able a painter as Fielding is not. His Squire Western and Parson Adams are exquisite, his Allworthy is vapid: deny him strong pigments of individualism, and he is unable to portray strong character. Scott, among British novelists, is, perhaps, in this respect most Shakspearian, though the Colonel Esmond of Thackeray is not to be forgotten; but even Scott's Dandie Dinmonts, or gentlemen in the rough, sparkle better than his polished diamonds. Yet in this respect the Waverley Novels are singularly and admirably healthful, comparing to infinite advantage with the rank and file of novels, wherein the "characters" are but bundles of quaintnesses, and the action is impossible.

Written history has somewhat of the same infirmity with fictitious literature, though not always by the fault of the historian. Far too little can it tell us respecting those of whom we desire to know much; while, on the other hand, it is often extremely liberal of information concerning those of whom we desire to know nothing. The greatest of men approach a pure personality, a pure representation of man's imperishable nature; individual peculiarity they far less abound in; and what they do possess is held in transparent solution by their manhood, as a certain amount of vapor is always held by the air. The higher its temperature, the more moisture can the atmosphere thus absorb, exhibiting it not as cloud, but only as immortal azure of sky: and so the greater intensity there is of the pure quality of man, the more of individual peculiarity can it master and transform into a simple heavenliness of beauty, of which the world finds few words to say. Men, in general, have, perhaps, no more genius than novelists in general,—though it seems a hard speech to make,—and while profoundly *impressed* by any manifestation of the pure genius of man, can *observe* and *relate* only peculiarities and exceptional traits. Incongruities are noted; congruities are only felt. If a two-headed calf be born, the newspapers hasten to tell of it; but brave boys and beautiful girls by thousands grow to fulness of stature without mention. We know so little of Homer and Shakspeare partly because they were Homer and Shakspeare. Smaller men might afford more plentiful materials for biography, because their action and character would be more clouded with individualism. The biography of a supreme poet is the history of his kind. He transmits himself by pure vital impression. His remembrance is committed, not to any separable faculty, but to a memory identical with the total being of men. If you would learn his story, listen to the sprites that ride on crimson steeds along the arterial highways, singing of man's destiny as they go.

HINDRANCE

Much that is in itself undesirable occurs in obedience to a general law which is not only desirable, but of infinite necessity and benefit. It is not desirable that Tupper and Macaulay should be read by tens of thousands, and Wilkinson only by tens. It is not desirable that a narrow, selfish, envious Cecil, who could never forgive his noblest contemporaries for failing to be hunchbacks like himself, should steer England all his life as it were with supreme hand, and himself sail on the topmost tide of fortune; while the royal head of Raleigh goes to the block, and while Bacon, with his broad and bountiful nature,—Bacon, one of the two or three greatest and humanest statesmen ever born to England, and one of the friendliest men toward mankind ever born into the world,—dies in privacy and poverty, bequeathing his memory "to foreign nations and the next ages." But it is wholly desirable that he who would consecrate himself to excellence in art or life should sometimes be compelled to make it very clear to himself whether it be indeed excellence that he covets, or only plaudits and pounds sterling. So when we find our purest wishes perpetually hindered, not only in the world around us, but even in our own bosoms, many of the particular facts may indeed merit reproach, but the general fact merits, on the contrary, gratitude and gratulation. For were our best wishes not, nor ever, hindered, sure it is that the still better wishes of

Atlantic Monthly, May, 1862.

destiny in our behalf would be hindered yet worse. Sure it is, I say, that Hindrance, both outward and inward, comes to us not through any improvidence or defect of benignity in Nature, but in answer to our need, and as part of the best bounty which enriches our days. And to make this indubitably clear, let us hasten to meditate that simple and central law which governs this matter and at the same time many others.

And the law is, that every definite action is conditioned upon a definite resistance, and is impossible without it. We walk in virtue of the earth's resistance to the foot, and are unable to tread the elements of air and water only because they are too complaisant, and deny the foot that opposition which it requires. Precisely that, accordingly, which makes the difficulty of an action may at the same time make its possibility. Why is flight difficult? Because the weight of every creature draws it toward the earth. But without this downward proclivity, the wing of the bird would have no power upon the air. Why is it difficult for a solid body to make rapid progress in water? Because the water presses powerfully upon it, and at every inch of progress must be overcome and displaced. Yet the ship is able to float only in virtue of this same hindering pressure, and without it would not sail, but sink. The bird and the steamer, moreover,—the one with its wings and the other with its paddles,—apply themselves to this hindrance to progression as their only means of making progress; so that, were not their motion obstructed, it would be impossible.

The law governs not actions only, but all definite effects whatsoever. If the luminiferous ether did not resist the sun's influence, it could not be wrought into those undulations wherein light consists; if the air did not resist the vibrations of a resonant object, and strive to preserve its own form, the sound-waves could not be created and propagated: if the tympanum did not resist these waves, it would not transmit their suggestion to the brain; if any given object does not resist the sun's rays,—in other words, reflect them,—it will not be visible; neither can the eye mediate between any object and the brain save by a like opposing of rays on the part of the retina.

These instances might be multiplied *ad libitum,* since there is literally *no* exception to the law. Observe, however, what the law is, namely, that *some* resistance is indispensable,—by no means that this alone is so, or that all modes and kinds of resistance are of equal service. Resistance and Affinity concur for all right effects; but it is the former that, in some of its aspects, is much accused as a calamity to man and a contumely to the universe; and of this, therefore, we consider here.

Not all kinds of resistance are alike serviceable; yet that which is required may not always consist with pleasure, nor even with safety. Our most customary actions are rendered possible by forces and conditions that inflict weariness at times upon all, and cost the lives of many. Gravitation, forcing all men against the earth's surface with an energy measured by their weight avoirdupois, makes locomotion feasible; but by the same attraction it may draw one into the pit, over the precipice, to the bottom of the sea. What multitudes of lives does it yearly destroy! Why has it never occurred to some ingenious victim of a sluggish liver to represent Gravitation as a murderous monster revelling in blood? Surely there are woful considerations here that might be used with the happiest effect to enhance the sense of man's misery, and have been too much neglected!

Probably there are few children to whom the fancy has not occurred. How convenient, how fine were it to weigh nothing! We smile at the little wiseacres; we know better. How much better do we know? That ancient lament, that ever iterated accusation of the world because it opposes a certain hindrance to freedom, love, reason, and every excellence which the imagination of man can portray and his heart pursue,—what is it, in the final analysis, but a complaint that we cannot walk without weight, and that therefore climbing *is* climbing?

Instead, however, of turning aside to applications, let us push forward the central statement in the interest of applications to be made by every reader for himself,—since he says too much who does not leave much more unsaid. Observe, then, that objects which so utterly submit themselves to man as to become testimonies and publications of his inward conceptions serve even these most exacting and monarchical purposes only by opposition to them, and, to a certain extent, in the very measure of that opposition. The stone which the sculptor carves becomes a fit vehicle for his thought through its resistance to his chisel; it sustains the impress of his imagination solely through its unwillingness to receive the same. Not chalk, not any loose and friable material, does Phidias or Michel Angelo choose, but ivory, bronze, basalt, marble. It is quite the same whether we seek expression or uses. The steam must be damned before it will drive wheels; the steam compressed ere it will compel the piston. In fine, Potentiality combines with Hindrance to constitute active Power. Man, in order to obtain instrumentalities and uses, blends his will and intelligence with a force that vigorously seeks to pursue its own separate free course; and while this resists him, it becomes his servant.

But why not look at this fact in its largest light? For do we not here touch upon the probable reason why God must, as it were, be offset by World, Spirit by Matter, Soul by Body? The Maker must needs, if it be lawful so to speak, heap up in the balance against His own pure, eternal freedom these numberless globes of cold, inert matter. Matter is, indeed, movable by no fine persuasions: brutely faithful to its own law, it cares no more for Æschylus than for the tortoise that breaks his crown; the purpose of a cross for the sweetest saint it serves no less willingly than any other purpose,—stiffly holding out its arms there, about its own wooden business, neither more nor less, centred utterly upon itself. But is it not this stolid self-centration which makes it needful to Divinity? An infinite energy required a resisting or doggedly indifferent material, itself *quasi* infinite, to take the impression of its life, and render potentiality into power. So by the encountering of body with soul is the product, man, evolved. Philosophers and saints have perceived that the spiritual element of man is hampered and hindered by his physical part: have they also perceived that it is the very collision between these which strikes out the spark of thought and kindles the sense of law? As the tables of stone to the finger of Jehovah on Sinai, so is the firm marble of man's material nature to the recording soul. But even Plato, when he arrives at these provinces of thought, begins to limp a little, and to go upon Egyptian crutches. In the incomparable apologues of the "Phædrus" he represents our inward charioteer as driving toward the empyrean two steeds, of which the one is virtuously attracted toward heaven, while the other is viciously drawn to the earth; but he countenances the inference that the earthward proclivity of the latter is to be accounted pure misfortune. But to the universe there is neither fortune nor misfortune; there is only the reaper, Destiny, and his perpetual harvest. All that occurs on a universal scale lies in the line of a pure success. Nor can the universe attain any success by pushing past man and leaving him aside. That were like the prosperity of a father who should enrich himself by disinheriting his only son.

Principles necessary to all action must of course appear in moral action. The moral imagination, which pioneers and produces inward advancement, works under the same conditions with the imagination of the artist, and must needs have somewhat to work *upon*. Man is both sculptor and quarry,—and a great noise and dust of chiselling is there sometimes in his bosom. If, therefore, we find in him somewhat which does not immediately and actively sympathize with his moral nature, let us not fancy this element equally out of sympathy with his pure destiny. The impulsion and the resistance are alike included in the design of our being. Hunger—to illustrate—respects food, food only. It asks leave to be hunger neither of your conscience, your sense of personal dignity, nor indeed of your humanity in any form; but exists by its own permission, and pushes with brute directness toward its own ends. True, the soul may at last so far prevail as to make itself felt even in the stomach; and the true gentleman could as soon relish a lunch of porcupines' quills as a dinner basely obtained, though it were of nightingales' tongues. But this is sheer conquest on the part of the soul, not any properly gastric inspiration at all; and it is in furnishing opportunity for precisely such conquest that the lower nature becomes a stairway of ascent for the soul.

And now, if in the relations between every manly spirit and

the world around him we discover the same fact, are we not by this time prepared to contemplate it altogether with dry eyes? What if it be true, that in trade, in politics, in society, all tends to low levels? What if disadvantages are to be suffered by the grocer who will not sell adulterated food, by the politician who will not palter, by the diplomatist who is ashamed to lie? For this means only that no one can be honest otherwise than by a productive energy of honesty in his own bosom. In other words,—a man reaches the true welfare of a human soul only when his bosom is a generative centre and source of noble principles; and therefore, in pure, wise kindness to man, the world is so arranged that there shall be perpetual need of this access and reinforcement of principle. Society, the State, and every institution, grow lean the moment there is a falling off in this divine fruitfulness of man's heart, because only in virtue of bearing such fruit is man worthy of his name. Honor and honesty are constantly consumed *between* men, that they may be forever newly demanded *in* them.

We cannot too often remind ourselves that the aim of the universe is a personality. As the terrestrial globe through so many patient æons climbed toward the production of a human body, that by this all-comprehending, perfect symbol it might enter into final union with Spirit, so do the uses of the world still forever ascend toward man, and seek a continual realization of that ancient wish. When, therefore, Time shall come to his great audit with Eternity, persons alone will be passed to his credit. "So many wise and wealthy souls,"—that is what the sun and his household will have come to. The use of the world is not found in societies faultlessly mechanized; for societies are themselves but uses and means. They are the soil in which persons grow; and I no more undervalue them than the husbandman despises his fertile acres because it is not earth, but the wheat that grows from it, which comes to his table. Society is the culmination of all uses and delights; persons, of all results. And societies answer their ends when they afford two things: first, a need for energy of eye and heart, of noble human vigor; and secondly, a generous appreciation of high qualities, when these may appear. The latter is, indeed, indispensable; and whenever noble manhood ceases to be recognized in a nation, the days of that nation are numbered. But the need is also necessary. Society must be a consumer of virtue, if individual souls are to be producers of it. The law of demand and supply has its applications here also. New waters must forever flow from the fountain-heads of our true life, if the millwheel of the world is to continue turning; and this not because the supernal powers so greatly cared to get corn ground, but because the Highest would have rivers of His influence forever flowing, and would call them men. Therefore it is that satirists who paint in high colors the resistances, but have no perception of the law of conversion into opposites, which is the grand trick of Nature,—these pleasant gentlemen are themselves a part of the folly at which they mock.

As a man among men, so is a nation among nations. Very freely I acknowledge that any nation, by proposing to itself large and liberal aims, plucks itself innumerable envies and hatreds from without, and confers new power for mischief upon all blindness and savagery that exist within it. But what does this signify? Simply that no nation can be free longer than it nobly loves freedom; that none can be great in its national purposes when it has ceased to be so in the hearts of its citizens. Freedom must be perpetually won, or it must be lost; and this because the sagacious Manager of the world will not let us off from the disciplines that should make us men. The material of the artist is passive, and may be either awakened from its ancient rest or suffered to sleep on; but that marble from which the perfections of manhood and womanhood are wrought quits the quarry to meet us, and converts us to stone, if we do not rather transform that to life and beauty. Hostile, predatory, it rushes upon us; and we, cutting at it in brave self-defence, hew it above our hope into shapes of celestial and immortal comeliness. So that angels are born, as it were, from the noble fears of man,—from an heroic fear in man's heart that he shall fall away from the privilege of humanity, and falsify the divine vaticination of his soul.

Hence follows the fine result, that in life to hold your own is to make advance. Destiny comes to us, like the children in their play, saying, "Hold fast all I give you"; and while we nobly detain it, the penny changes between our palms to the wealth of cities and kingdoms. The barge of blessing, freighted for us by unspeakable hands, comes floating down from the head-waters of that stream whereon we also are afloat; and to meet it we have only to wait for it, not ourselves ebbing away, but loyally stemming the tide. It may be, as Mr. Carlyle alleges, that the Constitution of the United States is no supreme effort of genius; but events now passing are teaching us that every day of fidelity to the spirit of it lends it new preciousness; and that an adherence to it, not petty and literal, but at once large and indomitable, might almost make it a charter of new sanctities both of law and liberty for the human race.

MR. BUCKLE AS A THINKER

The recent death of Henry Thomas Buckle calls a new attention
to his published works. Pathetic it will seem to all that he should
be cut off in the midst of labors so large, so assiduous and adventurous; and there are few who will not feel inclined to make
up, as it were, to his memory for this untimely interruption of
his pursuits, by assigning the highest possible value to his actual
performance. Additional strength will be given to these disposi-
tions by the impressions of his personal character. This was, indeed, such as to conciliate the utmost good-will. If we except
occasional touches of self-complacency, which betray, perhaps, a
trifling foible, it may be said that everything is pleasing which
is known concerning him. His devotion, wellnigh heroic, to
scholarly aims; his quiet studiousness; his filial virtue; his genial
sociability, graced by, and gracing, the self-supporting habit of
his soul; his intrepidity of intellect, matched by a beautiful boldness and openness in speech; the absence, too, from works so
incisive, of a single trace of truculence: all this will now be remembered; and those are unamiable persons, in whom the remembrance does not breed a desire to believe him as great in
thought as he was brave, as prosperous in labor as he was
persevering.

But however it may be with others, certainly he who has under-
taken the duties of a scholar must not yield too readily to these

Atlantic Monthly, January, 1863.

amiable wishes. He, as a sworn soldier of Truth, stands sacredly
bound to be as free from favor as from fear, and to follow steadily
wherever the standards of his imperial mistress lead him on.
And so performing his lawful service, he may bear in mind that
at last the interests of Truth are those of every soul, be it of
them that we number with the dead, or that are still reckoned
among these that we greet as living. Let us not be petty in our
kindness. Over the fresh grave of a scholar let us rise to that high
and large friendliness which respects more the scope of every
man's nature than the limited measure of any man's performance, and sides bravely with the soul of the departed, even
though it be against his fame. Who would not choose this for
himself? Who would not whisper from his grave, "My personal
weaknesses let those spare who can; my work do not praise, but
judge; and never think in behalf of my mortal fame to lower
those stars that my spirit would look up to yet and forever"?

As a man and scholar, Mr. Buckle needs no forbearance; and
men must commend him, were it only in justice to themselves.
Such intellectual courage, such personal purity, such devotion
to ideal aims, such a clean separation of boldness from bitterness,—in thought, no blade more trenchant, in feeling, no heart
more human,—when these miss their honor and their praise,
then will men have forgotten how to estimate fine qualities.

Meanwhile, as a thinker, he must be judged according to the
laws of thought. Here we are to forget whether he be living or
dead, and whether his personal traits were delightful or disagreeable. Here there is but one question, and that is the question
of truth.

And as a thinker, I can say nothing less than that Mr. Buckle
signally failed. His fundamental conceptions, upon which reposes the whole edifice of his labor, are sciolistic assumptions
caught up in his youth from Auguste Comte and other one-eyed
seers of modern France; his generalization, multitudinous and
imposing, is often of the card-castle description, and tumbles at
the touch of an inquisitive finger; and his cobweb logic, spun
chiefly out of his wishes rather than his understanding, is indeed
facile and ingenious, but of a strength to hold only flies. Such,

at any rate, is the judgment passed upon him in the present paper; and if it is stated roundly, the critic can be held all the better to its justification, and the more freely condemned, should these charges not be sustained.

But while in the grand topography of thought and in the larger processes of reasoning the failure of Mr. Buckle, according to the judgment here given, is complete, it is freely admitted that as a writer and man of letters he has claims not only to respect, but even to admiration. His mental fertility is remarkable, his memory marvellous, his reading immense, his mind discursive and agile, his style pellucid as water and often vigorous, while his *subordinate* conceptions are always ingenious and frequently valuable. Besides this, he is a genuine enthusiast, and sees before him that El Dorado of the understanding where golden knowledge shall lie yellow on all the hills and yellow under every footfall,——where the very peasant shall have princely wealth, and no man shall need say to another, "Give me of thy wisdom." It is this same element of romantic expectation which stretches a broad and shining margin about the spacious page of Bacon; it is this which wreathes a new fascination around the royal brow of Raleigh; it is this, in part, which makes light the bulky and antiquated tones of Hakluyt; and the grace of it is that which we often miss in coming from ancient to modern literature. Better it is, too, than much erudition and many "proprieties" of thought; and one may note it as curious, that Mr. Buckle, seeking to disparage imagination, should have written a book whose most winning and enduring charm is the appeal to imagination it makes. Moreover, he is an enthusiast in behalf of just that which is distinctively modern: he is a white flame of precisely those heats which smoulder now in the duller breast of the world in general; he worships at all the pet shrines; he expresses the peculiar loves and hatreds of the time. Who is so devout a believer in free speech and free trade and the let-alone policy in government, and the coming of the Millennium by steam? Who prostrates himself with such unfeigned adoration before the great god, "State-of-Society," or so mutters, for a mystic *O'm,* the word "Law"? Then how delightful it is, when he traces the whole ill of the world to just those things which we now all agree to detest,—to theological persecution, bigotry, superstition, and infidelity to Isaac Newton! In fine, the recent lessons of that great schoolboy, the world, or those over which the said youth now is poring or idling or blubbering, Mr. Buckle has not only got by heart, not only recites them capitally, but believes with assurance that they are the sole lessons worth learning in any time; and all the inevitable partialities of the text-book, all the errors and *ad captandum* statements with which its truth is associated, he takes with such implicit faith, and believes in so confidently as part and parcel of our superiority to all other times, that the effect upon most of us cannot be otherwise than delectable.

Unhappily, the text-book in which he studied these fine lessons chanced to be the French edition, and, above all, the particular compilation of Auguste Comte,—Comte, the one-eyed Polyphemus of modern literature, enormous in stature and strength, but a devourer of the finer races in thought, feeding his maw upon the beautiful offspring of the highest intelligence, whom the Olympians love. Therefore it befell that our eager and credulous scholar unlearned quite as much as he learned, acquiring the wisdoms of our time in the crudest and most liberal commixture with its unwisdoms. And thus, though his house is laboriously put together, yet it is built upon the sand; and though his bark has much good timber, and is well modelled for speed, yet its keel is wholly rotten, so that whosoever puts to sea therein will sail far more swiftly to bottom than to port.

And precisely this, in lieu of all else, it is my present purpose to show: that the keel of his craft is unsound,—that his fundamental notions are fundamental falsities, such as no thinker can fall into without discredit to his powers of thought. Fortunately, he has begun by stating and arguing these; so that there can be no question either what they are, or by what considerations he is able to support them.

The foundation-timber of Mr. Buckle's work consists of three pieces, or propositions, two of which take the form of denial. First, he denies that there is in man anything of the nature of

Free-Will, and attributes the belief in it to vulgar and childish ignorance. Secondly, and in support of the primary negation, he denies that there is any oracle in man's bosom,—that his spirit has any knowledge of itself or of the relationships it sustains: in other words, denies the validity of Consciousness. Thirdly and lastly, he attempts to show that all actions of individuals originate not in themselves, but result from a law working in the general and indistinguishable *lump* of society,—from laws of like nature with that which preserves the balance of the sexes; so that no man has more to do with his own deed than the mother in determining whether her child shall be male or female. By the two former statements man is stripped of all the grander prerogatives and characteristics of personality; by the last he is placed as freight, whether dead or alive it were hard to say, in the hold of the self-steering ship, "Society." These propositions and the reasons, or unreasons, by which they are supported, we will examine in order.

1. *Free-Will*. The question of free-will has at sundry times and seasons, and by champions many and furious, been disputed, till the ground about it is all beaten into blinding dust, wherein no reasonable man can now desire to cloud his eyes and clog his lungs. It is, indeed, one of the cheerful signs of our times, that there is a growing relish for clear air and open skies, a growing indisposition to mingle in old and profitless controversies. It commonly happens in such controversies, as it undoubtedly has happened in the dispute about free-will, that both parties have been trying to pull up Life or Spirit by the roots, and make a show, *à la* Barnum, of all its secrets. The enterprise was zealously prosecuted, but would not prosper. In truth, there are strict and jealous limits to the degree in which man's mind can become an object to itself. By silent consciousness, by an action of reason and imagination sympathetic with pure inward life, man may *feel* far down into the sweet, awful depths and mysteries of his being; and the results of this inward intimation are given in the great poems, the great art and divine philosophy of all time, and in the commanding beliefs of mankind; but so soon as one begins to come to his own existence as an outsider and stranger,

and attempts to bear away its secret, so soon he begins to be balked.

Mr. Buckle, however, has assumed in a summary and authoritative way to settle this question of free-will; and, without entering into the dust and suffocation of the old interminable dispute, we may follow him far enough to see whether he has thrown any light upon the matter, or has only thrown light upon his own powers as a thinker.

His direct polemic against the doctrine of Free-Will consists simply of an attempt to identify it with the notion of Chance in physics. The notion of Chance, he says, is the same with that of Free-Will; the doctrine of Necessary Connection with the dogma of Predestination. This statement has certainly an imposing air. But consider it. To assert the identity of chance and free-will is but another way of saying that pure freedom is one and the same with absolute lawlessness,—that where freedom exists, law, order, reason do not. If this be a misconception, as it surely is a total and fatal misconception, of the nature of freedom, then does the statement of our author, with all that rests upon it, fall instantly and utterly to the ground.

It is a misconception. Freedom and lawlessness are not the same. To make this finally clear, let us at once give the argument the widest possible scope; since the largest way of looking at the matter, as indeed it often happens, will prove also the nearest and simplest. In the universe as a whole Will does certainly originate, since there is, undoubtedly, origination somewhere. Freely, too, it must arise, for there is nothing behind it to bring it under constraint: indeed, all origination is by its nature free. But our philosopher tells us that wherever there is a pure and free origination of will, there is lawlessness, caprice, chance. The universe, therefore, should be a scene, not of absolute order, but of absolute disorder; and since it is not such, we have nothing for it but to say that either the logic of the universe, or that of Mr. Buckle, is very much awry.

In the universe, Will freely originates, but forever in unison with divine Reason; and the result is at once pure necessity and pure freedom: for these, if both be, as we say, absolutely *pure,* are one and the same. A coercing necessity is impure, for it is at war with that to which it applies; only a necessity in sweetest affinity with that which it governs is of the purest degree; and this is, of course, identical with the highest and divinest freedom.

And here we approach the solution of our problem, so far as it can be solved. Freedom and free-will exist only in virtue of reason, only in connection with the rational soul. In a rough account of man, and leaving out of sight all that is not strictly relevant to the present point, we discriminate in him two natures. One of these comprises the whole body of organic desires and energies, with all that *kind* of intellect by which one perceives the relation of things to his selfish wishes. By this nature, man is a selfish and intellectual animal; a polyp with arms that go round the world; a sponge with eyes and energies and delights; a cunning *ego,* to whom all outside of himself is but for a prey. But aloft over this, and constituting the second nature, into whose kingdom one should be born as by a second birth, is the sovereign eye and soul of Reason, discerning Justice and Beauty and the Best, creating in man's bosom an ideal, redeeming him out of his littleness, bringing him into fellowship with Eternal Truth, and making him universal. Now between these two natures there is, for there must be, a mediating term, a power by which man *enacts* reason, and causes doing to accord with seeing. This is will, and it must, from its very nature, be free; for to say that it is a mere representative of the major force in desire is simply to say that it does not exist. A mediation without freedom in the mediator is something worse than the mediation of Holland between England and the United States in the dispute concerning the North-East Boundary.

So far, now, as the sovereign law and benefaction of the higher nature, through a perfect mediation of the will, descends upon the lower, so far man enters into free alliance with that which is sovereign in the universe, and is himself established in perfected freedom. The right action of free-will is, then, freedom in the making. But by this entrance into the great harmonies of the world, by this loyalty to the universal reason which alone makes one free, it must be evident that the order of the world is graced and supported rather than assailed.

But how if free-will fail of its highest function? Must not the order of the world then suffer? Not a whit. Universal Reason prevails, but in two diverse ways: she may either be felt as a mere Force or Fate, or she may be recognized and loved and obeyed as an Authority. Wherever the rational soul, her oracle, is given, there she proffers the privilege of knowing her only as a divine authority,—of free loyalty, of honorable citizenship in her domains. But to those who refuse this privilege she appears as fate; and though their honor is lost, hers is not; for the order of the world continues to be vindicated. The just and faithful citizen, who of his own election obeys the laws, illustrates in one way the order of society and the supremacy of moral law. The villain in the penitentiary illustrates the order of society and the supremacy of moral law in quite another way. But order and law are illustrated by both, though in ways so very different. So one may refuse to make reason a free necessity in his own bosom; but then the constable of the universe speedily taps him upon the shoulder, and law is honored, though he is disgraced.

Now Mr. Buckle supposed that order in the world and in history could be obtained only by sacrificing the freedom of the individual; and that he so supposed determines his own rank as a thinker. There is no second question to be asked concerning a candidate for the degree of master in philosophy who begins by making this mistake.

But does some one, unwilling so soon to quit the point, require of me to explain *how* will can originate in man? My only answer is, I do not know. Does the questioner know *how* motion originates in the universe? It does or did originate; science is clear in assigning a progress, and therefore a beginning, to the solar system: can you find its origin in aught but the self-activity of Spirit, whose *modus operandi* no man can explain? *All* origination is inscrutable; the plummet of understanding cannot sound it; but wherefore may not one sleep as sweetly, knowing that the wondrous fact is near at hand, in the bosoms of his contempo-

raries and in his own being, as if it were pushed well out of sight
into the depths of primeval time? To my mind, there is something thoroughly weak and ridiculous in the way that Comte
and his company run away from the Absolute and Inexplicable,
fearing only its nearness; like a child who is quite willing there
should be bears at the North Pole, but would lie awake of nights,
if he thought there were one in the nearest wood. And it is the
more ridiculous because Mystery is no bear; nor can I, for one,
conceive why it should not be to every man a joy to know that all
the marvel which ever was in Nature is in her now, and that the
divine inscrutable processes are going on under our eyes and in
them and in our hearts.

Doubtless, however, many will adhere to the logic that has
satisfied them so long and so well,—that it is impossible the will
should move otherwise than in obedience to motives, and that,
obeying a motive, it is not free. Why should we not, then, amuse
ourselves a little with these complacent motive-mongers? They
profess a perfect explanation of mental action, and make it the
stigma of a deeper philosophy, that it must leave somewhat in all
action of the mind, and therefore in a doctrine of the will, un-
explained. Let, now, these good gentlemen explain to us how a
motive ever gets to be a motive. For there is precisely the same
difficulty in initiating motion here as elsewhere. You look on a
peach; you desire it; and you are moved by the desire to pluck or
purchase it. Now it is plain that you could not desire this peach
until you had perceived that it was a desirable fruit. But you
could not perceive that the fruit was desirable until you had
experienced desire of it. And here we are at the old, inexplicable
seesaw. It must appear desirable in order to be desired; it must
be desired in order to appear desirable: the perception must
precede the desire, and the desire must precede the perception.
These are foolish subtilties, but all the fitter for their purpose.
Our motive-mongering friends should understand that they can
explain no farther than their neighbors,—that by enslaving the
will they only shift the difficulty, not solve it.

Anything but this shallow sciolism! More philosophical a
thousand times than the knowing and facile metaphysic which

makes man a thing of springs and pivots and cogs, are the notions of old religionists, which attributed human action in large part to preventing, suggesting, and efficient "grace," or those of older poets, who gave Pallas Athene for a counsellor to Odysseus, and Krishna for a teacher to the young Aryan warrior,—which represent human action, that is, as issuing in part out of the Infinite. A thousand times more *philosophical,* as well as ten thousand times more inspiring, I say, are the metaphysics of Imagination,—of scriptures and great poems and the *live* human heart,—than the cut-and-dried sciolisms which explain you a man in five minutes, and make everything in him as obvious as the movements of a jumping-jack.

To deny, then, the existence of free-will is, in my judgment, a grave error; but to deny it on the ground of its identity with chance is more than an ordinary error, however grave; it is a poison in the blood of one's thought, conveying its vice to every part and function of the system. And herewith we pass to the next head.

2. *Consciousness.* It has been the persuasion of wise men in various ages, and is the persuasion of many, as wise, doubtless, as their neighbors, now, that the soul has a native sense of its quality and perpetual relations. By Plato this sense, in some of its aspects, was named Reminiscence; by modern speakers of English it is denoted as Consciousness. This, according to its grades and applications, is qualified as personal, moral, intellectual, or, including all its higher functions, as intuitive or spiritual. Of this high spiritual sense, this self-recognition of soul, all the master-words of the language—God, Immortality, Life, Love, Duty—are either wholly, or in all their grander suggestions, the product. Nothing, indeed, is there which confers dignity upon human life and labor, that is not primarily due to the same source. In union with popular and unconscious imagination, it generates mythology; in union with imagination and reason, it gives birth to theology and cosmogony; in union with imagination, reason, and experience, it is the source of philosophy; in union with the same, together with the artistic sense and high degrees of imaginative sympathy, it creates epic poetry and art. Its total outcome,

however, may be included under the term Belief. And it results from an assumed validity of consciousness, that universal belief is always an indication of universal truth. At the same time, since this master-power finds expression through faculties various in kind and still more various in grade of development, its outcome assumes many shapes and hues,—just as crystallized alumina becomes here ruby and there sapphire, by minute admixtures of different coloring substances.

We assume the validity of this prime source of belief. Why not? Here is a great natural product, human belief; we treat it precisely as we do other natural products; we judge, that, like these, it has its law and justification. We assume that it is to be studied as Lyell studies the earth's crust, or Agassiz its life, or Müller its languages. As our author shuns metaphysical, so do we shun metapsychical inquiries. We do not presume to go behind universal fact, and inquire whether it has any business to be fact; we simply endeavor to see it in its largest and most interior aspect, and then accept it without question.

But M. Comte made the discovery that this great product of man's spiritual nature is nothing but the spawn of his self-conceit: that it is purely gratuitous, groundless, superfluous, and therefore in the deepest possible sense lawless. Mr. Buckle follows his master, for such Comte really is. Proclaiming Law everywhere else, and, from his extreme partiality to the word, often lugging it in, as it were, by the ears, he no sooner arrives at these provinces than he instantly faces the other way, and denies all that he has before advocated. Of a quadruped he will question not a hair, of a fish not a scale; everywhere else he will accept facts and seek to coördinate them; but when he arrives at the great natural outcome and manifestation of man's spirit, then it is in an opposite way that he will not question; he simply lifts his eyebrows. The fact has no business to be there! It signifies nothing!

Why this reversal of position? First, because, if consciousness be allowed, free-will must be admitted; since the universal consciousness is that of freedom to choose. But there is a larger reason. In accordance with his general notions, personality must be degraded, denuded, impoverished,—that so the individual may lie passive in the arms of that society whose laws he is ambitious to expound. Having robbed the soul of choice, he now deprives it of sight; having denied that it is an originating source of will, he now makes the complementary denial, that it is a like source of knowledge; having first made it helpless, he now proceeds to make it senseless. And, indeed, the two denials belong together. If it be true that the soul is helpless, pray let us have some kind drug to make it senseless also. Nature has dealt thus equally with the stone; and surely she must design a like equality in her dealings with man. Power and perceiving she will either give together, or together withhold.

But how does our author support this denial? By pointing to the great varieties in the outcome of consciousness. There is no unity, he says, in its determinations: one believes this, another that, a third somewhat different from both; and the faith that one is ready to die for, another is ready to kill him for. And true it is that the diversities of human belief are many and great; let not the fact be denied nor diminished.

But does such diversity disprove a fundamental unity? All modern science answers, No. How much of outward resemblance is there between a fish and a philosopher? Is not the difference here as wide as the widest unlikenesses in human belief? Yet Comparative Anatomy, with none to deny its right, includes philosopher and fish in one category: they both belong to the vertebrate sub-kingdom. See what vast dissimilarities are included in the unity of this vertebrate structure: creatures that swim, creep, walk, fly; creatures with two feet, with four feet, with no feet, with feet and hands, with hands only, with neither feet nor hands; creatures that live in air only, or in water only, or that die at once in water or air; creatures, in fine, more various and diverse than imagination, before the fact, could conceive. Yet, throughout this astonishing, inconceivable variety, science walks in steady perception of a unity extending far toward details of structure. The boor laughs, when told that the forefoot of his horse and his own hand are essentially the same member. A "Positive Philosopher" laughs, when told that through Fetichism and Lutheranism there runs a thread of unity,—that human belief has its law, and may be studied in the spirit of science. But it is more than questionable whether the laugh is on their side.*

But our author does not quit this subject without attempting to adduce a specific instance wherein consciousness proves fallacious. Success, however, could hardly be worse; he fails to establish his point, but succeeds in discrediting either his candor or his discrimination. "Are we not," he says, "in certain circumstances, conscious of the existence of spectres and phantoms; and yet is it not generally admitted that such beings have no existence at all?" Now I should be ashamed to charge a scholar, like Mr. Buckle, with being unaware that consciousness does not apply to any matter which comes properly under the cognizance of the senses, and that the word can be honestly used in such applications only by the last extreme of ignorant or inadvertent latitude. *Conscious* of the existence of spectres! One might as lawfully say he is "conscious" that there is a man in the moon, or that the color of his neighbor's hair is due to a dye. Mr. Buckle is undoubtedly honest. How, then, could he, in strict philosophical discussion, employ the cardinal word in a sense flagrantly and even ludicrously false, in order to carry his point? It is partly to be attributed to his controversial ardor, which is not only a heat, but a blaze, and frequently dazzles the eye of his understanding; but partly it is attributable also to an infirmity in the understanding itself. He shows, indeed, a singular combination of intellectual qualities. He has great external precision, and great

---

* Comte did, indeed, profess to furnish a central law of belief. It is due, he said, to the tendency of man to flatter his own personality by foisting its image upon the universe. This, however, is but one way of saying that it is wholly gratuitous,— that it has no root in the truth of the world. But universal truth and universal law are the same; and therefore that which arises without having any root in eternal verity is lawless in the deepest possible sense,—lawless not merely as being irregular in its action, but in the deeper and more terrible sense of being in the universe without belonging there. To believe, however, that any product of universal dimensions can be generated, not by the truth of the universe, but by somewhat else, is to believe in a Devil more thoroughly than the creed of any Calvinist allows. But this is quite in character. Comte was perhaps the most superstitious man of his time; superstition runs in the blood of his "philosophy"; and Mr. Buckle, in my opinion, escapes and denounces the black superstitions of ignorance only to fall into the whited superstitions of sciolism.

inward looseness and slipperiness of mind: so that, if you follow
his words, no man's thought can be clearer, no man's logic more
firm and rapid in its march; but if you follow strictly the *conceptions,* the clearness vanishes, and the logic limps, nay, sprawls.
It is not merely that he writes better than he thinks, though this
is true of him; but the more characteristic fact is that he is a
master in the forms of thought and an apprentice in the substance. Read his pages, and you will find much to admire; read
under his pages, and you will find much not to admire.

It appears from the foregoing what Mr. Buckle aims to accomplish at the outset. His purpose is to effect a thorough degradation of Personality. Till this is done, he finds no clear field
for the action of social law. To discrown and degrade Personality
by taking away its two grand prerogatives,—this is his preliminary labor, this is his way of procuring a site for that edifice of
scientific history which he proposes to build.

But what an enormous price to pay for the purchase! If there
is no kingdom for social law, if there is no place for a science of
history, till man is made unroyal, till the glory is taken from his
brow, the sceptre from his right hand, and the regal hopes from
his heart, till he is made a mere serf and an appanage of that
ground and territory of circumstance whereon he lives and
labors,—why, then a science of history means much the same
with an extinction of history, an extinction of all that in history
which makes it inspiring. The history of rats and mice is interesting, but not to themselves,—interesting only to man, and this
because he is man; but if men are nothing but rats and mice, pray
let them look for cheese, and look out for the cat, and let goose-
quills and history alone.

But the truth is that Person and Society are mutually supporting facts, each weakened by any impoverishment of its reciprocal
term. Whenever a *real* history of human civilization is written,
they will thus appear. And Mr. Buckle, in seeking to empty one
term in order to obtain room for the other, was yielding conces-
sions, not to the pure necessities of truth, but to his own infirmity
as a thinker.

Having, however, taken the crown and kingdom from Personality, our philosophical Warwick proceeds to the coronation of his favorite autocrat, Society. His final proposition, which indeed is made obscurely, and as far as possible by implication, is this:—

3. *That Society is the Real Source of Individual Action.* A proposition made obscurely, but argued strenuously, and altogether necessary for the completion of his foundation. He attempts proof by reference to the following facts:—that in a given kingdom there occur, year after year, nearly the same number of murders, suicides and letters mailed without direction, and that marriages are more frequent when food is low and wages high, and so conversely. This is the sum total of the argument on which he relies here and throughout his work: if this proves his point, it is proven; if otherwise, otherwise.

To begin with, I admit the facts alleged. They are overstated; there *is* considerable departure from an exact average: but let this pass. I will go farther, and admit, what no one has attempted to show, that an average in these common and outward matters proves the like regularity in all that men do and think and feel. This to concentrate attention upon the main question.

And the main question is, What do these regular averages signify? Do they denote the dominancy of a social fate? "Yea, yea," cry loudly the French fatalists; and "Yea, yea," respond with firm assurance Buckle & Co. in England; and "Yea," there are many to say in our own land. Even Mr. Emerson must summon his courage to confront "the terrible statistics of the French statisticians." But I live in the persuasion that these statistics are extremely innocent, and threaten no man's liberty. Let us see.

Take first the instance of forgetfulness. In the United Kingdom some millions of letters are annually mailed; and of these, one in a certain number of thousands, "making allowance," as our author innocently says, "for variation of circumstances," is found to be mailed without a superscription. Now provision for a forgetting is made in every man's individual constitution. Partly for permanent and final forgetting; in this way we get rid of vast quantities of trash, which would suffocate us, if we could not obtain riddance. Partly also for temporary forgetting; by means of which we become oblivious to everything but the matter in hand, and, by a sole concentration upon that, act intensely and efficaciously. Then, as all particular constitutions have their debilities, this provision for temporary obliviousness may become an infirmity, and in some is an habitual and chronic infirmity.

Let us now assume an individual man, and suppose ourselves able to analyze perfectly his mental condition. From his temperament, constitution, and habit, we shall then be able also to infer with precision the measure of his *liability* to lapse of memory. Place him, now, in a world by himself; give him a life of several centuries' duration; and secure him through life from essential change of constitution. Divide, then, his life into centuries; count the instances of forgetfulness in each century; and in each century they will be found nearly the same. The Law of Probability determines this, and enables us to speak with entire confidence of a case so supposed. Here, then, is the continuous average; but it surely indicates no subjection of the individual soul to a law of society; for there is no society to impose such law,—there is only the constitution of the individual.

Now, instead of one individual, let us suppose a hundred; and let each of these be placed on a separate planet. Obtain in respect to each one the measure of his liability to infirm lapse of memory, and add these together. And now it will appear that the average outward result which one man gave in one hundred years one hundred men will give in one year. The law of probability again comes in, and, matching the irregularities of one by those of another, gives in this case, as in the former, an average result. Here, then, is Mr. Buckle's average without the existence of a society, and therefore without any action of social law. Does another syllable need to be said?

Perhaps, however, it will be objected that I redeem the individual from a fate working in the general whole of society, only to subject him to an equal fate working in his own constitution. There is undoubtedly a certain *degree* of fate expressed in each man's temperament and particular organization. But mark the difference. Mr. Buckle's social fate subjects each man totally, and in effect robs him of personality; the fate which works in his own constitution subjects him *only in that proportion which his abnormal liability bears to the total force of his mind.* One letter in ten thousand, say, is mailed without direction. Our historian of civilization infers hence that each individual is *totally* subject to a social fate. My inference is, that, on the average, each individual is *one ten-thousandth part* subject to a fate in his private constitution. There is the difference, and it does not seem to me insignificant. Our way to the cases of crime is now somewhat more clear; for it is already established beyond cavil that the mere fact of an average, to which, without any discriminations, our philosopher appeals with such confidence, proves nothing for his purpose.

The case of murders, however, differs from the foregoing in one important particular. The persons who are detected in the commission of this crime are commonly, by their punishment, withdrawn from the number of active criminals; and consequently the average is kept up, not by the same persons, but in part by different ones. Here is, therefore, more appearance of the mediation of compulsory social law; and indeed the action of social forces in the case I am far more disposed to assert than to question. What we are to inquire, however, is not whether social forces contribute to this result, but whether they are *such* forces as supersede and annihilate individual will. Let us see.

All men are liable to collisions of passion and interest with their neighbors and contemporaries. All desire to remove the obstructions thus opposed. All would labor for this end with brute directness, that is, by lawless violence and cunning, were it not for the rational and moral elements in their nature, which suggest noble pieces of abstinence and self-restraint, thus securing a certain freedom, a certain superiority to the brute pressure of interest and impulse. These rational and moral elements are in variable counterpoise with the ruder desires,—sometimes commanding them with imperial ease, sometimes overcoming them by struggle, sometimes striving with them feebly and vainly, or even ceasing to strive.

Suppose, now, a nation of thirty millions. Of these, twenty-nine millions, let us say, are never consciously tempted to commit a felony. Why? For want of opportunity? Not at all; good men, whom the police do not watch, have more opportunties for crime than those whose character causes them to be suspected. Is it because wrathful passion, the love of money, and other incentives to aggression are unknown to them? To none are they wholly unknown. Why, then, this immunity from temptation? Simply because their choices, or characters,—for character is but structural choice,—run in favor of just and prudent courses with a tide so steady and strong as to fill all the river-beds of action, and leave no room for worse currents. In other words, the elements that make men free hold, in this respect, easy sovereignty in their souls. Below these millions, suppose nine hundred thousand who might be open to such temptation, but for the influence of good customs, which are the legacies left by good men dead, and kept in force by the influence of just men who are living. In these, the freedom-making elements still keep the throne, and preserve regal sway; but they are like sovereigns who might be dethroned, but for the countenance of more powerful neighbors. Below these, the liability to actual commission of violence begins to open; but there are, we will suppose, ninety thousand in whom it is practically suppressed by the dangers which, in civilized communities, attend upon crime. These men have that in them which *might* make them felons, but for penal laws, prisons, and the executioner. But below these are ten thousand who have a liability *in excess* of all restraining influences whatsoever; and the result of this liability, in accordance with the law of probability already mentioned, is two hundred murders in a year.* Now here the action of fate does not *begin* until you reach the lowest ten thousand. Even here, freedom is not extinguished; the rational and moral elements that confer it are weak, but they are not necessarily dead or inoperative; for, in conjunction with lower restraints, they actually make the number of crimes not ten thousand, but two hundred. True it is, that these are partially enslaved, partially subject to fate; but they are enslaved not by any inscrutable law of society, comparable with "that which preserves the balance of the sexes"; they are "taken captive by their

* It may be said that this is a mere arguing by supposition. But the supposition here has respect only to the *numbers*.

own lusts," as one of our philosopher's "ignorant men" said many years ago. But above these the enslaving liability begins to disappear, and freedom soon becomes, so far as this test applies, supreme.

Thus for one year we apply a measure of the liability to crime, and obtain a result which is inexpressibly far from sustaining Mr. Buckle's inference; since it shows that the fatal force is to all freeing forces as two hundred to thirty millions,—and shows, moreover, that this fate, instead of inclosing in its toils every man in the nation, and utterly depriving all of freedom, actually touches at all but a small number, and only diminishes, not destroys, the freedom of these. Next year we apply the same measure to nearly the same persons, in the presence of nearly the same restraints; and find, of course, the result to be nearly the same. But this result no more proves universal enslavement in the second year than it did in the first. And so of the third, fourth, or fortieth application of the measure.

But a portion of these murderers are yearly withdrawn: ought not the number of crimes to diminish? It would do so, but for that law of social propagation which is ever and everywhere active. But this law, which connects men and generations, and tends to make history a unit, is not a part of fate alone; it carries just so much fate and so much freedom as there are to be carried. It changes nothing; it is simply a vehicle, and transports freight, —precious stones or ballast stones, as the case may be. Therefore, in unveiling a single year, and seeing precisely what this fact of two hundred murders means, we find its meaning for any possible succession of years. It shows certain measures of fate working in the bosoms of certain numbers of men; but that there is a fate inhabiting society as such, and holding every man and woman in its unfeeling hand, must be proven, if at all, by other facts than these.

Mr. Buckle generalizes with marvellous facility, but often with an infatuation, or even fatuity, equally marvellous. Specious and audacious generalization is, however, a vice of thinking more attractive to most than any virtue,—above all, if it flatter their wishes and opinions. There are few to appreciate an exquisite

temperance, an exquisite virgin modesty, continence, and reserve, whether in thought or art. The great masters disappoint,
the great showmen dazzle, at first sight; the multitudes crave
sensations and sudden effects. Even among thoughtful men, there
are, in this galloping age, too many who prefer to frequent a
philosophical slop-shop, where they can be fitted to a full suit in
five minutes; and they willingly forgive some bagging and
wrinkling, some ripping of seams and dropping-off of buttons,
in consideration of promptitude in the supply. Nor is this un-
natural. Ordinary travel goes by steam; does it not seem a little
hard that thought should have to journey still in the ancient
fashion? And so far as the mass of readers is concerned, this appetite for fast thinking and reckless generalization is a cheerful
token: it is a gainful substitute for that hiding away from the
blaze of intellect, that terror of large results in thought, which
has harbored in the Vatican since the days of Galileo, and even in
Protestant lands may sometimes be found, like the graveyard, in
the neighborhood of churches. A relish for premature and extrav-
agant generalization may be pardoned in the mass of readers;
but in the writer? "It must needs be that offences come; but woe
to that man by whom the offence cometh!"

Mr. Buckle finds some general book-facts, and, never trying to
think down to their roots, he seizes upon their specious aspect,
and thence rushes out into a generalization, which, rightly understood, sweeps Personality off the earth. Not such is the spirit of
science; not such the manner of its masters. Look at Newton investigating colors. What effort for nearness, nearness, nearness to
his facts! What solicitation for entrance to their households and
sanctuaries! See Agassiz or Tyndall investigating the flow of
glaciers. Here is no catching at book-aspects of the matter, and
launching instantly into generalization. No, these men must get
within eyeshot, within hand-reach, of the facts, and know first
precisely and intimately what these are. Yet the generalizations
for which they were seeking a basis were trivial in comparison
with those which our author hurtles out after a glance at M.
Quetelet. "A continuous average of so many murders a year; then
so many *must* happen; then somebody *must* commit them; then

free-will is a figment, and society is the source of all action which we call individual."

Intemperate and infatuated generalization, if supported by a certain ability, is an attractive vice. Yet he who indulges in this will be sure to leave upon his brilliant and exciting pages statements that are simply ludicrous. Our philosopher furnishes an instance of this in his treatment of the matter of marriage. If wages be low and food high, marriages are less frequent; if the converse be the case, they are more frequent. What conclusion would common sense base upon this fact? Why, of course, that the number of marriages is definitely *influenced* by the ease with which sustenance is obtained. But this is a commonplace result; there is nothing in it bold, brilliant, striking; besides, it does not make man the slave of outward influences. Accordingly, Mr. Buckle generalizes from it as follows:—"Marriages, instead of having *any connection* with personal feelings, are completely controlled by the price of food and the rate of wages." He does not distinguish between a definite modifying influence and a controlling cause. His facts prove the former; he asserts the latter. Let us see how this procedure would work elsewhere. There is "a definite relation," in our author's words, between the force and direction of the winds and the rise or fall of the sea upon our coast: therefore tidal rise and fall, "instead of having any connection" with the influence of the moon, are "completely controlled" by the direction and force of the wind! There is a "definite relation" between the straightness or want of straightness in a railroad and the speed of the train: *ergo,* the speed of the train, "instead of having any connection" with the locomotive and the force of steam, is "completely controlled" by the line of the road! It is by no means difficult to philosophize after this fashion; but if we are to have many professors of such philosophy, let the mediæval cap-and-bells, by all means, be reproduced.

Again, having stated the fact of an approximation to a continuous average of suicides, and having assumed for this a cause operating in the indivisible whole of society, he goes on to say, "And the power of this larger law is so irresistible, that neither the love of life nor the fear of another world can avail anything toward even checking its operation." How, pray, does Mr. Buckle know? What shadow of a fact has he to justify this vaunting of his "larger law"? Has he ever known the love of life and the awe of another world to be suspended? Has he afterwards seen their action restored, and ascertained that in their presence and in their absence the ratio of suicides remained the same? These questions answer themselves. But when a writer who loudly professes and fully believes himself to proceed purely upon facts adventures statement so groundless, so gratuitous and reckless as this, who can pass to the next paragraph in full confidence of his intellectual rectitude? If you retain, as in this case I do retain, assurance of his moral rectitude,—of his intention to be fair,— to what conclusion can you come more charitable than this, that his partiality to his own notions is so vigorous as not only to overslaugh his sense of logical truth, but to supersede the necessity of other grounds for believing these notions and for urging them?

Only our author's first chapter has been dealt with; firstly, because in this are enunciated those radical conceptions which he afterwards argues not *to,* but *from;* and secondly, because it has been the writer's desire, avoiding all vagrant and indecisive criticism, to have a fair grapple, and come to some clear result,— like that of a wrestler, who frankly proffers himself to throw or be thrown. It only remains to indicate, so far as may be, a comprehensive estimate of Mr. Buckle as a thinker.

And at last it must be said in plain words that he is to be regarded as an adventurer in the kingdoms of thought,—though the word must be freed from all customary flavors of charlatanry and wickedness. One of the boldest and cleverest of his class; a man, too, of probity, of dignity and character, amiable, estimable; but *intellectually* an adventurer nevertheless. The grand masters in thought are those to whom the subtilest and most purely universal principles are nearest and most habitual, coming to the elucidation of all minutest matters no less than to that of the greatest,—as those forces which hold the solar system together apply themselves, as on the same level, to a mote wandering in the air; and because to these masters first principles, through all their changes of seeming, through all their ranging by analogy up and down, are never disguised, but are always near and clear and sure, they can admit the action of all modifying principles without imperilling the great stabilities of truth; so that in their thought, as in Nature, the dust-particle shall float and fly with the wind, and yet gravitation shall hold particle and world in firm, soft, imperial possession. And next to these are the inventors, guided by a fine felicity of intelligence to special discoveries and admirable combinations, often surpassing in this way the masters themselves. And then come the wise and great scholars, who learn quickly what has been discovered, and follow the masters not by sight only, as a greyhound, but by long inferences; and these also do noble work. And after these follow the broader company of useful, able, eloquent men, applying, explaining, illustrating, and preparing the way for schools and commerce and the newspaper. Finally comes a man with a genius for boldness more than for anything else, so that he has a pleasant feeling of himself only when he gives himself the sense of being startling, novel, venturesome, and therefore goes off in his thought as in a balloon: and of such man,—being daring, ingenious, agile, and not being profound,—this will be the unfailing characteristic, that he substitutes and asserts secondary principles, which are obvious, outward, and within his reach, for primary principles, which are deep, subtile, inward, and beyond his reach; he will swing loose from the principles which are indeed prime and imperial in Nature, and will boldly assert secondary principles as fundamental: this man is the intellectual adventurer.

And this is Mr. Buckle. The first fact with regard to man is his possession of a rational soul, and consequently of that liberation of will without which, despite the existence of reason, he could not be in act a reasonable being. But the secondary fact in this connection is that man's freedom is modified by pedigree, by temperament, by influences almost numberless, and that he is included in laws, so that, if he falls away from reason, he falls into the hands of fate. And this secondary or modifying congeries of facts our author announces as primary.

The first fact with regard to the soul is that it is intelligent and vocal,—that it is not merely a subject, but also an organ, of THAT WHICH KNOWS in the universe. The modifying fact is that its voice is commonly obscure, and the language it shall use and the logic of its utterance prescribed by the accident of time, place, and other circumstances; so that it has the semblance of voices many and contradictory. And this modifying fact Mr. Buckle announces, with much assurance and complacency, as primary.

The first fact in the world of man is Personality. The secondary fact is Society,—secondary, but reciprocal, and full of import. And Mr. Buckle begins with making Personality acephalous, and ends with appending its corpse to Society, to be galvanized into seemings of life. And if you follow him through his book, you find this inversion constantly maintained,—and find, moreover, that it is chiefly this revolutionary audacity which makes his propositions so startling and his pages to many so fascinating.

Therefore an adventurer. This is concerning *him* the primary fact. But the modifying fact is that he has the manners of a gentleman, the heart of a humanitarian, the learning of a scholar, the pen of a ready writer, the outside or *shell* of a philosophical genius, excellent admixtures of sense, and an attractive hatred of ecclesiastical and political barbarisms.

He has great surface-reach, but no inward breadth. He invariably takes the liberal side with regard to practical and popular questions; he invariably takes the illiberal side in respect to questions of philosophy. In politics and in social feeling he is cosmopolitan; in questions of pure thought he is cockney. Here he is a tyrant; he puts out the soul's eyes, and casts fetters about its feet; here he is hard, narrow, materialistic, mechanical,—or, in a word, English. For—we may turn aside to say—in philosophy no nation is so straitened, illiberal, and hard of hearing as England, except, perhaps, China. Its tympanum is sadly thickened at once with materialism and conceit; and the consequence is that a thinker there is either ignored into silence, like Wilkinson, or driven to bellow, like Carlyle, or to put rapiers and poignards into his speech, like Ruskin. Carlyle began speaking sweetly and humanly, and was heard only on this side the ocean; then he came

to his bull-of-Bashan tones, and was attended to on his own side
the water. It is observable, too, that, if a thinker in America goes
beyond the respectable dinner-table depth, your true Englishman takes it for a personal affront, and hastens to make an ass of
himself in the "Saturday Review."

Apply to Mr. Buckle any test that determines the question of
pure intellectual power, and he fails to sustain it. Let us proceed
to apply one.

No man is an able thinker who is without power to comprehend that law of reciprocal opposites, on which the world is built.
For an example of this: the universe is indeed a *uni*-verse, a pure
unit, emanating, as we think, from a spirit that is, in the words of
old Hooker, "not only one, but very oneness," simple, indivisible, and therefore total in all action; and yet this universe is
various, multifarious, full of special character, full even of fierce
antagonisms and blazing contradictions. Infinite and Finite,
Same and Diverse, Eternal and Temporary, Universal and
Special,—here they are, purest opposites, yet mutual, reciprocal,
necessary to each other; and he is a narrow man who cannot stand
in open relations with both terms, reconciling in the depths of
his life, though he can never explain, the mystery of their friendship. He who will adhere only to the universal, and makes a blur
of the special, is a rhapsodist; he who can apprehend only the
special, being blind and callous to the universal, is a chatterer
and magpie. From these opposites we never escape; Destiny and
Freedom, Rest and Motion, Individual and Society, Origination
and Memory, Intuition and Observation, Soul and Body,—you
meet them everywhere; and everywhere they are, without losing
their character of opposites, nay, in very virtue of their opposition, playing into and supporting each other.

But, from the fact that they *are* opposites, it is always easy to
catch up one, and become its partisan as against the other. It is
easy in such advocacy to be plausible, forcible, affluent in words
and apparent reasons; also to be bold, striking, astonishing. And
yet such an advocate will never speak a word of pure truth. "He
who knows half," says Goethe, "speaks much, and says nothing to
the purpose; he who knows all inclines to act, and speaks seldom

or late." With such partisanship and advocacy the world has been liberally, and more than liberally, supplied. Such a number of Eurekas have been shouted! So often it has been discovered that the world is no such riddle, after all,—that half of it is really the whole! No doubt all this was good boy's-play once; afterwards it did to laugh at for a while; then it ceased to be even a joke, and grew a weariness and an affliction; and at length we all rejoiced when the mighty world-pedagogue of Chelsea seized his ferule, and roared, over land and sea, "Silence, babblers!"

If only Mr. Buckle had profited by the command! For, follow this writer where you will, you find him the partisan of a particular term as against its fraternal opposite. It is Fate *against* Free-Will; Society *against* the prerogatives of Personality; Man *against* Outward Nature (for he considers them only as antagonistic, one "triumphing" over the other); Intellect *against* the Moral Sense; Induction *against* Deduction and Intuition; Knowledge *against* Reverence; and so on and on to the utter weariness of one reader, if of no more. For what can be more wearying and saddening than to follow the pages of a writer who is fertile, ingenious, eloquent, rich in right feeling, in reading and courage, and yet who, in chapter after chapter of effective paragraphs, and tome after tome of powerful chapters, is merely persuading you that half is the whole? And if your duty as a scholar require you to peruse the book fully, instead of casting it aside, your mind at length fairly *aches* for the sense of poise and soundness, were it only for a single page. But no; it is always the same succession of perspicuous and vigorous sentences, all carrying flavors of important truth, and none utterly true. For the half *is* really half; but it simply is *not* the whole, be as eloquent about it as one may.

Such, then, is the estimate here given of Mr. Buckle's laborious and powerful work. Meantime, with every secondary merit which such a work *could* possess this is replete; while its faults are only such as were inseparable from the conjunction of such ambitions with such powers. He may whet and wield his blade; but he puts no poison on its edge. He may disparage reverence; but he is not himself irreverent. He may impugn the convictions that most men love; but, while withholding no syllable of dissent and reprehension, he utters not a syllable that can insult or sting. And all the while his pages teem with observations full of point, and half full of admirable sense and suggestion.

After all, we owe him thanks,—thanks, it may be, even for his errors. The popular notions of moral liberty are probably not profound, and require deepening. The grand fact that we name Personality *is* grand and of an unsounded depth only because in it Destiny and Freedom meet and become one. But the play into this of Destiny and Eternal Necessity is, in general, dimly discerned. The will is popularly pronounced free, but is thought to originate, as it were, "between one's hat and his boots"; and so man loses all largeness of relation, and personality all grandeur. Now blisters, though ill for health, may be wholesome for disease; and doctrines of Fate, that empty every man of his soul, may be good as against notions of moral liberty that make one's soul of a pin's-head dimension. It may be well, also, that the doctrine of Social Fate should be preached until all are made to see that Society *is* a fact,—that it is generative,—that personal development cannot go on but by its mediation,—that the chain of spiritual interdependence cannot be broken, and that in proportion as it is weakened every bosom becomes barren. In this case also Mr. Buckle may be medicinal. We owe him thanks also for refreshing our expectation of a science of civilization,—for affirming the venerableness of intellect, which recent teachers have undervalued,—for vindicating the uses of doubt,—and, finally, for a specimen of intellectual intrepidity of which one could wish there were less need. And withal how royally he presumes upon a welcome for candid confession of his thought! Such a presumption could be created in his soul only by a great magnanimity; and the evidence of this on his pages sheds a beauty about all his words.

But he is not an Œdipus. He has guessed; and the riddle awaits another comer. A science of history he has not established; the direction in which it lies he has not pointed out; and if Hegel and his precursors have failed to indicate such a science, the first clear step toward it remains yet to be taken. And should some majestic genius—for no other will be sufficient for the task—at length arise to lay hold upon the facts of man's history, and exercise over them a Newtonian sway, he will be the last man on the planet to take his initial hint from Auguste Comte and the "Positive Philosophy." This mud-mountain is indeed considerably heaped up, but it is a very poor Pisgah nevertheless; for it is a mountain in a pit, whose top does not rise to an equality with the broad common levels, far less with the high table-lands and skyward peaks and summits of intelligence.

THE LAW OF COSTS

Our Nation is now paying the price, not only of its vice, but also of its virtue,—not alone of its evil doing, but of its noble and admirable doing as well. It has of late been a customary cry with a certain class, that those who cherish freedom and advocate social justice are the proper authors of the present war. No doubt there is in this allegation an ungracious kind of truth; that is, had the nation been destitute of a political faith and of moral feeling, there would have been no contest. But were one lying ill of yellow-fever or small-pox, there would be the same sort of lying truth in the statement, that the *life* in him, which alone resists the disease, is really its cause; since to yellow-fever, or to any malady, dead bodies are not subject. There is no preventive of disease so effectual as death itself,—no place so impregnable to pestilence as the grave. So, had the vitality gone out of the nation's heart, had that lamp of love for freedom and justice and of homage to the being of man, which once burned in its bosom so brightly, already sunk into death-flicker and extinction, then in the sordid and icy dark that would remain there could be no war of like nature with this that today gives the land its woful baptism of blood and tears. Oh, no! there would have been peace— *and* putrefaction: peace, but without its sweetness, and death, but without its hopes.

In one important sense, however, this war—hateful and horrible though it be—is the price which the nation must pay for its ideas and its magnanimity. If you take a clear initial step toward any great end, you thereby assume as a debt to destiny the pursuit and completion of your action; and should you fail to meet this debt, it will not fail to meet you, though now in the shape of retribution and with a biting edge. The seaman who has signed shipping-papers owes a voyage, and must either sail or suffer. The nation which has recognized absolute rights of man, and in their name assumed to shed blood, has taken upon itself the burden of a high destination, and must bear it, if not willingly, reluctantly, if not in joy and honor, then in shame and weeping.

Our nation, by the early nobility of its faith and action, assumed such a debt to destiny, and now must pay it. It needed not to come in this shape: there need have been no horror of carnage,—no feast of vultures, and carnival of fiends,—no weeping of Rachel, mourning for her children, and refusing to be comforted, because they are not. There was required only a magnanimity in proceeding to sustain that of our beginning,— only a sympathy broad enough to take our little planet and all her human tribes in its arms, deep enough to go beneath the skin in which men differ, to the heart's blood in which they agree— only pains and patience, faith and forbearance,—only a national obedience to that profound precept of Christianity which prescribes service to him that would be greatest, making the knowledge of the wise due to the ignorant, and the strength of the strong due to the weak. The costs of freedom would have been paid in the patient lifting up of a degraded race from the slough of servitude; and the nation would at the same time have avoided that slough of lava and fire wherein it is now ingulfed.

It was not to be so. History is coarse; it gets on by gross feeding and fevers, not by delicacy of temperance and wisdom of regimen. Our debt was to be paid, not in a pure form, but mixed with the costs of unbelief, cowardice, avarice. Yet primarily it is the cost, not of meanness, but of magnanimity, that we are now paying,—not of a base skepticism, but of a noble faith. For, in truth, normal qualities and actions involve costs no less than vicious and abnormal. Such is the law of the world; and it is this law of the costs of worthiness, of knowledge and nobility, of all memorable being and doing, that I now desire to set forth. Having obtained the scope and power of the law, having considered it also as applying to individuals, we may proceed to exhibit its bearing upon the present struggle of our Republic.

The general statement is this,—that whatever has a worth has also a cost. "The law of the universe," says a wise thinker, "is, Pay and take." If you desire silks of the mercer or supplies at the grocery, you, of course, pay money. Is it a harvest from the field that you seek? Tillage must be paid. Would you have the river toil in production of cloths for your raiment? Only pay the due modicum of knowledge, labor, and skill, and you shall bind its hand to your water-wheels, and turn all its prone strength into pliant service. Or perhaps you wish the comforts of a household. By payment of the due bearing of its burdens, you may hope to obtain it,—surely not otherwise. Do you ask that this house may be a true home, a treasury for wealth of the heart, a little heaven? Once more the word is *pay*,—pay your own heart's unselfish love, pay a generous trustfulness, a pure sympathy, a tender consideration, and a sweet firm-heartedness withal. And so, wherever there is a gaining, there is a warning,—wherever a well-being, a well-doing,—wherever a preciousness, a price of possession; and he who scants the payment stints the purchase; and he that will proffer nothing shall profit nothing; but he that freely and wisely gives shall receive as freely.

But these *desiderata* which I have named are all prices either of ordinary use, of comfort, or felicity; and it is generally understood that happiness is costly: but virtue? Virtue, so far from costing anything, is often supposed to be itself a price that you pay for happiness. It is told us that we shall be rewarded for our virtue; what moralistic commonplace is more common than this? But rewarded for your virtue you are not to be; you are to pay for it; at least, payment made, rather than received, is the principal fact. He who is honest for reward is a knave without reward. He who asks pay for telling truth has truth only on his tongue and a double lie in his heart. Do you think that the true artist strives to paint well that he may get money for his work? Or rather, is not his desire to pay money, to pay anything in reason, for the sake of excellence in his art? And, indeed, what is worthier than Worth? What fitter, therefore, to be paid for? And that payment is made, even under penal forms, every one may see. For what did Raleigh give his lofty head? For the privilege of being Raleigh, of being a man of great heart and a statesman of great mind, with a King James, a burlesque of all sovereignty, on the throne. For what did Socrates quaff the poison? For the privilege of that divine sincerity and penetration which characterized his life. For what did Kepler endure the last straits of poverty, his children crying for bread, while his own heart was pierced with their wailing? For the privilege—in his own noble words—"of reading God's thoughts after Him,"—God's thoughts written in stellar signs on the scroll of the skies. And Cicero and Thomas Cromwell, John Huss and John Knox, John Rogers and John Brown, and many another, high and low, famed and forgotten, must they not all make, as it were, penal payment for the privilege of being true men, truest among true? And again I say, that, if one knows something worthier than Worth, something more excellent than Excellence, then only does he know something fitter than they to be paid for.

Payment *may* assume a penal form: do not think this its only form. And to take the law at once out of the limitations which these examples suggest, let me show you that it is a law of healthy and unlamenting Nature. Look at the scale of existence, and you will see that for every step of advance in that scale payment is required. The animal is higher than the vegetable; the animal, accordingly, is subject to the sense of pain, the vegetable not; and among animals the pain may be keener as the organization is nobler. The susceptibility not only to pain, but to vital injury, observes the same gradation. A little girdling kills an oak; but some low fungus may be cut and troubled and trampled *ad libitum,* and it will not perish; and along the shores, farmers year after year pluck sea-weed from the rocks, and year after year it springs again lively as ever. Among the lowest orders of animals you shall find a creature that, if you cut it in two, straightway duplicates its existence and floats away twice as happy as before;

but of the prick of a bodkin or the sting of a bee the noblest of men may die.

In the animal body the organs make a draft from the general vigors of the system just in proportion to their dignity. The eye, —what an expensive boarder at the gastric tables is that! Considerable provinces of the brain have to be made over to its exclusive use; and it will be remembered that a single ounce of delicate, sensitive brain, full of mysterious and marvellous powers, requires more vital support than many pounds of common muscle. The powers of the eye are great; it has a right to cost much, and it does cost. Also we observe that in this organ there is the exceeding susceptibility to injury, which, as we have observed, invariably accompanies powers of a lofty grade.

Noble senses cost much; noble susceptibilities cost vastly more. Compare oxen with men in respect to the amount of feeling and nervous wear and tear which they severally experience. The ox enjoys grass and sleep; he feels hunger and weariness, and he is wounded by that which goes through his hide. But upon the nerve of the man what an incessant thousandfold play! Out of the eyes of the passers-by pleasures and pains are rained upon him; a word, a look, a tone thrills his every fibre; the touch of a hand warms or chills the very marrow in his bones. Anticipation and memory, hope and regret, love and hate, ideal joy and sorrow and shame, ah, what troops of visitants are ever present with his soul, each and all, whether welcome guests or unwelcome, to be nourished from the resources of his bosom! And out of this high sensibility of man must come what innumerable stabs of quick agony, what slow, gasping hours of grief and pain, that to the cattle upon the hills are utterly unknown! But do you envy the ox his bovine peace? It is precisely that which makes him an ox. It is due to nothing but his insensibility,—by no means, as I take occasion to assure those poets who laud outward Nature and inferior creatures to the disparagement of man,—by no means due to composure and philosophy. The ox is no great hero, after all, for he will bellow at a thousandth part the sense of pain which from a Spartan child wrings no tear nor cry.

Yes, it is precisely this sensibility which makes man human.

Were he incapable of ideal joy and sorrow, he, too, were brute. It is through this delicacy of conscious relationship, it is through this openness to the finest impressions, that he can become an organ of supernal intelligence, that he is capable of social and celestial inspirations. High spiritual sensibility is the central condition of a noble and admirable life; it is the hinge on which turn and open to man the gates of his highest glory and purest peace. Yet for this he must pay away all that induration of brutes and boors which sheds off so many a wasting excitement and stinging chagrin, as the feathers of the water-fowl shed rain.

In entering, therefore, upon any noble course of life, any generous and brave pursuit of excellence, understand, that, so far as ordinary coin is concerned, you are rather to pay, than to be paid, for your superiorities. Understand that the pursuit of excellence must indeed be brave to be prosperous,—that is, it is always in some way opposed and imperilled. Understand, that, with every step of spiritual elevation which you attain, some part of your audience and companionship will be left behind. Understand, that, if you carry lofty principles and philosophic intelligence into camps, these possessions will in general not be passed to your credit, but will be charged against you; and you must surpass your inferiors in their own kinds of virtue to regain what of popular regard these cost you. Understand, that, if you have a reverence for theoretical and absolute truth, less of common fortune will come to you in answer to equal business and professional ability than to those who do care for money, and do not care for truth. Are you a physician? Let me tell you that there is a possible excellence in your profession which will rather limit than increase your practice; yet that very excellence you must strive to attain, for your soul's life is concerned in your doing so. Are you a lawyer? Know that there is a depth and delicacy in the sense of justice, which will sometimes send clients from your office, and sometimes tie your tongue at the bar; yet, as you would preserve the majesty of your manhood, strive just for that unprofitable sense of justice,—unprofitable only because infinitely, rather than finitely, profitable. In a stormy and critical time, when much is ending and much beginning, and a great land is heaving and quivering with commingled agonies of dissolution and throes of new birth, are you a statesman of earnestness and insight, with your eye on the cardinal question of your epoch, its answer clearly in your heart, and your will irrevocably set to give it due enunciation and emphasis? Expect calumny and affected contempt from the base; expect alienation and misconstruction and undervaluing on the part of some who are honorable. Are you a woman rich in high aims, in noble sympathies and thrilling sensibilities, and, as must ever be the case with such, not too rich in a meet companionship? Expect loneliness, and wear it as a grace upon your brow; it is your laurel. Are you a true artist or thinker? Expect to go beyond popular appreciation; *go* beyond it, or the highest appreciation you will not deserve. In fine, for all excellence expect and *seek* to pay.

No one ever held this law more steadily in view than Jesus; and when ardent young people came to him proposing pupilage, he was wont at once to bring it before their eyes. It was on such an occasion that he uttered the words, so simple and intense that they thrill to the touch like the string of a harp, "The foxes have holes, and the birds of the air have nests; but the Son of Man hath not where to lay his head." Of like suggestion his question of the king going to war, who first sitteth down and consulteth whether he be able, and of the man about to build a house, who begins by counting the cost.

The cost,—question of this must arise; question of this must on all sides either be honestly met or dishonestly eluded. For observe, that attempt to escape payment for the purest values, no less than for the grossest, *is* dishonest. If one seek to compass possession of ordinary goods without compensation, we at once apply the opprobrious term of *theft* or *fraud*. Why does the same sort of attempt cease to be fraudulent when it is carried up to a higher degree and applied to possessions more precious? If he that evades the revenue law of the State be guilty of fraud, what of him who would import Nature's goods and pay no duties? For Nature has her own system of impost, and permits no smuggling. There was a tax on truth ere there was one on tea or on silver plate. Character, genius, high parts in history are all assessed upon. Nature lets out her houses and lands on liberal terms; but resorts to distraint, if her dues be not forthcoming. Be sure, therefore, that little success and little honor will wait upon any would-be thieving from God. He who attempts to purloin on this high scale has set all the wit of the universe at work to thwart him, and will certainly be worsted sorely in the end.

The moment, therefore, that any man is found engaged in this business, how to estimate him is clear. Daniel O'Connell tried the experiment of being an heroic patriot and making money by it. It is conceded by his friends that he applied to his private uses, to sustaining the magnificence of his household, the rent-moneys sweated from the foreheads of Irish peasants. But, they say, he had sacrificed many ambitions in taking up the *rôle* of a patriot; and he felt entitled to revenues as liberal as any indulgence of them could have procured him! The apology puts his case beyond all apology. He who—to employ the old phraseology—seeks to exact the same bribe of God that he might have obtained from the Devil is always the Devil's servant, no matter whose livery he wears. Had one often to apply the good word *patriot* to such men, it would soon blister his mouth. I find, in fact, no vice so bad as this spurious virtue, no sinners so unsavory as these mock saints.

To nations, also, this comprehensive law applies. Would you have a noble and orderly freedom? Buy it, and it is yours. "Liberty or death," cried eloquent Henry; and the speech is recited as bold and peculiar; but, by an enduring ordinance of Nature, the people that does not in its heart of hearts say, "Liberty or death," cannot have liberty. Many of us had learned to fancy that the stern tenure by which ancient communities held their civilization was now become an obsolete fact, and that without peril or sacrifice we might forever appropriate all that blesses nations; but by the iron throat of this war Providence is thundering down upon us the unalterable law, that man shall hold no ideal possession longer than he places all his lower treasures at its command.

But there was a special form of cost, invited by the virtue of our national existence; and it is this in particular that we are now paying,—paying it, I am sorry to say, in the form of retribution because the nation declined to meet it otherwise. But the peculiarity of the case is, as has been affirmed, that it was chiefly the virtue and nobility of the nation which created this debt at the outset.

And now what is the peculiar virtue and glory of this nation? Why, that its national existence is based upon a recognition of the absolute rights and duties of humanity. Theoretically this is our basis; practically there is a commixture; much of this cosmopolitan faith is mingled with much of confined self-regard. But the theoretical fact is the one here in point: since the question now is not of the national *un*faith or infidelity, but of the national faith. And beyond a question, the real faith of the nation, so far as it has one, is represented by its formal declaration, made sacred by the shedding of blood. Our belief really is not in the special right or privilege of Americans, but in the prerogative of man. This prerogative we may have succeeded well or ill in stating and interpreting; the fact, that our appeal is to this, alone concerns us here.

Now this national attitude, so far as history informs me, is unprecedented. The true-born son of Albion, save as an exceptional culture enlarges his soul, believes religiously that God is an Englishman, and that the interests of England precede those of the universe. When, therefore, he sees anything done which depletes the pocket of England, it affects him with a sense of infidelity in those to whom this loss is due. England professes to have a *national* religion; she has, and in a deeper sense than is commonly meant.

We will not disparage England overmuch; she has done good service in history. We will not boast of ourselves; the actual politics of this country have been, in no small part, base and infidel to a degree that is simply sickening. Nevertheless, it remains true that the fundamental idea of the State here represents a new phase of human history. Every European nationality had taken shape and character while yet our globe was not known to be a globe, while before the eyes of all lookers land and sea faded away into darkness and mystery; and it was not possible that common human sympathy should take into its arms a world of which it could not conceive. But a national spirit was here generated when the ocean had been crossed, when the earth had been rounded, when, too, Newton had, as it were, circumnavigated the solar system,—when, therefore, there could be, and must be, a new recognition of humanity. Our country, again, was peopled from the minorities of Europe, from those whom the spirit of the new time had touched, and taken away their content with old institutions,—a population restless, uncertain, yeasty, chaotic, it might be, full of the rawness of new conditions, mean and magnanimous by turns, as such people are wont, but all leavened more or less with a sentiment new in history,—all leavened with a kind of whole-world feeling, a sense of the oneness of humanity, and, as derived from this, a sense of absolute rights of man, of prerogatives belonging to human nature as such.

The truth of all this has been brought under suspicion by the flatulent oratory of our Fourth-of-Julys; but truth it remains. Our nation did enunciate a grand idea never equally felt by any other. Our nation has said, and said with the sword in its right hand, "Every man born into this world has the right from God to make the most and best of his existence, and society is established only to further and guard this sacred right." We thus established a new scale of justice; we raised a demand for the individual which had not been so made before. Freedom and order were made one; both were identified with justice, simple, broad, equal, universal justice. The American idea, then, what is it? *The identification of politics with justice,* this it is. With justice, and this, too, not on a scale of conventional usage, but on the scale of natural right. That, as I read, is the American idea,—making politics moral by their unity with natural justice, justice world-old and world-wide.

This conception—obscurely seen and felt, and mixed with the inevitable amount of folly and self-seeking, yet, after all, this conception—our nation dared to stand up and announce, and to consecrate it by the shedding of blood, calling God and all good men to witness. The deed was grand; the hearts of men everywhere were more or less its accomplices; all the tides of history ran in its favor; kings, forgetting themselves into virtue and

generosity, lent it good wishes or even good arms; it was successful; and on its primary success waited such prosperities as the
world has seldom seen.

But, because the deed was noble, great costs must needs attend
it, attend it long. And first of all the cost of *applying our principle within our own borders*. For, when a place had been obtained
for us among nations, we looked down, and, lo! at our feet the
African—in chains. A benighted and submissive race, down-
trodden and despised from of old, a race of outcasts, of Pariahs,
covered with the shame of servitude, and held by the claim of
that terrible talisman, the word *property,*—here it crouched at
our feet, lifting its hands, imploring. Yes, America, here is your
task now; never flinch nor hesitate, never begin to question now;
thrust your right hand deep into your heart's treasury, bring
forth its costliest, purest justice, and lay its immeasurable bounty
into this sable palm, bind its blessing on this degraded brow. Ah,
but America did falter and question. "How can I?" it said.
"This is a Negro, a *Negro!* Besides, he is PROPERTY!" and so
America looked up, determined to ignore the kneeling form.
With pious blasphemy it said, "He is here providentially; God
in His own good time will dispose of him"; as if God's hour for
a good effect were not the earliest hour at which courage and
labor can bring it about, not the latest to which indolence and
infidelity can postpone it. Then it looked away across oceans to
other continents, and began again the chant, "Man is man; natural right is sacred forever; and of politics the sole basis is universal justice." Joyfully it sang for a while, but soon there began
to come up the clank of chains mingling with its chant, and the
groans of oppressed men and violated women, and prayers to
Heaven for another justice than this; and then the words of its
chant grew bitter in the mouth of our nation, and a sickness came
in its heart, and an evil blush mounted and stood on its brow;
and at length a devil spoke in its bosom and said, "The negro has
no rights that a white man is bound to respect"; and ere the
words were fairly uttered, their meaning, as was indeed inevitable, changed to this,—"A Northern 'mudsill' has no rights

that a Southern gentleman is bound to respect"; and soon guns were heard booming about Sumter, and a new chapter in our history and in the world's history began.

Our nation refused allegiance to its own principles, refused to pay the lawful costs of its virtue and nobility; therefore it is sued in the courts of destiny, and the case is this day on trial.

The case is plain, the logic clear. Natural right is sacred, or it is not. If it is, the negro is lawfully free; if it is not, you may be lawfully a slave. Just how all this stands in the Constitution of the United States I do not presume to say. Other heads, whose business it is, must attend to that. Every man to his vocation. I speak from the stand-point of philosophy, not of politics; I attend to the logic of history, the logic of destiny, according to which, of course, final judgment will be rendered. It is not exactly to be supposed that the statute of any nation makes grass green, or establishes the relationship between cause and effect. The laws of the world are considerably older than our calendar, and therefore date yet more considerably beyond the year 1789. And by the laws of the world, by the eternal relationship between cause and effect, it stands enacted beyond repeal, and graven upon somewhat more durable than marble or brass, that the destiny of this nation for more than one century to come hinges upon its justice to that outcast race,—outcast, but not henceforth to be cast out by us, save to the utter casting down of ourselves. Once it might have been otherwise; now we have made it so. Justice to the African is salvation to the white man upon this continent. Oh, my America, you must not, cannot, shall not be blind to this fact! America, deeper in my love and higher in my esteem than ever before, newly illustrated in worth, newly proven to be capable still, in some directions, of exceeding magnanimity, open your eyes that your feet may have guidance, now when there is such need! Open your eyes to see, that, if you deliberately deny justice and human recognition to one innocent soul in all your borders, you stab at your own existence; for, in violating the unity of humanity, you break the principle that makes you a nation and alive. Give justice to black and white, recognize man as man; or the constituting idea, the vital faith, the crystallizing principle of the nation perishes, and the whole disintegrates, falls into dust.

I invite the attention of conservative men to the fact that in this due paying of costs lies the true conservation. I invite them to observe, that, as every living body has a principle which makes it alive, makes it a unit, harmonizing the action of its members,—as every crystal has a unitary law, which commands the arrangement of its particles, the number and arrangement of its faces and angles,—so it is with every orderly or living state. To this also there is a central, clarifying, unifying faith. Without this you may collect hordes into the brief, brutal empire of a Chingis Khan or Tamerlane; but you can have no firm, free, orderly, inspiring national life.

Whenever and wherever in history this central condition of national existence has been destroyed, there a nation has fallen into chaos, into imbecility, losing all power to produce genius, to generate able souls, to sustain the trust of men in each other, or to support any of the conditions of social health and order. Even advances in the right line of progress have to be made slowly, gradually, lest the shock of newness be too great, and break off a people from the traditions in which its faith is embodied; but a mere recoil, a mere denial and destruction of its centralizing principle, is the last and utmost calamity which can befall any nation.

This is no fine-spun doctrine, fit for parlors and lecture-rooms, but not for counting-rooms and congressional halls. It is solid, durable fact. History is full of it; and he is a mere mole, and blinder than midnight, who cannot perceive it. The spectacle of nations falling into sudden, chronic, careless imbecility is frequent and glaring enough for even wilfulness to see; and the central secret of this sad phenomenon, so I am *sure,* has been suggested here. When the socializing faith of a nation has perished, the alternative for it becomes this, that it can be stable only as it is stagnant, and vigorous only as it is lawless.

Of this I am sure; but whether Bullion Street can be willing to understand it I am not so sure. Yet, if it cannot, or some one in its behalf, grass will grow there. And why should it refuse heed? Who is more concerned? Does Bullion Street desire chaos? Does it wish that the pith should be taken out of every statute, and the chief value from every piece of property? If not, its course is clear. This nation has a vital faith,—or had one,—well grounded in its traditions. Conserve this; or, if it has been impaired, renew its vigor. This faith is our one sole pledge of order, of peace, of growth, of all that we prize in the present, or hope for the future. That it is a noble faith, new in its breadth, its comprehension and magnanimity,—this would seem in my eyes rather to enhance than diminish the importance of its conservation. Yet the only argument against it is, that it *is* generous, broad, inspiring; and the only appeal in opposition to it must be made to the coldness of skepticism, the suicidal miserliness of egotism, or the folly and fatuity of ignorance.

Our nation has a political faith. Will you, conservative men, conserve this, and so regain and multiply the blessing it has already brought? or will you destroy it, and wait till, through at least a century of tossing and tumult, another, and that of less value is grown? A faith, a crystallizing principle for many millions of people is not grown in a day; if it can be grown in a century is problematical. The fact, and the choice, are before you.

Our nation *had* a faith which it cherished with sincerity and sureness. If half the nation has fallen away from this,—if half the remaining moiety is doubtful, skeptical about it,—if, therefore, we are already a house divided against itself and tottering to its fall,—to what is all due? Simply to the fact that no nation can long unsay its central principle, and yet preserve it in faithfulness and power,—that no nation can long preach the sanctity of natural right, the venerableness of man's nature, and the identity of pure justice with political interest, from an auction-block on which men and maidens are sold,—that, in fine, a nation cannot continue long with impunity to play within its own borders the part both of Gessler and Tell, both of Washington and Benedict Arnold, both of Christ and of him that betrayed him.

We must choose. For our national faith we must make honest

payment, so conserving it, and with it all for which nations may hope; or else, refusing to meet these costs, we must suffer the nation's soul to perish, and in the imbecility, the chaos, and shame that will follow, suffer therewith all that nations may lawfully fear.

What good omens, then, attend our time, now when the first officer of the land has put the trumpet to his mouth and blown round the world an intimation that, to the extent of the nation's power, these costs will begin to be paid, this true conservation to be practised! The work is not yet done; and the late elections betoken too much of moral debility in the people. But my trust continues firm. The work will be done,—at least, so far as we are responsible for its doing. And then! Then our shame, our misery, our deadly sickness will be taken away; no more that poison in our politics; no more that degradation in our commercial relations; no more that careful toning down of sentiment to low levels, that it may harmonize with low conditions; no more that need to shun the company of all healthful and heroic thoughts, such as are fit, indeed, to brace the sinews of a sincere social order, but sure to crack the sinews of a feeble and faithless conventionalism. Base men there will yet be, and therefore base politics; but when once our nation has paid the debt it owes to itself and the human race, when once it has got out of its blood the venom of this great injustice, it will, it must, arise beautiful in its young strength, noble in its new-consecrated faith, and stride away with a generous and achieving pace upon the great highways of historical progress. Other costs will come, if we are worthy; other lessons there will be to learn. I anticipate a place for brave and wise restrictions,—for I am no Red Republican,— as well as for brave and generous expansions. Lessons to learn, errors to unlearn, there will surely be; tasks to attempt, and disciplines to practise; but once place the nation in the condition of *health,* once get it at one with its own heart, once get it out of these aimless eddies into clear sea, out of these accursed "doldrums," (as the sailors phrase it,) this commixture of broiling calm and sky-bursting thundergust, into the great trade-winds of natural tendency that are so near at hand,—and I can trust it to meet all future emergency. All the freshest blood of the world is flowing hither: we have but to wed this with the life-blood of the universe, with eternal truth and justice, and God has in store no blessing for noblest nations that will not be secured for ours.

A LETTER
TO THOMAS CARLYLE

Sir,—You have Homered it of late in a small way, one sees. You profess to sing the purport of our national struggle. "South chooses to hire its servants for life, rather than by the day, month, or year; North bludgeons the Southern brain to prevent the same": that, you say, is the American Iliad in a Nutshell. In a certain sense, more's the pity, it must be supposed that you speak correctly; but be assured that this is the American Iliad in no other nutshell than your private one,—in those too contracted cerebral quarters to which, with respect to our matters, your powerful intelligence, under such prolonged and pitiless extremes of dogmatic compression, has at last got reduced.

Seriously, not in any trivial wilfulness of retort, I accuse you of a narrowness and pettiness of understanding with regard to America. Give me leave to "wrestle a fall" with you on this theme. And as I can with but twoscore years match your threescore and five, let me entreat of your courtesy to set that circumstance aside, and to constitute me, for the nonce, your equal in age and privilege of speech. For I must wrestle to-day in earnest!

You are a great nature, a great writer, and a man of piercing intellect: he is a jack or a dunce that denies it. But of you, more than of most men at all your equals in intellectual resource, it may be said that yours is not a spherical or universal, but a special

Atlantic Monthly, October, 1864.

and linear intelligence,—of great human depth and richness, but special nevertheless. Of a particular order of truths you are an incomparable champion; but always you are the champion and on the field, always your genius has its visor down, and glares through a loop-hole with straitened intentness of vision. A particular sort of errors and falsities you can track with the scent of a blood-hound, and with a speed and bottom not surpassed, if equalled; but the Destinies have put the nose of your genius to the ground, and sent it off for good and all upon a particular trail. You sound, indeed, before your encounter, such a thrilling war-note as turns the cripple's crutch to an imaginary lance; you open on your quarry with such a cry as kindles a huntsman's heart beneath the bosoms of nursing mothers. No living writer possesses the like fascination. Yet, in truth, we should all have tired of your narrow stringency long ago, did there not run in the veins of your genius so rich and ruddy a human blood. The profoundness of your interest in man, and the masterly way in which you grasp character, give to your thought an inner quality of centrality and wholeness, despite the dogmatic partiality of its shaping at your hands. And so your enticement continues, intensely partial though it be.

Continues,—but with growing protest, and growing ground for it. For, to speak the truth, by your kind permission, without reserve, you are beginning to suffer from yourself. You are threatening to perish of too much Thomas Carlyle. I venture to caution you against that tremendous individual. He is subduing your genius to his own special humors; he is alloying your mental activity, to a fearful degree, with dogmatic prepossession; he is making you an intellectual *routinier,* causing thereby an infiltration of that impurity of which all routine at last dies. For years we that love you most have seen that you were ceasing more and more to hold open, fresh relations with truth,—that you were straitening and hardening into the linear, rigid eagerness of the mere propagandist. You have, if I may so speak, been turning all your front-head into back-head, giving to your cerebral powers the characters of preappointed, automatic action, which are proper to the cerebellum. It cannot be denied that you have thus acquired a remarkable, machine-like simplicity, force, and constancy of mental action,— your brain-wheels spinning away with such a steam-engine whirr as one cannot but admire; but, on the other hand, as was inevitable, you have become astonishingly insensitive to all truths, save those with which you are established in organic connection; nor could the products of Manchester mills be bargained for beforehand with more certainty than the results of your intellectual activity. You can be silent,—I venture to assert so much; but if you speak at all, we know perfectly well what description of fabric *must* come from your loom.

It does not, therefore, surprise us, does not clash with our sense of your native greatness, that for our particular Iliad you prove a very nutshell Homer indeed. For I must not disguise it from you that this is exactly the case. It was *Homerus in nuce* first; and the pitiful purport of the epic results less from any smallness in the action celebrated than from that important law, not, perhaps, wholly new to your own observation, which forbids a pint-measure to contain more than a pint, though you dip it full from the ocean itself.

You are great, but not towards us Americans. Towards us you are little and insignificant and superfluous. Your eyes, though of wondrous efficacy in their way, blink in our atmosphere like those of an owl in broad sunlight; and if you come flying here, it is the privilege of the smallest birds—of which you are quite at liberty to esteem me one—to pester you back into your mediæval twilight.

Shall I try to tell you why you can have no right to judge us and our affairs? By your leave, then, and briefly.

There is a spiritual nature of man, which is ever and everywhere the same; and, through the necessary presence of this in every human being, there is a common sense and a common conscience, which make each man one with all others. Here in America we are seeking to give the force of political sovereignty to this common and unitive nature,—assuming that all political problems are at last questions of simple justice, courage, good sense, and fellow-feeling, which any sound heart and healthy intelligence may appreciate.

On the other hand, there is the truth of spiritual Rank or Degree,—that one man may be immensely superior in human quality to another. This is the truth that is most powerfully present to your mind, and you would constitute government strictly, if not solely, in the light of it. To this you are impelled by the peculiar quality of your genius, which is so purely *biographical,* so inevitably drawn to special personalities, that you can hardly conceive of history otherwise than as a record of personal influence.

We assume, then, as a basis, common sense; you, uncommon sense. We assume Unity or Identity; you assume Difference, and seek to reconstitute unity only through mastership on the one hand and reverent obedience on the other. We do not deny Difference; we recognize the truth of spiritual Degree; we merely *elect the common element as the material out of which to constitute, and the force by which to operate, the State.*

Now my judgment is, that either the truth of a common Manhood or the truth of spiritual Rank may be made primary in a State, and that with admirable results, provided it be duly allied and tempered with its opposite. For these opposites I hold to be correlative and polaric, each required by the other. But chasm is worse than indistinction; and he that breaks the circle of human fellowship is more mischievous than he who blurs the hues of gradation.

I affirm, then, that America has a grand spiritual fact at the base of her political system. But you are the prophet of an opposite order of truths. And you are so intensely the partisan of your pole, that you have not a moment's patience with anything else, above all with an opposite partiality. And wanting sympathy and patience with it, you equally want apprehension of its meaning.

But this is not all. An awful shadow accompanies the brilliant day of your genius. That dark humor of yours, that woful demon from whose companionship, by the law of your existence, you cannot be free, tolls funeral-bells and chants the dirges of death in your ears forever. What your faith does not take with warmth to its bosom it must spurn violently away; where you cannot hope strongly, you must vehemently despair; what your genius does not illumine to your heart it must bury as in shadows of eternal night. It being, therefore, of the nature of your mind to shine powerfully on the eminences of mankind, it became in consequence no less its nature to call up over the broad levels a black fog that even its own eye could not penetrate. Thus with you, if I understand you rightly, the *common* and the *fateful* are nearly one and the same; the Good is to you an exceptional energy which struggles up from the level forces of the universe. Is not your conception of human existence nearly this: a perpetual waste deluge, and here and there some Noah in his ark above it?

There is noble truth to be seen from this point of view,—truth to which America also will have to attend. But being intensely limited to this sole point of view, you are *utterly* without eye for the whole significance of our national life. You are not only *at* the opposite pole from us, but your whole heart and intelligence are *included in* the currents of that polaric opposition.

Still further. I think, that, having made out its scheme of thought, your mind soon contracts a positive demand *even for the evil conditions* which, in your estimation, made that scheme necessary. To illustrate. A man is roused at night, and sent flying for a physician in some sudden and terrible emergency. He returns, broken-winded, to learn that it was altogether a false alarm. It is quite possible that his first emotion, on receiving this intelligence, will not be pleasure, but indignation; he may feel that somebody ought to *be* sick, since he has been at such pains. Pardon me, if I think your position not wholly dissimilar. It seems to me to have become an imperative requisition of your mind that nine-tenths of mankind should be fools. They *must* be so; else you have no place for them in your system, and know not what to do with them. As fools, you have full arrangements made for their accommodation. Some hero, some born ruler of men, is to come forth (out of your books) and reduce them to obedience, and lord it over them in a most useful manner. But if they will not be fools, if they contumaciously refuse to be fools, they disturb the necessary conditions of kingship, and, of course, deserve much reprobation. I do not, therefore, feel myself unjust to you in saying, that, the better the American people behave, *in consistency with their political traditions and customary modes of thought,* the less you are able to be pleased with them. If they demean themselves as fools and incapables, (as they sometimes do,) they bring grist to your mill; but if they show wisdom, courage, and constancy, they leave you to stand at your mill-doors and grumble for want of toll,—as in the nutshell-epic aforesaid.

Well, there are many foolish and some wise, and I, for one, could heartily wish both classes more justly placed; for he who styles me an extreme intrepid democrat pays me a compliment to which I have no claim. While, then, by "kingship" you meant something human and noble, while I could deem the command you coveted for strong and wise men to be somewhat which should *lift the weak and unwise above the range of their own force and intelligence,* I held your prophesying in high esteem, and readily pardoned any excesses of expression into which your prophetic *afflatus* (being Scotch) might betray you.

But your appetite for kingship seems to have gained in strength while it lost in delicacy and moral significance, till it has become an insatiable craving, which disdains not to batten on very vile garbage. If one rule, and another be ruled, and if the domination be open, frank, and vigorous, you seem to feast on the fact, be this domination as selfish in its nature and as brutal in its form as it may. Whether its aim be to uplift or to degrade its subjects, whether it be clean or filthy, of heaven or of hell, a stress of generous purpose or a mere emphasis of egotism,—what pause do you make to inquire concerning this? The appearance is, that any sovereignty, in these democratic days, is over-welcome to your hunger to admit of pause; and a rule, whose undisguised aim is, not to supplement the strength of the weak, but to pillage them of its product, not to lend the ignorant a wisdom above their own, but to make their ignorance perpetual as a source of pecuniary profit to their masters, may reckon upon your succors whenever succors are needed.

Hence your patronage of our slavery. Hence your effort to commend it by a description so incomparably false, that, though one should laugh derision at it from Christmas to Candlemas, he would not laugh enough. "Hiring servants for life,"—that is the most intrepid *lucus a non lucendo* of the century. It fairly takes one's breath away. It is stunning, ravishing. One can but cry, on recovering his wind,—Hear, O Caucus, and give ear, O Mock-Auction! ye railway Hudsons, tricksters, impostors, ye demagogues that love the people in stump-speeches at $___ per year, ye hired bravos of the bar that stab justice in the dark, ye Jesuit priests that "lie for God," listen all, and learn how to do it! What are your timid devices, compared with this of be-numbing your adversary at the start by an outright electric shock of untruth? But a man must be supported by a powerful sense of sincerity to be capable of a statement so royally false that the truth itself shall look tame and rustic beside it.

You have spoken ill of a certain sort of German metaphysic; but I perceive that you have now become a convert to it. The final *arcanum* of that, I think, is, Something = Nothing. You give this abstraction a concrete form; your axiom is, No Hire = Hire for Life. To deny that laborers have any property of their own toil, and to allow them their poor peck of maize and pound of bacon per week, not at all as a wage for their work, but solely as a means of converting corn into cotton, and cotton into seats in Congress and summers at Saratoga,—that, according to the Chelsea metaphysic, is "hiring them for life"! To deny laborers any legal *status* as persons, and any social *status* as human souls,— to give them fodder for food, and pens for homes,— to withhold from them the school, the table, and the sanctities of marriage,— if that is not "hiring them for life," what is it? To affirm, by consistent practice, that no spiritual, no human value appertains to the life of laboring men and women,—to rate them in their very persons as commercial values, measuring the virtue of their existence with coin, as cloths are measured with a yardstick,— this, we all see, is "hiring them for life"! To take from women the LEGAL RIGHT to be chaste,—to make it a *capital offence* for a woman of the laboring caste to defend her own person by blows, for any "husband" or father of the laboring caste to defend wife or daughter with blows, against the lust of another caste, and, having made them thus helpless before outrage, to close the judicial tribunals against their testimony, and refuse them the faintest show of redress,—truly, it is very kind of you to let us know that this is the simplest piece of "hiring for life," for without that charitable assistance the fact would surely have eluded our discovery. How could we have found it out without your assistance, when, after that aid has been rendered, the fact continues to seem so utterly otherwise as to reflect even upon your generous information the colors of an unexampled untruth?

No-Hire + Dehumanization of the Laborer = Life-Hire? We never should have dreamt of it!

Within the past year, a document has come into my hands which they may thank their stars who are not required to see. It is the private diary of a most eminent and respectable slaveholder, recently dead. The chances of war threw it into the hands of our troops, and the virtue of a noble surgeon rescued it from defiling uses, and sent it to me, as one whose duty bound him to know the worst. Of its authenticity there is not a shadow of question. And such a record of pollution,—of wallowing, to which the foulness of swine is as the life of honey-bees harboring in the bosoms of roses,—I deliberately suppose can never have got into black and white before. Save in general terms, I can hardly speak of it; but one item I must have the courage to suggest more definitely. Having bidden a young slave-girl (whose name, age, color, etc., with the shameless precision that marks the entire document, are given) to attend upon his brutal pleasure, and she silently remaining away, he writes,—"Next morning ordered her a dozen lashes for disobedience." * For disobedience, observe! She had been "hired for life"; the great Carlyle had witnessed the bargain; and behold, she has broken the contract! She must be punished; Mr. Carlyle and his co-cultivator of the virtue of obedience (*par nobile fratrum*) will see to it that she is duly punished. She shall go to the whipping-post, this disobedient virgin; she shall have twelve lashes, (for the Chelsea gods are

---

* The writer is known to the publishers of the "Atlantic Monthly": he is one whose word is not and cannot be called in question; and he pledges his word that the above is exact and *proven* fact. Horace Mann, years ago, made public some similar cases.

severe, and know the use of "beneficent whip,") —twelve lashes on the naked person,—blows with the terrible slave-whip, beneath which the skin purples in long, winding lines, then breaks and gushes into spirts of red blood, and afterwards cicatrizes into perpetual scars; for disobedience is an immorality not to be overlooked!

Yes, Thomas Carlyle, I hold you a party to these crimes. *You,* YOU are the brutal old man who would flog virgins into prostitution. You approve the system; you volunteer your best varnish in its commendation; and this is an inseparable and *legal* part of it. Legal, I say,—legal, and not destructive of respectability. That is the point. In ordering such lashes, that ancient miscreant (for old he already was) neither violated any syllable of the slave-code, nor forfeited his social position. He was punishing "disobedience"; he was administering "justice"; he was illustrating the "rights of property"; he was using the lawful "privileges of gentlemen."

No doubt, deeds of equal infamy are done in the dens of New York. But in New York they *are* infamous. In New York they are indeed done in *dens,* by felons who flee the eye of the policeman,—unless, to be sure, the police have been appointed by a certain *alter ego* of yours in negro-hatred, whilom chief magistrate and disgrace of that unfortunate city. But under your life-service *régime* things are managed in a more enlightened way. There they who have liberty—and *sometimes* use the liberty— to torture women into beastly submissions, do not hide from the laws, they make the laws. There such a personage as the one mentioned may be a *gentleman,* a man of high standing, "one of the most respectable men in the State" (Florida).

And this, just *this,*—for surely you will not be a coward, and dodge consequences,—you name a scheme of life-hire. This you esteem so much superior to our democratic way of holding each man and woman to be the shrine of rights which have an infinite sanctity, and of adjudging it the chief duty of the State to annex to these rights the requisite force for their practical assertion.

Is it, then, You, or is it some burglarious Devil that has broken into your bosom and stolen your soul, who is engaged in plastering over this infernal fester with smooth euphemisms? Are You verily the mechanic who is engaged in veneering these out-houses of hell with rosewood? Is it your very and proper Self that stands there sprinkling *eau-de-Cologne* on the accursed reek of that pit of putrescence, so to disguise and commend it to the nostrils of mankind? Is it in very deed Thomas Carlyle, Thomas the Great, who now volunteers his services as male lady's-maid to the queen-strumpet of modern history, and offers to her sceptred foulness the benefit of his skill at the literary rouge-pots? You? Yes? I give you joy of your avocations! Truly, it was worth the while, having such a cause, to defame a noble people in the very hour of their life-and-death struggle!

Well, you have made your election; now I make mine. It is my deliberate belief that no man ever gave heartier love and homage to another than I to you; but while one woman in America may be *lawfully* sent to the whipping-post on such occasion, I will hold your existence and name, if they come between me and her rescue, but as the life of a stinging gnat! I love you,—but cannot quite sacrifice to you the sanctity of womanhood, and all the honor and all the high hopes of a great nation. Your scheme of "life-hire" will therefore have to undergo very essential modifications, such as will not only alter, but *reverse,* its most characteristic features, before I can esteem either it or the advocacy of it anything less than abominable.

But where are you now with relation to that Thomas Carlyle whose "Sartor Resartus" I read twenty years ago afoot and on horseback, sleeping with it under my pillow and wearing it in my pocket till pocket and it were worn out,—I alone there in the remote solitudes of Maine? We have both travelled far since then; but whither have you been travelling? The whole wide heaven was not too wide for you then; but now you can be jolly in your "nutshell." Then, you held spiritual, or human, values to be final, infinite, absolute, and could gibe in your own incomparable way at the besotted conventionalism which would place commercial values above them; now, who chants with such a roaring, pious nasal at that apotheois of Property which our modern commercial slavery essentially is? Then, with Schiller, you desired, as a basis of political society, something better than a doctrine of personal *rights,* something more noble, human, unitary, something more opposed to egoistic self-assertion, namely, a doctrine of *powers* and their consequent *duties;* now, a scheme of society which is the merest riot or insurrection of property-egotism reckons you among its chiefest advocates. Then, you struck heroically out for a society more adequate to the spiritual possibilities of man; now, social infidelity *plus* cotton and polite dining would seem to suffice for you.

Ah, Heaven! is anything sadder than to see a grand imperial soul, long worthy and secure of all love and honor, at length committing suicide, not by dying, but by living? Ill it is when they that do deepest homage to a great spirit can no longer pray for the increase of his days; when there arises in their hearts a pleasure in the growing number of his years expressly as these constitute a deduction from the unknown sum total of those which have been appointed him; and when the utmost bravery of their affection must breathe, not *Serus,* but cɪᴛo in *cœlum redeas!* O royal Lear of our literature, who have spurned from your love the dearest daughter of your thought, is it only left us to say, "How friendly is Death,—Death, who restores us to free relations with the whole, when our own fierce partialities have imprisoned and bound us hand and foot"?

Royal you are, royal in pity as in purpose; and you have done, nay, I trust may still be doing, imperishable work. If only you did not hate democracy so bitterly as to be perpetually prostrated by the recoil of your own gun! Right or wrong in its inception, this aversion has now become a chronic ailment, which drains insatiably at the fountains of your spiritual force. I offer you the suggestion; I can do no more.

To have lost, in the hour of our trial, the fellowship of yourself, and of others in England whom we most delighted to honor, is a loss indeed. Yet we grieve a thousand times more for you than for ourselves; and are not absorbed in any grief. It is clear to us that the Eternal Providence has assigned us our tasks, not by your advice, nor by vote of Parliament,—astonishing to sundry as that may seem. Your opinion of the matter we hold, therefore, to be quite beside the matter; and drivel, like that of your nutshell-epic, by no means tends to make us wish that Providence had acted upon European counsel rather than upon His Own! Moreover, we are *very* busy in these days, and can have small eye to the by-standers. We are busy, and are likely to be so long; for the peace that succeeds to such a war will be as dangerous and arduous as the war itself. We have as little time, therefore, to grieve as to brag or bluster; we must work. We neither solicit nor repel your sympathy; we must work,—work straight on, and let all that be as it can be.

We seek not to conceal even from *you* that our democracy has great weaknesses, as well as great strength. Mean, mercenary, and stolid men are not found in England alone; they are ominously abundant here also. We have lunatic radicalisms as well as sane, idiotic conservatisms as well as intelligent. Too much for safety, our politics are purulent, our good men over-apt to forget the objects of government in a besotted devotion to the form. It is possible we may yet discover that universal suffrage can be a trifle too universal,—that it should pause a *little* short of the state prison. New York must see to it that the thief does not patronize the judge, and sit in the prisoner's box as on the bench of a higher court. Our democracy has somewhat to learn; it *knows* that it has somewhat to learn, and says cheerfully, "What is the use of living without learning?"

What can we do but meet the future with an open intelligence and a stout heart? And this I say,—I, who am almost an extreme dissenter from extreme democracy,—if our people bring to all future emergencies those qualities of earnestness, courage, and constancy which they have thus far contributed to the present, they will disgrace neither themselves nor their institutions; and it will be their honor more than once to extort some betrayal of dissatisfaction from those who, like yourself, are happiest to see a democracy behaving, not well, but ill.

"Peter of the North," then, has made up his mind. He is re-solved on having three things:—

First, a government; a real government; a government not to be whistled down the wind by any jack (or jeff) who chooses to secede; a government that will not dawdle with hands in pockets while this continent is converted into a maggot-swarm of ten-acre empires;

Secondly, a government whose purpose, so far as it can act, shall be to forward *every* man on the path of his proper humanity;

Thirdly, a government constituted and operated, so far as shall finally prove possible, by the common intelligence and common conscience of the whole people.

This is Peter's business at present: he is intently minding his business; and has been heard to mutter in his breast that "it might be as well if others did the same." What "others," pray?

COMMUNICATION

Whether virtue can be taught is a question over which Plato lingers long. And it is a curious illustration of the different eyes with which different men read, that some students of Plato are confident he answers the question in the affirmative, while others are equally sure that he gives it an unqualified negative. "Plato," says Schwegler, "holds fast to the opinion that virtue is science, and therefore to be imparted by instruction." "We are told," says Burgess, one of Bohn's translators, "that, as virtue is not a science, it cannot, like a science, be made a subject of teaching." Professor Blackie, again, an open-minded and eloquent scholar, cannot doubt that virtue may be verbally imparted, nor, therefore, that the great Athenian thinker so believed and affirmed.

What is the voice of common sense and the teaching of history touching this matter? Can a liberal and lofty nature be included in words, and so passed over to another? Elevation of character, nobility of spirit, wealth of soul,—is any method known, or probably ever to be known, among men, whereby these can be got into a text-book, and then out of the text-book into a bosom wherein they had no dwelling before? Alas, is not the story of the world too full of cases in which the combined eloquence of verbal instruction, vital influence, and lustrous example, aided even by all the inspirations of the most majestic and moving presence, have failed utterly to shape the character of disciples? Did Alcibiades profit greatly by the conversation of Socrates? Was Judas extremely ennobled by the companionship of Jesus?

Atlantic Monthly, October, 1864.

Was it to any considerable purpose that the pure-minded, earnest, affluent Cicero strewed the seeds of Stoic culture upon the wayside nature of his son? Did Faustina learn much from Antoninus Pius, or Commodus from Marcus Aurelius?

I think we must assume it as the judgment of common sense that there neither is nor is likely to be any educational mortar wherein a fool may be so brayed that he shall come forth a wise man. The broad, unequivocal sentence of history seems to be that whoever is not noble by nature will hardly be rendered so by art. Education can do much; it can foster nobilities, it can discourage vices; but literal conveyance of lofty qualities, can it effect that? Can it create opulence of soul in a sterile nature? Can it cause a thin soil to do the work of a deep one? We have seen harsh natures mellowed, violent natures chastened, rough ones refined; but who has seen an essentially mean nature made largehearted, self-forgetful, fertile of grandest faiths and greatest deeds? Who has beheld a Thersites transformed into an Achilles? Who a Shylock, Iago, or Regan changed into an Antonio, Othello, or Cordelia, or a Simon Magus into a Paul? What virtue of nature is in a man culture may bring out; but to put nature into any man surpasses her competence.

Nay, it would even seem that in some cases the finest openings and invitations for what is best in man must operate inversely, and elicit only what is worst in him. Every profoundest truth, when uttered with fresh power in history, polarizes men, accumulating atheism at one pole, while collecting faith and resolve at the other. As the sun bleaches some surfaces into whiteness, but tans and blackens others, so the sweet shining of Truth illumines some countenances with belief, but some it darkens into a scowl of hate and denial. The American Revolution gave us George Washington; but it gave us also Benedict Arnold. One and the same great spiritual emergency in Europe produced Luther's Protestantism and Loyola's Jesuitism. Our national crisis has converted General Butler; what has it done for Vallandigham?

It were easy to show that the deepest intelligence of the world concurs with common sense in this judgment. Its declaration ever is, in effect, that, though Paul plant and Apollos water, yet fruit can come only out of divine and infinite Nature,—only, that is, out of the native, incommunicable resources of the soul. "No man can come to me," said Jesus, "except the Father draw him." "To him that hath shall be given." The frequent formula, "He that hath ears to hear, let him hear," is a confession that no power of speech, no wisdom of instruction, can command results. The grandest teacher, like the humblest, can but utter his word, sure that the wealthy and prepared spirits will receive it, and equally sure that shallow, sterile, and inane natures will either not receive it at all, or do so to extremely little purpose.

And such, as I read, is the judgment of Plato; though, ever disposed to explore the remote possibilities of education, he discusses the subject in a tentative spirit, as if vaguely hoping that more might, through some discovery in method, be accomplished by means of doctrine. But in the "Republic" his permanent persuasion is shown. He there bases his whole scheme of polity, as Goethe in the second part of "Wilhelm Meister," bases his scheme of education, upon a primary inspection of natures, in which it is assumed that culture must begin by humbly accepting the work of Nature, forswearing all attempt to add one jot or tittle to the native virtue of any human spirit.

It is always, however, less important for us to know what another thinks upon any high matter than to know what is our own deepest and inevitable thought concerning it; for, as the man himself thinketh, not as another thinketh for him, so is he; his own thoughts are forces and engines in his nature; those of any other are at best but candidates for these profound effects. I propose, therefore, that we throw open the whole question of man's benefit to man by means of words. Let us inquire—if possible, with somewhat of courage and vigor—what are the limits and what the laws of instructive communication.

And our first discovery will be that such communication has adamantine limitations. The off-hand impression of most persons would probably be that we are able to make literal conveyance of our thought. But, in truth, one could as soon convey the life out of his veins into the veins of another as transfer from his own mind to that of another any belief, thought, or perception whatsoever.

Words are simply the signs, they are not the vehicles, of thought. Like all signs, they convey nothing, but only suggest. Like all signs, they are intelligible to none but the initiated. One man, having a certain mental experience, hoists, as it were, a signal, like ships at sea, whereby he would make suggestion of it to another; and if in the mental experience of that other be somewhat akin to this, which, by virtue of that kindred, can interpret its symbol, then only, and to the extent of such interpretation, does communication occur. But the mental experience itself, the thought itself, does not pass; it only makes the sign.

If, for example, I utter the word *God,* it conveys nothing out of my mind into the mind of you, the reader; it simply appeals to your conception of divinity. If I attempt to explain, then every word of the explanation must be subject to the same conditions; not one syllable of it can do more than merely appeal to somewhat already in your mind. For instance, suppose I say, *God is love;* what then is done? The appeal is shifted to another sign; that is all. What my own soul, fed from the vital resources and incited by the vital relationships of my life, has learned of love, that my thought may connect with the word; but of all this nothing passes when it is uttered; and the sound, arriving at your ear, can do no more than invite you to summon and bring before the eye of your consciousness that which your own soul, out of its divine depths and through the instruction of vital relationship, has learned and has privily whispered to you of this sacred mystery, love. Just so much as each one, in the inviolable solitudes of his own consciousness, has learned to connect with this, or with any great word, just that, and never a grain more, it can summon. And if endeavor be made to explain any such by others, the explanation can come no nearer; it can only send words to your ear, each of which performs its utmost office by inviting you to call up and bring before your cognizance this or that portion of your mental experience. But always what answers the call is your mental experience, no less yours, no less wedded to your life, than the blood in your arteries; it cannot be that of any other.

And the same is true, or nearly the same, respecting the most obvious outside matters. Suppose one to make merely this statement, *I see a house*. Now, if the person addressed has ever had experience of the act of vision, if he has ever seen anything, he will know what *see* means; otherwise not. If, again, he has ever seen a house, he will know what *house* denotes; not otherwise. Or suppose, that, not knowing, he ask what a house is, and that the first speaker attempt to explain by telling him that it is such and such a structure, built of brick, wood, or stone; then it is assumed that he has seen stone, wood, or brick, that he has seen the act of building, or at least its result;—and in fine, the explanation, every syllable of it, can do no more than appeal to perceptions of which the questioner is assumed to have had experience.

We do, indeed, gain an approximate knowledge of things we have never seen. For example, I have an imperfect notion of a banian-tree, though I have never seen one; but it is only by having seen other trees, and by having also had the perceptions to which appeal is made in describing the peculiarities of the banian. So he who is born blind may learn so much concerning outward objects as the senses of touch, hearing, smell, and taste can impart to him; and he may profit by verbal information to such extent as these perceptions enable him. But the perception itself, and so thought, faith, and in fine all mental experience whatsoever, whether of high order or low, whether relating to objects within us or to objects without, take place only in the privacy of our own minds, and are in their substance not to be transferred.

Observe with precision what is here said. The mental experience of each man, if it be of any spiritual depth, has transacted itself in his nature in virtue, to a most important degree, of spiritual relationship with other human beings. There never was an act of development in any man's soul that did not imply a humanity, and involve the virtue of social affinity. I should be dumb, but for the ears of others; I should be deaf, that is, my human ear would be closed, but for human voices; and there is no particle of human energy, and no tint of human coloring, for which we are not, in part, indebted to vital human fellowship. Nevertheless, of this experience, though in the absence of social connection it could not have occurred, not one jot nor tittle can be made over to another by means of words. It can hoist its verbal signal, and the like experience in other souls may interpret the sign; it can do no more.

Men may, indeed, *commune;* that is, they may by verbal conference enter mutually into a sense of an already existing unity of inward experience; and there are other and eminent uses of words, of which more anon; but here let it be noted with sufficient emphasis that of minds there can be no mixture, and that speech can make no substantive conveyance of any mental product from one mind to another. Each soul must draw from its native fountains; though we must never forget that without conversation and social relationship its divine thirst would not have been excited.

Therefore, in the midst of all warmest and quickest verity of social nearness, there is a kind of sacred and inviolable solitude of the soul. We speak across to each other, as out of different planets in heaven; and the closest intimacy of souls is like that of double stars which revolve about each other, not like that of two lumps of clay which are squeezed and confounded together.

So much, then, concerning the limits of verbal communication. Words, we say, are not vehicles. No perception, no mental possession, passes from mind to mind. You can impart to another no piece of knowledge whose main elements were not already in his mind, no thought which was not substantially existent in his consciousness before your voice began to seek his ear. Instructors may, indeed, put a pupil in the way to obtain fresh perceptions, and more rarely a wise man may put an apt disciple in the way to obtain deeper insights; but, after all, the learner must *learn;* the learner must for himself behold the fact, with the eyes of body or of soul; and he must behold it as it is in itself, not merely as it is in words.

Hence the new scheme of school-education. Agassiz says, in substance,——"If you would teach a boy geography, take him out on the hills, and make the earth herself his instructor. If you would teach him respecting tigers or turtles, *show* him tiger or turtle. Take him to a Museum of Natural History; let him always, so far as possible, learn about facts from the facts themselves." Judicious and important advice. And the basis of it we find in what has been set forth above, namely, that words convey no perception, whether of physical or of spiritual truth.

It follows, therefore, that only he whose soul is eloquent within him will gain much from any eloquence of his fellow. Only he whose heart is a prophet will hear the prophet. A divine preparation of the nature, divine activities of the soul, precede all high uses of communication. Though Demosthenes or Phillips speak, it is the hearer's own spirit that convinces him. Conviction cannot be forced upon one from without. Hence the well-known futility of belligerent controversy. No possible logic will lead a man ahead of his own intelligence; neither will any take from him the persuasions which correspond to his mental condition. A good logical *pose* may sometimes serve to lower the crest of an obstreperous sophist, as boughs of one species of ash are said to quell the rattlesnake; but with both these sinuous animals the effect is temporary, and the quality of the creature remains unchanged.

Even though one be sincerely desirous of advancing his intelligence, it is seldom, as Mr. Emerson has somewhere said, of much use for him to carry his questions to another. He of whom insight is thus asked may be sage, eloquent, apt to teach; but it will commonly be found, nevertheless, that his words, for some reason, do not seem to suit the case in hand: admirable words they are, perhaps, for some cases closely analogous to this, it may be for all such cases, and it is a thousand pities that the present one does not come within their scope; but this, as ill luck will have it, is that other case which they do *not* fit.

And yet, despite these iron limits, communication is not only one of the especial delights, but also one of the chief uses, of human life. As every spiritual activity implies fellowship, so does almost every thought, almost every result of spiritual activity, imply some speech of our fellows. Voices and books,—who would be himself without them? I do not believe myself to have now in my mind one valuable thought which owes nothing to the written or spoken thought of other men, living or dead.

How, then, is it that the speech of our fellows renders us aid? What are to us the uses of the words of others?

And here be it first of all frankly acknowledged, that there is much speech of no remarkable import, in itself considered, which yet serves good ends. There is much speech whose office is simply to refresh the sense of fellowship. It will not make a good leading article; but the leading article which subserves equal uses is not to be contemned. So much are men empowered by each other, that any careless, kindly chat which gives them the sense of cordial nearness gives also warmth and invigoration. Better than most ambitious conversation is the light, happy, bubbling talk which means at bottom simply this:——"We are at home together; we believe in each other." Words are good, if they only festoon love and trust. Words are good, if they merely show us that worthy natures do not suspect us, do not lock their closets when we are in the house, do not put their souls in dress-costume to meet us, but leave their thoughts and hearts naked in our presence, and are not ashamed. Be it mine sometimes to sit with my friend when our mere nearness and unity of spirit are felt by us both to be so utterly eloquent, that, without silence, we forbear to set up any rivalry to them by grave and meditated speech,—— observing, it may be, a falling leaf toyed with by the wind, and speaking words that drop from the lips like falling leaves, and float down a zephyr that knows not which way to blow. Some of the sweetest and most fruitful hours of life are these in which we speak half-articulate nothings, merely airing the sense of fellowship, and so replete with this wealth of vital intimacy that we have room for nothing more.

But our aim is to regard communication as an instruction, and to consider the more explicit and definite uses of words.

And of these the first, and one of the chief, is based upon the very limitations which have been set forth,——upon the very fact that words are *not* vehicles. I have said that there is a certain divine solitude of the soul; and of this solitude the uses are infinitely great. The absolute soul of humanity, we hold, seeks to insphere itself in each person, though in each giving itself a peculiar or individual representation; and only as this insphering takes place are the ends of creation attained, only so is man made indeed a *human* life. Therefore must we draw out of that, out of that alone; therefore truth is permitted to come to us only out of these infinite depths, albeit incitement, invitation, and the ability to draw from these native fountains may be due to social connection. Because our life is really enriched only as the absolute soul gives itself to us, therefore will it suffer us no otherwise than by its gift to supply our want. And as it cannot give itself to us save in response to a felt want, a seeking, an inward demand, it belongs to the chief economies of our life to bring us to this attitude of inward request, to this call and claim upon the resources of our intelligence.

Now words come to us as empty vessels, which we are to fill from within; and in making for this purpose a requisition upon the perpetual contents of reason, conscience, and imagination, we open a valve through which new spiritual powers enter, and add themselves to our being. If the word *God* be sometimes spoken simply and spontaneously, a youth who hears it will be sure upon some day, when the sense of the infinite and divine stirs vaguely within him, to ask himself what this word means, to require his soul to tell him what is the verity corresponding thereto; and precisely this requisition is what the soul desires, for only when sought may its riches be found. The utilities of words in this kind are deserving of very grave estimation. Words teach us much, but they teach less by what is in them than by what is not in them,—less by what they give to us than by what they demand from us.

It is, therefore, one of the grand services of communication to bring us to the limits of communication, making us feel, that, ere it can go farther, there must occur in us new stretches of thought, new energies of hope, faith, and all noble imagining. It were well, therefore, that, among other things, we should sometimes thank God for our ignorance and weakness,—thank Him for what we do *not* understand and are not equal to; for with every fresh recognition of these, with every fresh approach to the borders of our intelligence, we are prepared for new requisitions upon the soul. As in a pump the air is exhausted in order that the water may rise, so a void in our intelligence *caused by its own energy* precedes every enrichment. Hence he who will not admit to his heart the sense of ignorance will always be a fool; he who is perpetually filled with self-sufficiency will never be filled with much else. And from this point of view one may discern the significance of that doctrine of humility which belongs equally to Socratic thinking and Christian believing.

It follows, too, that we need not laboriously push and foist upon the young our faith and experience. Aside from direct vital influence, which is a powerful propagandist, our simple, natural, inevitable speech will cause them to do much better than learn from us, it will cause them to learn from their own souls. And however uncertain may be a harvest from questions asked of others, a great question rightly put to one's self not only must be fruitful, but carries in it a capacity for infinite fruitfulness; while the longer and more patiently and persistently one can wait for an answer, the richer his future is to be. I am sure of him who can put to his heart the great questions of life, and wait serenely and vigilantly for a response, one, two, ten years, a lifetime, well-nigh an eternity, if need be, not falling into despondencies and despairing skepticisms because the universe forbears to babble and tattle its secret ere yet he half or a thousandth part guesses how deep and holy that secret is, but quietly, heroically asking and waiting. And toward this posture of asking the profound and vital words assist us by being heard,—which is their first eminent use to us.

Secondly, they serve us greatly, when they simply cause a pre-existing community of thought to be mutually recognized. It is much to bring like to like, brand to brand, believing soul to believing soul. As several pieces of anthracite coal will together make a powerful heat, but separately will not burn at all, so in the conjunction of similar faiths and beliefs there is a wholly new effect; it is not at all the mere sum of the forces previously in operation, but a pure product of union. "My confidence in my own belief," said Novalis, "is increased *infinitely* the moment another shares it with me. The reason is obvious. You and I have grown up apart, and have never conferred together; our temperaments, culture, circumstances are different; we have come to have certain thoughts which seem to us true and deep, but each of us doubts whether these thoughts may not be due to his peculiarities of mind, position, and influence. But to-day we come together, and discover, that, despite these outward diversities in which we are so widely unlike, our fundamental faiths are one and the same; the same thoughts, the same beliefs have sprung into life in our separate souls. Instantly is suggested a unity underlying our divided being, a law of thought abiding in mind itself,—not merely in your mind or mine, but in the mind and soul of man. What we arrive at, therefore, is not merely the sum of you and me, the aggregate of two men's opinions, but the universal, the absolute, and spiritually necessary. Such is always the suggestion which spontaneous unity of faith carries with it; hence it awakens religion, and gives total peace and rest."

But the faiths which are to be capable of these divine embraces must indeed be spontaneous and native. Hence those who create factitious unity of creed render these fructifications impossible. If we agree, not because the absolute soul has uttered in both of us the same word, but because we have both been fed with dust out of the same catechism, our unity will disgust and weary us rather than invigorate. Dr. Johnson said he would compel men to believe as he and the Church of England did, "because," he reasoned, "if another differs from me, he weakens my confidence in my own scheme of faith, and so injures me." Now this speech is good just so far as it asserts social dependence in belief; it is bad, it is idiotic or insane, so far as it advocates the substitution of a factitious and artificial unity for one of spiritual depth and reality. The fruits of the tree of life are not to be successfully thieved. In dishonest hands they become ashes and bitterness. He who has more faith in an Act of Parliament than in God and the universe may be a good conventional believer; but, in truth, the choice he makes is the essence of all denial and even of all atheism and blasphemy.

Let each, then, bring up out of his own soul its purest, broadest, simplest faith; and when any ten or ten thousand find that the same faith has come to birth in their several souls, each one of them all will be exalted to a divine confidence, and will make new requisitions upon the soul which he has so been taught to trust. Thus, though we tell each nothing new, though we merely demonstrate our unity of consciousness, yet is the force of each many times multiplied,—dimless certitude and dauntless courage being bred in hearts where before, perhaps, were timorous hesitation and wavering.

The third service of words may be compared to the help which the smith renders to the fire on his forge. True it is that no blowing can enkindle dead coals, and make a flame where was no spark. True it is that both spark and bellows will be vain, if the fuel is stone or clay. And so no blowing will enkindle a nature which does not bring in itself the fire to be fanned and the substance that may support it. But in our being, as at the forge, the flame that languishes may be taught to leap, and the spark that was hidden may be wrought into blaze.

Simple attraction and encouragement,—there is somewhat of the marvellous in their effects. Physiologists tell us, that, if two liquids in the body are separated by a moist membrane, and if one of these fluids be in motion and the other at rest, that which rests will of its own accord force its way through the membrane and join the one which flows. So it is in history. Any man who represents a spiritual streaming will command and draw into the current of his soul those whose condition is one of stagnancy or arrest. Now courage and belief are streamings forward; skepticism and timidity are stagnancies; panic, fear, and destructive denial are streamings backward. True, now, it is, that any swift flowing, forward or backward, attracts; but progressive or affirmative currents have this vast advantage, that they are health, and therefore the healthy humanity in every man's being believes in them and belongs to them; and they accordingly are like rivers, which, however choked up temporarily and made refluent, are sure in the end to force their way; while negative and backward currents are like pestilences and conflagrations, which of necessity limit themselves by exhaustion, if not mastered by happier means.

We may, indeed, note it as a nicety, that the membrane must be moist through which this transudation is to take place; and I admit that there are men whose enveloping sheath of individualism and egotism is so hard and dry, so little interpenetrated by candor and the love of truth, as to be nearly impervious to noble persuasion; and were whole Missouris of tidings from the highest intelligence rushing past them, they would still yawn, and say, "Do you get any news?" as innocently as ever.

Nevertheless, history throbs with the mystery of this influence. A little girl sleeping by her mother's side awoke in a severe thunder-storm, and, nestling in terror near to the mother, and shrinking into the smallest possible space, said, trembling, "Mother, are you afraid?" "No, my dear," answered the lady, calmly. "Oh, well," said the child, assuming her full proportions, and again disposing herself for sleep, "if you're not afraid, I'm not afraid," and was soon slumbering quietly. What volumes of gravest human history in that little incident! So infinitely easy are daring and magnanimity, so easy is transcendent height of thought and will, when exalted spiritually, when imperial valor and purpose breathe and blow upon our souls from the lips of a living fellow! Not, it may be, that anything new is said. That is not required. What another now thrills, inspires, transfigures us by saying, we probably knew before, only dared not let ourselves think that we knew it. The universe, perhaps, had not a nook so hidden that therein we could have been solitary enough to whisper that divine suggestion to our own hearts. But now some childlike man stands up and speaks it to the common air, in serenest unconsciousness of doing anything singular. He has said it,—and lo, he lives! By the help of God, then, we too, by word and deed, will utter our souls.

Get one hero, and you may have a thousand. Create a grand impulse in history, and no fear but it will be reinforced. Obtain your champion in the cause of Right, and you shall have indomitable armies that charge for social justice.

More of the highest life is suppressed in every one of us than ever gets vent; and it is this inward suppression, after making due account of all outward oppressions and injuries, which constitutes the chief tragedy of history. Daily men cast to the ground the proffered beakers of heaven, from mere fear to drink. Daily they rebuke the divine, inarticulate murmer that arises from the deeps of their being,—inarticulate only because denied and reproved. And he is greatest who can meet with a certain pure intrepidity those suggestions which haunt forever the hearts of men.

No greater blunder, accordingly, was ever made than that of attempting to render men brave and believing by addressing them as cowards and infidels. Garibaldi stands up before his soldiers in Northern Italy, and says to them, (though I forget the exact words,) "I do not call you to fortune and prosperity; I call you to hardship, to suffering, to death; I ask you to give your toil without reward, to spill your blood and lie in unknown graves, to sacrifice all for your country and kind, and hear no thanks but the *Well done* of God in heaven." Did they cower and go back? Ere the words had spent their echoes, every man's will was as the living adamant of God's purpose, and every man's hand was as the hand of Destiny, and from the shock of their onset the Austrians fled as from the opening jaws of an earthquake. Demosthenes told Athens only what Athens knew. He merely blew upon the people's hearts with their own best thoughts; and what a blaze! True, the divine fuel was nearly gone, Athens wellnigh burnt out, and the flame lasted not long; but that he could produce such effects, when half he fanned was merest ashes, serves all the more to show how great such effects may be.

Before passing to the last and profoundest use of communication, I must not omit to mention that which is most obvious, but not most important,—the giving of ordinary informations and instructions. These always consist in a suggestion to another of new combinations of his notions, new societies in his mind. Thus, if I say, *Fire burns,* I simply assert a connection between fire and burning,—the notion of both these being assumed as existing in the mind of the person addressed. Or if I say, *God is just,* I invite him to associate in his mind the sentiment of justice and the sense of the infinite and omnipotent. Now in respect to matters of mere external form we usually confide in the representations of others, and picture to ourselves, so far as our existing perceptions enable us, the combinations they affirm,—provided always these have a certain undefined conformity with our own experience. But in respect to association, not of mere notions, but of *spiritual elements in the soul,*—of truths evolved by the spiritual nature of man,—the case is quite different. Thus, if the fool who once said in his heart, "There is no God," should now say openly, (of course by some disguising euphemism,) "God is an egotist," I may indeed shape an opinion accordingly, and fall into great confusion in consequence; but my spiritual nature does not consent to this representation; no *real* association takes place within me between the sense of the divine and the conception of egotism. Such opinion may have immense energy in history, but it has no efficiency in the eliciting and outbuilding of our personal being; these representations, however we may trust and base action upon them, serve us inwardly only to such degree as our spiritual nature can ally itself with them and find expression in them. It is simply impossible for any man to associate the idea of divinity with the conception of selfishness; but he may associate the notion of Zeus or Allah or the like with that or any other conception of baseness, and out of the result may form a sort of crust over his spiritual intelligence, which shall either imprison it utterly, or force it to oblique and covert expression. And of this last, by the way,—and we may deeply rejoice over the fact,—history is full.

Yet in this suggestion toward new societies in the soul, in this formal introduction to each other of kindred elements in the consciousness, there may be eminent service. It is only formal, it does not make friendship, it leaves our spirits to their own action; but it may prepare the way for inward unities and communities whose blessedness neither speech nor silence can tell.

Finally, there is an effect of words profounder and more creative than any of these. As a brand which burns powerfully may at last ignite even green wood, so divine faiths, alive and awake in one soul, may appeal to the mere elements, to mere possibilities, of such faiths in other souls, and at length evoke them by that appeal. The process is slow; it requires a celestial heat and persistency in the moving spirit; it is one of the "all things" that are possible only with God: but it occurs, and it is the most sacred and precious thing in history.

Every human soul has the absolute soul, has the whole truth, significance, and virtue of the universe, as its lawful and native resource. Therefore says Jesus, "The kingdom of heaven is within you"; therefore Antoninus, "Look inwards, within is the fountain of truth"; therefore Eckart, "Ye have all truth potentially within you." All ideas of truth dwell in every soul, but in every soul they are at first wrapped in deep sleep, in an infinite depth of sleep; while the base incense of brutish lives is like chloroform, or the fumes of some benumbing drug, to steep them ever more and more in oblivion. But to awaken truth thus sleeping in the soul is the highest use of discipline, the noblest aim of culture, and the most eminent service which man can render to man. The scheme of our life is providentially arranged with reference to that end; and the thousand shocks, agitations, and moving influences of our experience, the supreme invitations of love, the venom of calumny, and all toil, trial, sudden bereavement, doubt, danger, vicissitude, joy, are hands that shake and voices that assail the lethargy of our deepest powers. Now it is in the power of truth divinely awakened in one soul to assist its awakening in another. For as nothing so quickly arouses us from slumber as hearing ourselves called upon by name, so is it with this celestial inhabitant: whoever by virtue of elder brotherhood can rightly name him shall cause his spirit to be stirred and his slumber to be broken.

Let him, therefore, in whom any great truth is alive and awake, enunciate, proclaim it steadily, clearly, cheerily, with a serene and cloudless passion; and wherever a soul less mature than his own lies open to the access of his tones, there the eye-fast angels of belief and knowledge shall hear that publication of their own hearts, and, hearing, lift their lids, and rise into wakefulness and power.

Seldom, indeed, is any voice, though it be in its origin a genuine voice of the soul, pure and impartial enough, enough delivered from the masks of egotism and accident, to be greatly competent for these effects. Besides which, there are not a few that have closed their ears, lest they should hear, not a few that are even filled with base astonishment and terror, and out of this with base wrath, to find their deafness assailed. And still further, it must be freely owned that our natures have mysterious elections, and though one desire openness of soul as much as folly fears it, yet may it happen that some tint of peculiarity in the tone of a worthy voice shall render it to him opaque and unintelligible.

Yet let us not fear that the product of any sacred and spiritual sincerity will fail of sufficient uses. If a deep, cordial, and clarified nature will but give us his heart in a pure and boundless bravery of confession,—if, like autumn plants, that cast forth their seeds, winged with down, to the four winds of heaven, or like the blossoms of spring and early summer, that yield up their preciousness of pollen to the forage of bees, and even by being so robbed attain to the hearts of neighbor-blossoms, and accomplish that mystery of fructification which is to make glad the maturer year,—if so this inflorescence of eternity that we name a Noble Man will yield up the golden pollen of his soul, even to those that in visiting him seek but their own ends, and if so he will intrust winged words, words that are indeed spiritual *seeds*, purest, ripest, and most vital products of his being, to the winds of time,—he will be sure to reach some, and they to reach others, and there is no telling how far the seminal effect may go; there is no telling what harvests may yellow in the limitless fields of the future, what terrestrial and celestial reapers may go home rejoicing, bearing their sheaves with them, what immortal hungers may be fed at the feasts of earth and heaven, in final consequence of that lonely and faithful sowing. As in the still mornings of summer the earliest awakened bird hesitates to utter, yet utters, his solitary pipe, timidly rippling the silence, but is not long alone, for quickly the melodious throb begins to beat in every tree-top, and soon the whole rapturous grove gushes and palpitates into song, —even so, thus to appearance alone and unsupported, begins

that chant of belief which is destined to heave and roll in billows
of melodious confession over a continent, over a world. Thus
does a faith that has lain long silent in the hearts of nations sud-
denly answer to the note of its kind, astonishing all bystanders,
astonishing most of all the heart it inhabits. For, lo! the tree-tops
of human life are full of slumbering melodies, and if a song-
sparrow pipe sincerely on the hill-sides of Judea, saying, after his
own fashion of speech, "Behold, the divine dawn hath visited my
eyes," be sure that the forests of far-off America, then unknown,
will one day reply, and ten thousand thousand throats throbbing
with high response will make it mutually known all round the
world that this auroral beam is not for any single or private eye,
but that the broad amber beauty of spiritual morning belongs
to man's being, and that in man's heart, by virtue of its perennial
nature, is prophesied the day whose sun shall be God and its
earth heaven.

ICE AND ESQUIMAUX

≫≪≫≪≫≪≫≪≫≪≫≪≫≪≫≪≫≪≫≪

CHAPTER IV

AUTOCHTHONES

July 30.—At Hopedale, lat. 55° 30', we come upon an object of first-class interest, worthy of the gravest study,—an original and pre-Adamite man. In two words I give the reader a key to my final conclusions, or impressions, concerning the Esquimaux race.

Original: Shakspeare is a copyist, and England a plagiarism, in comparison with this race. The Esquimaux has done all for himself: he has developed his own arts, adjusted himself by his own wit to the Nature which surrounds him. Heir to no Rome, Greece, Persia, India, he stands there in the sole strength of his native resources, rich only in the traditionary accomplishments of his own race. Cut off equally from the chief bounties of Nature, he has small share in the natural wealth of mankind. When Ceres came to the earth, and blessed it, she forgot him. The grains, the domestic animals, which from the high plateaus of Asia descended with the fathers of history to the great fields of the world, to him came not. The sole domestic animal he uses, the dog, is not the same with that creature as known elsewhere: he has domesticated a wolf, and made a dog for himself.

Not only is he original, but one of the most special of men, related more strictly than almost any other to a particular aspect

Atlantic Monthly, April, 1865.

of Nature. Inseparable from the extreme North, the sea-shore, and the seal, he is himself, as it were, a seal come to feet and hands, and preying upon his more primitive kindred. The cetacean of the land, he is localized, like animals,—not universal, like civilized man. He is no inhabitant of the globe as a whole, but is contained within special poles. His needle does not point north and south; it is commanded by special attractions, and points only from shore to sea and from sea to shore in the arctic zone. Nor is this relation to particular phases of Nature superficial merely, a relation of expedient and convenience; it penetrates, saturates, nay, anticipates and moulds him. Whether he has come to this correspondence by original creation or by slow adjustment, he certainly does now correspond in his whole physical and mental structure to the limited and special surroundings of his life,—the seal itself or the eider-duck not more.

He is pre-Adamite, I said,—and name him thus not as a piece of rhetorical smartness, but in gravest characterization.

The first of human epochs is that when the thoughts, imaginations, beliefs of men become to them *objects,* on which further thought and action are to be adjusted, on which further thought and action may be based. So long as man is merely responding to outward and physical circumstances, so long he is living by bread alone, and has no history: It is when he begins to respond *to himself,*—to create necessities and supplies out of his own spirit,—to build architectures on foundations and out of materials that exist only in virtue of his own spiritual activity,—to live by bread which grows, not out of the soil, but out of the soul,—it is then, then only, that history begins. This one may be permitted to name the Adamite epoch.

The Esquimaux belongs to that period, more primitive, when man is simply responding to outward Nature, to physical necessities. He invents, but does not create; he adjusts himself to circumstances, but not to ideas; he works cunningly upon materials which he has *found,* but never on material which owes its existence to the productive force of his own spirit.

In going to look upon the man of this race, you sail, not merely over seas, but over ages, epochs, unknown periods of time,—sail beyond antiquity itself, and issue into the obscure existence that antedates history. Arrived there, you may turn your eye to the historical past of man as to a barely possible future. Palestine and Greece, Moses and Homer, as yet are not. Who shall dare to say that they can be? Surely that were but a wild dream! Expel the impossible fancy from your mind! Go, spear a seal, and be a reasonable being!—Never enthusiast had a dream of the future so unspeakably Utopian as actual history becomes, when seen from the Esquimaux, or pre-Adamite, point of view.

Swiss lakes are raked, Belgian caves spaded and hammered, to find relics of old, pre-historical races. Go to Labrador, and you find the object sought above ground. There he is, preserving all the characters of his extinct congeners,—small in stature, low and smooth in cranium, held utterly in the meshes of Nature, skilled only to meet ingeniously the necessities she imposes, and meeting them rudely, as man ever does till the ideal element comes in: for any fine feeling of even physical wants, any delicacy of taste, any high notion of comfort, is due less to the animal than to the spiritual being of man.

A little sophisticated he is now, getting to feel himself obsolete in this strange new world. He begins to borrow, and yet is unable radically to change; outwardly he gains a very little from civilization, and grows inwardly poorer and weaker by all that he gains. His day wanes apace; soon it will be past. He begins to nurse at the breasts of the civilized world; and the foreign aliment can neither sustain his ancient strength nor give him new. Civilization forces upon him a rivalry to which he is unequal; it wrests the seal from his grasp, thins it out of his waters; and he and his correlative die away together.

We reached Hopedale, as intimated above, on the morning of the 30th of July, at least a month later than had been hoped. The reader will see by the map that this place is about half way from the Strait of Belle Isle to Hudson's Strait. We were to go no farther north. This was a great disappointment; for the expecta-

tion of all, and the keen desire of most, had been to reach at least
Cape Chudleigh, at the opening of Hudson's Strait. Ice and storm
had hindered us: they were not the only hindrances.

"The Fates are against us," said one.

"It is true," answered the Elder,—"the Fates are against us: I
know of nothing more fatal than imbecility."

However, we should be satisfied; for here we have fairly
penetrated the great solitudes of the North. Lower Labrador is
visited by near forty thousand fishermen annually, and vessels
there are often more frequent than in Boston Bay. But at a point
not far from the fifty-fifth parallel of latitude you leave all these
behind, and leave equally the white residents of the coast: to
fishermen and residents alike the region beyond is as little known
as the interior of Australia. There their world comes to an end;
there the unknown begins. Knowledge and curiosity alike pause
there; toward all beyond their only feeling is one of vague dislike
and dread. And so I doubt not it was with the ordinary inhabitant
of Western Europe before the discovery of America. The unknown, breaking in surf on his very shores, did not invite him,
but dimly repelled. Thought about it, attraction toward it, would
seem to him far-fetched, gratuitous, affected, indicating at best a
feather-headed flightiness of mind. The sailors of Columbus
probably regarded him much as Sancho Panza does Don Quixote,
with an obscure, overpowering awe, and yet with a very definite
contempt.

On our return we passed two Yankee fishermen in the Strait
of Belle Isle. The nearer hailed.

"How far *down* [up] have you been?"

"To Hopedale."

"WHERE?"—in the tone of one who hears distinctly enough,
but cannot believe that he hears.

"Hopedale."

"H-o-p-e-d-a-l-e! Where the Devil's that?"

"A hundred and fifty miles beyond Cape Harrison." (Cape
Weback on the map.)

Inarticulate gust of astonishment in response.

"Where did he say?" inquires some one in the farther schooner.

"————! He's been to the North Pole!"

To him it was all North Pole beyond Cape Harrison, and he evidently looked upon us much as he might upon the apparition of the Flying Dutchman, or some other spectre-ship.

The supply-ship which yearly visits the Moravian stations on this coast anchored in the harbor of Hopedale ten minutes before us: we had been rapidly gaining upon her in our Flying Yankee for the last twenty miles. Signal-guns had answered each other from ship and shore; the missionaries were soon on board, and men and women were falling into each other's arms with joyful, mournful kisses and tears. The ship returned some missionaries after long absence; it brought also a betrothed lady, next day to be married: there was occasion for joy, even beyond wont on these occasions, when, year by year, the missionary-exiles feel with bounding blood the touch of civilization and fatherland. But now those who came on board brought sad tidings,—for one of their ancient colaborers, closely akin to the new comers, had within a day or two died. Love and death the world over; and also the hope of love without death.

Our eyes have been drawn to them; it is time to have a peep at Hopedale.

I had been so long looking forward to this place, had heard and thought of it so much as an old mission-station, where was a village of Christian Esquimaux, that I fully expected to see a genuine village, with houses, wharves, streets. It would not equal our towns, of course. The people were not cleanly; the houses would be unpainted, and poor in comparison with ours. I had taken assiduous pains to tone down my expectations, and felt sure that I had moderated them liberally,—nay, had been philosophical enough to make disappointment impossible, and open the opposite possibility of a pleasant surprise. I conceived that in this respect I had done the discreet and virtuous thing, and silently moralized, not without self-complacency, upon the folly of carrying through the world expectations which the fact, when seen, could only put out of countenance. "Make your expectations zero," I said with Sartor.

I need not put them *below* zero. That would be too cold an

anticipation to carry even to this latitude. Zero: a poor, shabby village these Christian Esquimaux will have built, even after nigh a century of Moravian tuition. Still it will be a real village, not a distracted jumble of huts, such as we had seen below.

The prospect had been curiously pleasing. True, I desired much to see the unadulterated Esquimaux. But that would come, I had supposed, in the further prosecution of our voyage. Here I could see what they would become under loving instruction,— could gauge their capabilities, and thus answer one of the prime questions I had brought.

A real Hopedale, after all this wild, sterile, hopeless coast! A touch of civilization, to contrast with the impression of that Labradorian rag-tag existence which we had hitherto seen, and which one could not call human without coughing! I like deserts and wilds,—but, if you please, by way of condiment or sauce to civilization, not for a full meal. I have not the heroic Thoreau-digestion, and grow thin after a time on a diet of moss and granite, even when they are served with ice. Lift the curtain, therefore, and let us look forthwith on your Hopedale.

"Hopedale? Why, here it is,—look!"

Well, I have been doing nothing less for the last half-hour. If looking could make a village, I should begin to see one. There, to be sure, is the mission-house, conspicuous enough, quaint and by no means unpleasing. It is a spacious, substantial, two-story edifice, painted in two shades of a peculiar red, and looking for all the world as if a principal house, taken from one of those little German toy-villages which are in vogue about Christmas, had been enormously magnified, and shipped to Labrador. There, too, and in similar colors, is the long chapel, on the centre of whose roof there is a belfry, which looks like two thirds of an immense red egg, drawn up at the top into a spindle, and this surmounted by a weathercock,—as if some giant had attempted to blow the egg from beneath, and had only blown out of it this small bird with a stick to stand on! Ah, yes! and there is the pig-sty,—not in keeping with the rest, by any means! It must be that they keep a pig only now and then, and for a short time, and house it any way for that little while. But no, it is not a piggery;

it is not a building at all; it is some chance heap of rubbish, which will be removed to-morrow.

The mission-station, then, is here; but the village must be else-where. Probably it is on the other side of this point of land on which the house and chapel are situated; we can see that the water sweeps around there. That is the case, no doubt; Hopedale is over there. After dinner we will row around, and have a look at it.

After dinner, however, we decide to go first and pay our re-spects to the missionaries. They are entitled to the precedence. We long, moreover, to take the loving, self-sacrificing men by the hand; while, aside from their special claims to honor, it will be *so* pleasant to meet cultivated human beings once more! They are Germans, but their head-quarters are at London; they will speak English; and if their vocabulary prove scanty, we will try to eke it out with bits of German.

We row ashore in our own skiff, land, and—Bless us! what is this now? To the right of the large, neat, comfortable mission-house is a wretched, squalid spatter and hotch-potch of—what in the world to call them? Huts? Hovels? One has a respect for his mother-tongue,—above all, if he have assumed obligations toward it by professing the function of a writer; and any term by which human dwellings are designated must be taken *cum grano salis,* if applied to these structures. "It cannot be that this is Christian Hopedale!" Softly, my good Sir; it can be, for it is!

Reader, do you ever say, "Whew-w-w"? There were three minutes, on the 30th of July last, during which that piece of inter-jectional eloquence seemed to your humble servant to embody the whole dictionary!

To get breath, let us turn again to the mission-mansion, which now, under the effect of sudden contrast, seems too magnificent to be real, as if it had been built by enchantment rather than by the labor of man. This is situated half a dozen rods from the shore, at a slight elevation above it, and looks pleasantly up the bay to the southwest. The site has been happily chosen. Here, for a wonder, is an acre or two of land which one may call level,— broader toward the shore, and tapering to a point as it runs back.

To the right, as we face it, the ground rises not very brokenly; giving a small space for the bunch of huts, then falls quickly to the sea; while beyond and toward the ocean islands twenty miles deep close in and shelter all. To the left go up again the perpetual hills, hills. Everywhere around the bay save here, on island and main, the immitigable gneiss hills rise bold and sudden from the water, now dimly impurpled with lichen, now in nakedness of rock surface, yet beautified in their bare severity by alternating and finely waving stripes of lightest and darkest gray,—as if to show sympathy with the billowy heaving of the sea.

Forward to the mansion. In front a high, strong, neat picket-fence incloses a pretty flower-yard, in which some exotics, tastefully arranged, seem to be flourishing well. We knock; with no manner of haste, and with no seeming of cordial willingness, we are admitted, are shown into a neat room of good size, and entertained by a couple of the brethren.

One of these only, and he alone among the missionaries, it appeared, spoke English. This was an elderly, somewhat cold and forbidding personage, of Secession sympathies. He had just returned from Europe after two years' absence, was fresh from London, and put on the true Exeter-Hall whine in calling ours "a n-dreadful n-war." He did not press the matter, however, nor in any manner violate the *rôle* of cold courtesy which he had assumed; and it was chiefly by the sudden check and falling of the countenance, when he found us thorough Unionist, that his sympathies were betrayed. Wine and rusks were brought in, both delicious,—the latter seeming like ambrosia, after the dough cannon-balls with which our "head cook at the Tremont House" had regaled us. After a stay of civil brevity we took our leave, and so closed an interview in which we had been treated with irreproachable politeness, but in which the heart was forbidden to have any share.

First, the missionaries; now the natives. The squat and squalid huts, stuck down upon the earth without any pretence of raised foundation, and jumbled together, corner to side, back to front, any way, as if some wind had blown them there, did not improve on acquaintance. The walls, five feet high, were built of poles some five inches in diameter; the low roof, made of similar poles, was heavily heaped with earth. What with this deep earth-covering, and with their grovelling toward the earth in such a flat and neighborly fashion, they had a dreadfully under-foot look, and seemed rather dens than houses. Many were ragged and rotten, all inconceivably cheerless. No outhouses, no inclosures, no vegetation, no relief of any kind. About and between them the swardless ground is all trodden into mud. Prick-eared Esquimaux dogs huddle, sneak, bark, and snarl around, with a free fight now and then, in which they all fall upon the one that is getting the worst of it. Before the principal group of huts, in the open space between them and the mansion, a dead dog lies rotting; children lounge listlessly, and babies toddle through the slutch about it. Here and there a full-grown Esquimaux, in greasy and uncouth garb, loiters, doing nothing, *looking* nothing.

I, for one, was completely overcrowed by the impression of a bare and aimless existence, and could not even wonder. Christian Hopedale! "Leave all hope, ye that enter here!"

At 5 P.M. the chapel-bell rings, and at once the huts swarm. We follow the crowd. They enter the chapel by a door at the end nearest their dens, and seat themselves, the women at the farther, the men at the hither extreme, all facing a raised desk at the middle of one side. Behind them, opposite this pulpit, is an organ. Presently, from a door at the farther end, the missionaries file in, some twelve in number; one enters the pulpit, the others take seats on either side of him facing the audience, and at a dignified remove. The conductor of the service now rises, makes an address in Esquimaux a minute and a half long, then gives out a hymn, —the hymns numbered in German, as numbers, to any extent, are wanting to the Esquimaux language. All the congregation join in a solid old German tune, keeping good time, and making, on the whole, better congregational music than I ever heard else-where,—unless a Baptist conventicle in London, Bloomsbury Chapel, furnish the exception. After this another, then another; at length, when half a dozen or more have been sung, mission-aries and congregation rise, the latter stand in mute and motion-less respect, the missionaries file out with dignity at their door;

and when the last has disappeared, the others begin quietly to disperse.

This form of worship is practised at the hour named above on each week-day, and the natives attend with noticeable promptitude. There are no prayers, and the preliminary address in this case was exceptional.

Sunday, July 31.—I had inquired at what hour the worship would begin this day, and, with some hesitancy, had been answered, "At half past nine." But the Colonel also had asked, and his interlocutor, after consulting a card, said, "At ten o'clock." At ten we went ashore. Finding the chapel-door still locked, I seated myself on a rock in front of the mission-house, to wait. The sun was warm (the first warm day for a month) ; the mosquitoes swarmed in myriads; I sat there long, wearily beating them off. Faces peeped out at me from the windows, then withdrew. Presently Bradford joined me, and began also to fight mosquitoes. More faces at the windows; but when I looked towards them, thinking to discover some token of hospitable invitation, they quickly disappeared. After half an hour, the master of the supply-ship came up, and entered into conversation; in a minute one of the brethren appeared at the door, and invited him to enter, but without noticing Bradford and myself. I took my skiff and rowed to the schooner. Fifteen minutes later the chapel-bell rang.

I confess to some spleen that day against the missionaries. When I expressed it, Captain French, the pilot, an old, prudent, pious man, "broke out."

"Them are traders," said he. "I don't call 'em missionaries; I call 'em traders. They live in luxury; the natives work for 'em, and get for pay just what they choose to give 'em. They fleece the Esquimaux; they take off of 'em all but the skin. They are just traders!"

My spleen did not last. There was some cause of coldness,—I know not what. The missionaries afterwards became cordial, visited the schooner, and exchanged presents with us. I believe them good men. If their relation to the natives assume in some degree a pecuniary aspect, it is due to the necessity of supporting the mission by the profits of traffic. If they preserve a stately distance toward the Esquimaux, it is to retain influence over them. If they allow the native mind to confound somewhat the worship of God with the worship of its teachers, it is that the native mind cannot get beyond personal relations, and must worship something tangible. That they are not at all entangled in the routine and material necessities of their position I do not assert; that they do not carry in it something of noble and self-forgetful duty nothing I have seen will persuade me.

August 1.—We go to push our explorations among the Esquimaux, and invite the reader to make one of the party. Enter a hut. The door is five feet high,—that is, the height of the wall. Stoop a little,—ah, there goes a hat to the ground, and a hand to a hurt pate! One must move carefully in these regions, which one hardly knows whether to call sub- or supra-terranean.

This door opens into a sort of porch occupying one end of the den; the floor, earth. Three or four large, dirty dogs lie dozing here, and start up with an aspect of indescribable, half-crouching, mean malignity, as we enter; but a sharp word, with perhaps some menace of stick or cane, sends the cowardly brutes sneaking away. In a corner is a circle of stones, on which cooking is done; and another day we may find the family here picking their food out of a pot, and serving themselves to it, with the fingers. Save this primitive fireplace, and perhaps a kettle for the dogs to lick clean, this porch is bare.

From this we crouch into the livingroom through a door two and a half or three feet high, and find ourselves in an apartment twelve feet square, and lighted by a small, square skin window in the roof. The only noticeable furniture consists of two board beds, with skins for bed-clothes. The women sit on these beds, sewing upon seal-skin boots. They receive us with their characteristic fat and phlegmatic good-nature, a pleasant smile on their chubby cheeks and in their dark, dull eyes,—making room for us on the bedside. Presently others come in, mildly curious to see the strangers,—all with the same aspect of unthinking, good-tempered, insensitive, animal content. The head is low and smooth; the cheek-bones high, but less so than those of American Indians; the jowl so broad and heavy as sometimes to give

the *ensemble* of head and face the outline of a cone truncated
and rounded off above. In the females, however, the cheek is so
extremely plump as perfectly to pad these broad jaws, giving,
instead of the prize-fighter physiognomy, an aspect of smooth,
gentle heaviness. Even without this fleshy cheek, which is not
noticeable, and is sometimes noticeably wanting, in the men,
there is the same look of heavy, well-tempered tameness. The
girls have a rich blood color in their swarthy cheeks, and some
of them are really pretty, though always in a lumpish, domestic-
animal style. The hands and feet are singularly small; the fingers
short, but nicely tapered. Take hold of the hand, and you are
struck with its *cetacean* feel; It is not flabby, but has a peculiar
blubber-like, elastic compressibility, and seems not quite of
human warmth.

See them in their houses, and you see the horizon of their life.
In these fat faces, with their thoughtless content, in this pent-up,
greasy, wooden den, the whole is told. The air is close and fetid
with animal exhalations. The entrails and part of the flesh of a
seal, which lie on the floor in a corner,—to furnish a dinner,—
do not make the atmosphere nor the aspect more agreeable. Yet
you see, that to them this is comfort, this is completeness of existence. If they are hungry, they seek food. Food obtained, they
return to eat and be comfortable until they are again hungry.
Their life has, on this earth at least, no farther outlook. It sallies,
it returns, but here is the fruition; for is not the seal-flesh dinner
there, nicely and neatly bestowed on the floor? Are they not
warm? (The den is swelteringly hot.) Are they not fed? What
would one have more?

Yes, somewhat more, namely, tobacco,—and also second-hand
clothes, with which to be fine in church. For these they will
barter seal-skins, dog-skins, seal-skin boots, a casual bear-skin,
bird-spears, walrus-spears, anything they have to vend,—con-
cealing their traffic a little from the missionaries. Colored glass
beads were also in request among the women. Ph——had
brought some large, well-made pocket-knives, which, being useful, he supposed would be desired. Not at all; they were fumbled

indifferently, then invariably declined. But a plug of tobacco,—ah, that now *is* something!

The men wear tight seal-skin trousers and boots, with an upper garment of the same material, made like a Guernsey frock. In winter a hood is added, but in summer they all go bareheaded,—the stiff, black hair chopped squarely off across the low forehead, but longer behind. The costume of the females is more peculiar,—seal-skin boots, seal-skin trousers, which just spring over the hips, and are there met by a body garment of seal-skin more lightly colored. Over this goes an astonishing article of apparel somewhat resembling the dress-coat in which unhappy civilization sometimes compels itself to masquerade, but—truth stranger than fiction!—*considerably* more ugly. A long tail hangs down to the very heels; a much shorter peak comes down in front; at the sides it is scooped out below, showing a small portion of the light-colored body-garment, which irresistibly suggests a very dirty article of lady-linen whereon the eyes of civilized decorum forbear to look, while an adventurous imagination associates it only with snowy whiteness. The whole is surmounted by an enormous peaked hood, in which now and then one sees a baby carried.

This elegant garment was evidently, copied from the skin of an animal,—so Ph——acutely suggested. The high peak of the hood represents the ears; the arms stand for the fore legs; the downward peak in front for the hind legs sewed together; the rear dangler represents the tail. I make no doubt that our dress-coat has the same origin, though the primal conception has been more modified. It is a bear-skin *plus* Paris.

Is the reader sure of his ribs and waistcoat-buttons? If so, he may venture to look upon an Esquimaux woman walking,—which I take to be the most ludicrous spectacle in the world. Conceive of this short, squat, chunky, lumpish figure in the costume described,—grease *ad libitum* being added. The form is so plump and heavy as very much to project the rear dangler at the point where it leaves the body, while below it falls in, and goes with a continual muddy slap, slap, against the heels. The effect of this, especially in the profile view, is wickedly laughable, but the gait makes it more so. The walk is singularly slow, un-elastic, loggy, and is characterized at each step by an indescriba-ble, sudden sag or *slump* at the hip. As she thus slowly and heavily *churns* herself along, the nether slap emphasizes each step, as it were, with an exclamation-point; while, as the foot advances, the shoulder and the whole body on the same side turn and sag forward, the opposite shoulder and side dragging back,—as if there were a perpetual debate between the two sides whether to proceed or not. It was so laughable that it made one sad; for this, too, was a human being. The gait of the men, on the contrary, is free and not ungraceful.

August 3.—An Esquimaux wedding! In the chapel,—Mor-avian ceremony,—so far not noticeable. Costume same as above, only of white cloth heavily embroidered with red. Demeanor perfect. Bride obliged to sit down midway in the ceremony, over-powered with emotion. She did so with a simple, quiet dignity, that would not have misbecome a duchess.

When the ceremony was ended, the married pair retired into the mission-house, and half an hour later I saw them going home. This was the curious part of the affair. The husband walked before, taking care not to look behind, doing the indifferent and unconscious with great assiduity, and evidently making it a mat-ter of serious etiquette not to know that any one followed. Four rods behind comes the wife, doing the unconscious with equal industry. She is not following this man here in front,—bless us, no, indeed!—but is simply walking out, or going to see a neighbor, this nice afternoon, and does not observe that any one precedes her. Following that man? Pray, where were you reared, that you are capable of so discourteous a supposition? It gave me a malicious pleasure to see that the pre-Adamite man, as well as the rest of us, imposes upon himself at times these difficult duties, *toting* about that foolish face, so laboriously vacant of precisely that with which it is brimming full.

To adjust himself to outward Nature,—that, we said, is the sole task of the primitive man. The grand success of the Esqui-maux in this direction is the *kayak*. This is his victory and his

school. It is a seal-skin Oxford or Cambridge, wherein he takes
his degree as master of the primeval arts. Here he acquires not
only physical strength and quickness, but self-possession also,
mental agility, the instant use of his wits,—here becomes, in fine,
a *cultivated* man.

It is no trifling matter. Years upon years must be devoted to
these studies. Oxford and Cambridge do not ask one more, nor
exhibit more degrees of success. Some fail, and never graduate;
some become illustrious for kayak-erudition.

This culture has also the merit of entire seriousness and sincerity. Life and death, not merely a name in the newspapers, are
in it. Of all vehicles, on land or sea, to which man intrusts himself, the kayak is safest and unsafest. It is a very hair-bridge of
Mohammed: security or destruction is in the finest poise of a
moving body, the turn of a hand, the thought of a moment.
Every time that the Esquimaux spears a seal at sea, he pledges his
life upon his skill. With a touch, with a moment's loss of balance,
the tipsy craft may go over; over, the oar, with which it is to be
restored, may get entangled, may escape from the hand, may—
what not? For all *what-nots* the kayaker must preserve instant
preparation; and with his own life on the tip of his fingers, he
must make its preservation an incidental matter. He is there, not
to save his life, but to capture a seal, worth a few dollars! It is his
routine work. Different from getting up a leading article, making
a plea in court, or writing Greek iambics for a bishopric!

Probably there is no race of men on earth whose ordinary
avocations present so constantly the alternative of rarest skill on
the one hand, or instant destruction on the other. And for these
avocations one is fitted only by a *scholarship,* which it requires
prolonged schooling, the most patient industry, and the most
delicate consent of mind and body to attain. If among us the
highest university-education were necessary, in order that one
might live, marry, and become a householder, we should but
parallel in our degree the scheme of their life.

Measured by post-Adamite standards, the life of the Esquimaux is a sorry affair; measured by his own standards, it is a piece
of perfection. To see the virtue of his existence, you must, as it

were, look at him with the eyes of a wolf or fox,—must look up from that low level, and discern, so far above, this skilled and wondrous creature, who by ingenuity and self-schooling has converted his helplessness into power, and made himself the plume and crown of the physical world.

In the kayak the Esquimaux attains to beauty. As he rows, the extremes of the two-bladed oar revolve, describing rhythmic circles; the body holds itself in airy poise, and the light boat skims away with a look of life. The speed is greater than our swiftest boats attain, and the motion graceful as that of a flying bird. Kayak and rower become to the eye one creature; and the civilized spectator must be stronger than I in his own conceit not to feel a little humble as he looks on.

We had racing one calm evening. Three kayaks competed: the prize—O Civilization!—was a plug of tobacco. How the muscles swelled! How the airy things flew! "Hi! Hi!" jockey the lookers-on: they fly swifter still. Up goes another plug,—another!—another!—and the kayaks half leap from the water. It was sad withal.

The racing over, there was a new feat. One of the kayakers placed himself in his little craft directly across the course; another stationed himself at a distance, and then, pushing his kayak forward at his utmost speed, drove it directly over the other! The high sloping bow rose above the middle of the stationary kayak on which it impinged, and, shooting up quite out of water, the boat skimmed over.

The Esquimaux is an honest creature. I had engaged a woman to make me a pair of fur boots, leaving my name on a slip of paper. L——, next day, roaming among the huts, saw her hanging them out to dry. Enamored of them, and ignorant of our bargain, he sought to purchase them; but at the first token of his desire, the woman rushed into the hut, and brought forth the slip of paper, as a sufficient answer to all question on that matter. L—— having told me of the incident, and informed me that he had elsewhere bargained for a similar pair, I was wicked enough to experiment upon this fidelity, desirous of learning what I could. Taking, therefore, some clothes, which I knew would be desired, and among them a white silk handkerchief bordered with blue, which had been purchased at Port Mulgrave, all together far exceeding in value the stipulated price, I sought the hut, and began admiring the said boots, now nearly finished. Instantly came forth the inevitable slip with L——'s name upon it. Making no sign, I proceeded to unroll my package. The good creature was intensely taken with its contents, and gloated over them with childish delight. But though she rummaged every corner to find somewhat to exchange with me for them, it evidently did not even enter her thoughts to offer me the boots. I took them up and admired them again; she immediately laid her hand on the slip of paper. So I gave her the prettiest thing I had, and left with a cordial *okshni* (good-bye).

This honesty is attributed to missionary instruction, and with the more color as the untaught race is noted for stealing from Europeans everything they can lay hands on. It is only, however, from foreigners that they were ever accustomed to steal. Toward each other they have ever been among the most honest of human beings. Civilization and the seal they regarded as alike lawful prey. The missionaries have not implanted in them a new disposition, but only extended the scope of an old and marked characteristic.

At the same time their sense of pecuniary obligation would seem not to extend over long periods. Of the missionaries in winter they buy supplies on credit, but show little remembrance of the debt when summer comes. All must be immediate with them; neither their thought nor their moral sense can carry far; they are equally improvident for the future and forgetful of the past. The mere Nature-man acts only as Nature and her necessities press upon him; thought and memory are with him the offspring of sensation; his brain is but the feminine spouse of his stomach and blood,—receptive and respondent, rather than virile and original.

Partly, however, this seeming forgetfulness is susceptible of a different explanation. They evidently feel that the mission-house owes them a living. They make gardens, go to church and save their souls, for the missionaries; it is but fair that they should be fed at a pinch in return.

This remark may seem a sneer. Not so; my word for it. I went to Hopedale to study this race, with no wish but to find in them capabilities of spiritual growth, and with no resolve but to see the fact, whatever it should be, not with wishes but with eyes. And, pointedly against my desire, I saw this,—that the religion of the Esquimaux is, nine parts in ten at least, a matter of personal relation between him and the missionaries. He goes to church as the dog follows his master,—expecting a bone and hoping for a pat in return. He comes promptly at a whistle (the chapel-bell) ; his docility and decorum are unimpeachable; he does what is expected of him with a pleased wag of the tail; but it is still, it is always, the dog and his master.

The pre-Adamite man is not distinctively religious; for religion implies ideas, in the blood at least, if not in the brain, as imagination, if not as thought; and ideas are to him wanting, are impossible. His whole being is summed and concluded in a relationship to the external, the tangible, to things or persons; and his relation to persons goes beyond animal instinct and the sense of physical want only upon the condition that it shall cling inseparably to them. The spiritual instincts of humanity are in him also, but obscure, utterly obscure, not having attained to a circulation in the blood, much less to intellectual liberation. Obscure they are, fixed, in the bone, locked up in phosphate of lime. Ideas touch them only as ideas lose their own shape and hide themselves under physical forms.

Will he outgrow himself? Will he become post-Adamite, a man to whom ideas are realities? I desire to say yes, and cannot. Again and again, in chapel and elsewhere, I stood before a group, and questioned, questioned their faces, to find there some prophecy of future growth. And again and again these faces, with their heavy content, with their dog-docility, with their expression of utter limitation, against which nothing in them struggled, said to me,—"Your quest is vain; we are once and forever Esquimaux." Had they been happy, had they been unhappy, I had hoped for them. They were neither: they were contented. A half-animal, African exuberance, token of a spirit obscure indeed, but rich and effervescent, would open for them a future. One sign of dim inward struggle and pain, as if the spirit resented his imprisonment, would do the same. Both were wanting. They ruminate; life is the cud they chew.

The Esquimaux are celebrated as gluttons. This, however, is but one half the fact. They can eat, they can also fast, indefinitely. For a week they gorge themselves without exercise, and have no indigestion; for a week, exercising vigorously, they live on air, frozen air, too, and experience no exhaustion. Last winter half a dozen appeared at Square-Island Harbor, sent out their trained dogs, drove in a herd of deer, and killed thirteen. They immediately encamped, gathered fuel, made fires, began to cook and eat,—ate themselves asleep; then waked to cook, eat, and sleep again, until the thirteenth deer had vanished. Thereupon they decamped, to travel probably hundreds of miles, and endure days on days of severe labor, before tasting, or more than tasting, food again.

The same explanation serves. These physical capabilities, not to be attained by the post-Adamite man, belong to the primitive races, as to hawks, gulls, and beasts of prey. The stomach of the Esquimaux is his cellar, as that of the camel is a cistern, wherein he lays up stores.

August 4.—This day we sailed away from Hopedale, heading homeward,—leaving behind a race of men who were to me a problem to be solved, if possible. All my impressions of them are summed in the epithet, often repeated, pre-Adamite. In applying this, I affirm nothing respecting their physical origin. All that is to me an open question, to be closed when I have more light than now. It may be, that, as Mr. Agassiz maintains, they were created originally just as they are. For this hypothesis much may be said, and it may be freely confessed that in observing them I felt myself pressed somewhat toward the acceptance of it as a definite conclusion. It may be that they have become what they are by slow modification of a type common to all races,— that, with another parentage, they have been made by adoption

children of the icy North, whose breath has chilled in their souls
the deeper powers of man's being. This it will be impossible for
me to deny until I have investigated more deeply the influence of
physical Nature upon man, and learned more precisely to what
degree the traditions of a people, constituting at length a definite
social atmosphere, may come to penetrate and shape their individual being. I do not pronounce; I wait and keep the eyes
open. Doubtless they are God's children; and knowing this, one
need no be fretfully impatient, even though vigilantly earnest, to
know the rest.

In naming them pre-Adamite I mean two things.

First, that they have stopped short of ideas, that is, of the point
where human history begins. They belong, not to spiritual or
human, but to outward and physical Nature. There they are a
great success.

Secondly, in this condition of mere response to physical Nature, their whole being has become shapen, determined, fixed.
They have no future. Civilization affects them, but only by
mechanical modification, not by vital refreshment and renewal.
The more they are instructed, the weaker they become.

They change, and are unchangeable.

Unchangeable: if they assume in any degree the ideas and
habits of civilization, it is only as their women sometimes put on
calico gowns over their seal-skin trousers. The modification is
not even skin-deep. It is a curious illustration of this immobility,
that no persuasion, no authority, can make them fishermen. Inseparable from the seashore, the Esquimaux will not catch a fish,
if he can catch a dinner otherwise. The missionaries, both as
matter of paternal care and as a means of increasing their own
traffic,—by which the station is chiefly sustained,—have done
their utmost to make the natives bring in fish for sale, and have
failed. These people are first sealers, then hunters; some attraction in the blood draws them to these occupations; and at last it
is an attraction in the blood which they obey.

Yet on the outermost surface of their existence they change,
and die. At Hopedale, out of a population of some two hundred,
twenty-four died in the month of March last! At Nain, where the

number of inhabitants is about the same, twenty-one died in the same month; at Okkak, also twenty-one. More than decimated in a month!

The long winter suffocation in their wooden dens, which lack the ventilation of the *igloe* that their untaught wit had devised, has doubtless much to do with this mortality. But one feels that there is somewhat deeper in the case. One feels that the hands of the great horologe of time have hunted around the dial, till they have found the hour of doom for this primeval race. Now at length the tolling bell says to them, "No more! on the earth no more!"

Farewell, geological man, *chef-d'œuvre*, it may be, of some earlier epoch, but in this a grotesque, grown-up baby, never to become adult! As you are, and as in this world you must be, I have seen you; but in my heart is a hope for you which is greater than my thought,—a hope which, though deep and sure, does not define itself to the understanding, and must remain unspoken. There is a Heart to which you, too, are dear; and its throbs are pulsations of Destiny.

MODERN SPECULATIVE
RADICALISM

For more than a century there has been a vast movement of mind in the Western world, which now receives the general name of radicalism. Or going back to the beginning, we should fix the date of its explicit appearance as the 31st October, 1517, when Martin Luther affixed certain daring theses to the gates of the castle church of Wittenberg. In the next century, it assumed shape in English and New English Puritanism; in the next, played a subordinate indefinable part in the American Revolution, while in France it had become meantime a speculative mania, warring in the name of reason upon all the higher antecedent experience of humanity, which mania, getting to be practical, broke out at length in the immeasurable frenzy of the Revolution of 1789. From this it retired discomfited, despairing, disgraced, glad to hide its head; and just when it seemed gone forever, lo! here it is again all over the Western world, sober, resolute, thoughtful, morally earnest, and, in its maturer phases, profoundly religious. It has had many characters; it has many still; and it is often opposed to itself. It may be advancing in one line of thought, while rather receding than advancing in another. Thus Protestantism at first strengthened monarchical power, while fighting the battle of the soul against the despotism of the church. It may be in a mature stage with respect to the problems of religion, for example, while in a stage less mature by some degrees with respect to those of politics; which I think a charac-

Radical, July, 1867.

teristic position in our country. But there is a general order in the movement, nevertheless. Thus in religion it was during the sixteenth and seventeenth centuries a movement strictly within the limits of a special theological tradition; with Spinoza and some minor names as exceptions in the latter century. In the eighteenth, it was a war of the understanding against, not tradition in its formal statements alone, but the spiritual experience of mankind in its innermost import; while, however, a very different spirit was arising with Lessing in Germany. In the nineteenth, it finds some difficulty in believing in anything but experience, and only in its higher forms dares confide enough in ideas to find what this experience of man, in the heart and essence of it, has really been.

I propose to consider modern radicalism in its attitude toward the higher problems of human life and the higher facts of human history. Nothing of this kind would now need to be done, had the well-known work of Mr. Lecky been adequate to its theme. But this able scholar, carrying in his head such a magazine of facts, and able to state them in a manner so lucid, and a spirit so pure, lacks intellectual grasp, and enriches the memory more than he helps the intelligence. My own inquiry, however, is very limited. I speak distinctively of speculative or theoretic radicalism only. I limit myself further to this in its religious aspect. And thirdly, only its characteristic *attitude* is here to be considered. A limited inquiry, but large enough for the occasion, it may be found.

First, we must ask what radicalism and what conservatism *are* in the most general idea of them. There is a sort of conservatism which stands only upon advantages held in possession. It says, "I have wealth, I have respectability, I am well off here, and well guaranteed for the hereafter. Any change, good or bad in itself, will be bad for me; change is my enemy; I bolt and bar my doors, and, so far as I can, the doors of the world against it." There is on the other hand a sort of radicalism which, with fine things in the mouth, means in the heart of it, "You are in place, and I am out; you have, and I want; any change gives me a chance, and the more chance the more sweeping it be." There is a conservatism which is only a moral laziness, and a radicalism which is little more than a moral itch. We pass these by; we pass by whatever in a higher state of mind is only accidental or only incidental; and, leaving all this behind, inquire concerning pure mental tendencies.

It has been found of late that in common clay there is concealed as its real basis, a fine metal, closely resembling silver, which, when a cheap process for its disengagement shall have been discovered, promises important uses. In the clay of our humanity, in the tendencies of sects and parties, hidden beneath their gross rivalries, there is another *aluminium,* finer still. I delight in nothing more than the discovery and disengagement of this pure metal. Clay is indeed but clay; I scrape it off my boots, like another; I have no wish to represent the actual fact as cleaner or handsomer than it really is; but if something pure, like silver, can be eliminated from it, or even if it be there, though not to be extricated, let us know, if possible, what it is.

The characteristic distinction between radicalism and conservatism I conceive to be this: the radical reposes in Mind, or to take the most comprehensive word, in Spirit, as living, active, free; the conservative reposes in antecedent experience, that is, in Spirit as embodied in history. The one says, "This is true and right, *for* I think it": the other, "This is true and right, *for* I found it here, and stated as such, on coming into the world."

The radical has a strong position. Listen to him, hear his profession of faith; it will not be found unattractive. "What reason, conscience, heart approve," he says, "I believe. If reason say, 'It is thus and so,' to me it is indeed thus and so, though kings decree, and councils decide, and traditions aver, and institutions represent the contrary. If conscience, rationally enlightened, say, 'Do thus and so,' I do it, though fires blaze in my pathway. If heart and faith, out of their living power, lift up a hope which is indeed a prayer to the heavens, I fly on their wings; no weight shall hold me down. The voice of the Spirit of Truth must indeed be represented for me by that of my own spirit: I accept the necessity, confident that the universal spirit will be true to me when I am true to myself. What indeed can I do but think my best? To distrust my own being,—is it not to distrust *more* than my own being? Is there not a blasphemy in the doubt? If my intelligence lie to me, who is responsible for the falsehood? I am bold enough to think according to my ability; but I am *not* bold enough to push a question of veracity against the eternal Principle of Thought itself!" Let the man so speaking be worthy of his words, and it were not easy to hate or despise him.

But the conservative also has his profession of faith, which may not seem the worst possible; let us listen to him. "I do not," he says, "distrust my own being; rather I distrust my own power to arrive at its postulates and determinations by an immediate exercise of consciousness. I am limited by my special temperament, if not by want of opportunity, culture, and intellectual power; truth is not so limited. At best, I am but one man, and dare not attempt to find in my own being all which belongs to that of humanity, in my own mind all which mind in its universality declares. Only all truth is wholly true; partial truth is partial falsehood; I will therefore be as little partial as I can be. Now, there is more reason embodied in the experience of humanity, than there is in me as an individual intelligence. Therefore I modestly refer myself to that, taking what comes *to* me rather than what could come *from* me, expressly as being the larger and richer in significance of the two. I will not shut myself up to my rood of ground when I may have the whole earth for my commons." Said simply and sincerely, this also would have force. Here, then, are two attitudes of mind precisely opposed, yet neither to be condemned outright. Spirit thinking, speaking, on the one hand; Spirit spoken, its thoughts embodied in visible facts, on the other;—both are venerable. But let us, as radicals, attend first to that position, whose unity with our own is least apparent.

It is undoubtedly true that more reason is involved in the recorded experience of humanity than any mind, however great, could evolve immediately from its own resources. The thought which has made a Christendom for us is a grander thought than the brightest individual could sit down and write out irrespective of that. It takes millions of ages to give the earth a fertile soil, and equally in humanity an enormous past to make a rich present. Even when thinking most freely, we are in point of fact drawing from wells dug for us by forgotten centuries. "An endless seeker with no past at my back?" Who spoke? was it Emerson or Socrates, America or Greece? Whichever, he has a very great past at his back, and not there in vain, who has arrived at this spirituality of purpose, this consecration of thought.

A new and even religious respect for embodied fact constitutes one chief element in the higher genius of this century. In the immeasurable scale of degrees, it is indeed only facts of a humble order, which as yet charm attention; but a beginning has been made. See cultivated, able men, faithfully putting out their eyes at the microscope over cell-germs and animalculæ,—looking at the infinite through a pin-hole, and discerning a great deal, too. See another, making prolonged studies of the mud-worm, and the house-fly. Two or three years ago Mr. Agassiz lectured in Boston before a highly cultivated and delighted audience upon a subject which some centuries ago might have been thought befitting only a philosopher in cap and bells,—upon the clam. All the principal newspapers had reporters there busily scratching; copious notes of the lecture appeared in print next day; the clam had become a matter of public interest, the clam had obtained admission to the best society,—and not in the shape of chowder. That lecture I reckon among the more significant events of American history: the future Bancroft should not forget it. This regard for fact, for embodied and defined Nature, has genius, has religion in it. John Stuart Mill thinks there may be a religion without a God. Yes, religion with only a clam,—*and* the infinite energy of Nature behind it and implied in it. We might almost call this the new fetish worship;—not by any means a mere repetition of the old, yet, like that, beginning at the bottom. Many men now-a-days get their best sense of the Ineffable in this way. The charm, the fascination, comes, not from the small object in itself, but from that Unnameable it suggests. Perhaps his clamship has not in and for himself got admitted to good society after all; he might find on presenting his card that clam *plus* Infinite Nature, and clam *qua* clam, are not considered as quite the same.

This touching reverence for embodied fact was characteristic of Thoreau, and constituted the vital essence of his genius. He did, it is true, limit himself to facts almost wholly inarticulate, having his blind side, and a very blind side indeed, but having also on another side such an eye, so sympathetic, so deep-seeing, as was given to few in his century,—indeed in some respects it was perhaps the best eye of the century. His life was a religion, a worship, and of the purest quality, nothing purer seen in our day; but it was a worship beginning at the bottom once more, following literally the *footsteps* of Spirit, its sign pedal, getting so near the soles of its feet.

I remember talking with him once, when he began to tell of finding arrow heads, with remnants of Indian tobacco pipes, and broken pottery, in the neighborhood. "When I come upon these things," he said, "I feel that I have indeed found something! This is genuine and unmistakeable; there is Nature in it, no cant, nor artifice, nor make-belief; it is solid and real as rock; and with such relics before me I could lose the houses of the village, the shops, the churches, and the post office, without missing them."

By way of offset, I began chanting the praises of the Westminster catechism. "Here," I said, "are arrow-heads of another sort, weapons used in a warfare with the embodical principle of evil,—quite as primitive in their way as those of your Indians, and somewhat *harder* than flint, I think. Here is the smoke of the bottomless pit rather than that of a tobacco pipe, suggesting a narcotic for nerves finer and more vital by far than those affected by the Indian weed. Broken pottery? Think of that cup of communion which men once quaffed, verily believing that they drank the blood of God. There is broken pottery for you! Broken, hopelessly broken, I admit; but suggesting such memories, such thoughts not to be spoken!"

The world must learn to reverence the higher facts, as it is just beginning to reverence the lower. Calvinism,—it is much more than a mere opinion, to be tried in an opinion scale, found wanting, and flung aside as a cheat. It is a vast out-birth from the heart of Nature, with profound, infinite thoughts in it, wherein,

however crudely stated, are the thoughts of eternal Spirit itself.
As matter of opinion I could accuse it; as fact, part of the spiritual
history of man, I *study* it, bringing to bear upon it the most
powerful sympathetic solvents I am master of, as Sir Humphrey
Davy applied the galvanic battery to soda and potassa. Without
Calvinism what were America, Great Britain, Western Europe
indeed, now? Causes are worthy of their effects, in history as
elsewhere.

The opinion-scale is not precisely the one to weigh the universe in. Weigh; but make allowances, and above all keep up a
just reverence for high human fact, sacred energies of man's
heart; else the opinion-scale will be more deceiving than any
blindest worship of custom. A gentleman found in his possession
a light guinea, and gave it to his Irish servant, saying, "This is
light weight, and will not pass; take it, and get what you can for
it." Happening to inquire about it a day or two later, he was told
by the servant with great glee, that, having to pay for a glass of
beer, he had slipped it between two half-pence, and so passed it
successfully off! The Voltaires act more honestly, but not otherwise more wisely. They find that Mosaicism, for example, does
not come up to the standard weight of good coin. "Ha! Light
weight! Fraud! We have been cheated, but no others shall be
cheated." And away it goes out at the window.

I am ashamed to think what pains, what appliances, the miners
in California use to crush quartz, that they may obtain from it
some minute fractional per centum of gold, when I compare
with this industry the manner in which some Buckle, amid storms
of applause, treats the history of man. History, forsooth, must be
all gold, and that, too, ready minted, perfect in weight, clear cut
in the impression, else it is "superstition," and fit only to furnish
a warning! But no, I am giving too much credit; the real point
of that complaint is that the gold is not *brass,*—that the transcendent elements of human experience appear in it at all.

Now, conservatism does service by simply clinging to the higher
facts of history, heroically persisting in the faith that these are of a
divine import. I have a pleasure in its pertinacity, and like to see

the irrepressible tides come flowing back upon the Mrs. Parting-ton-Voltaires, when, however honorable their impulse, they would treat what is grandest in man's record only with a broom. It is an attempt to sweep out Nature; which in the end will not be swept out.

But the radical on his side has somewhat to say. History is vitalized for us only, or at least chiefly, as it is resolved in thought. Remaining mere experience, embodied in custom, tradition, institution, and blindly reverenced as such, it may indeed shape men's conduct, but will not refresh their minds; it may impress moralities upon them, but will do so without making them inwardly, freely, vitally moral. Hegel says of China,—whose civilization is the most strictly traditional in the world,—that it exhibits a morality of the mass, which cannot be found in any individual, and an intelligence implied in the public order, that never becomes explicit and productive in personal consciousness. But where progress ends, decay sets in. The tree dies when it ceases to grow. Mere recital becomes at last automatic; the forces of man's spirit, no longer engaged, grow weak for want of exercise, or wander in aimless irregularities. So we may believe that M. Huc does not speak merely as a catholic missionary, when he declares Chinese civilization to be in a steady process of decomposition.

Facts are dead things until they are seen under the aspect of truth; and the truth must not be merely that they are, or were, facts. What is more insignificant than the clam to the clam digger? —though he has no doubt of its being really a clam. It is to one who regards it in the light of thought that the poor little creature has a suggestion which is not poor nor small. *Crush* your auriferous quartz, if you would obtain gold. "Clinging to fact?" the rigorous radical might say, glancing at his rival. "Clinging to it much like barnacles to a ship's bottom, always on the under side, and always where they were, no matter what voyage is made." And there is a conservatism, by which the sarcasm is not wholly unmerited.

Besides, it is only a limited and local, never a universal, experience which custom and tradition bring to our doors. In order to comprehend the experience of *humanity,* we must find its significance, its principles, its unity with living mind.

Our result, then, is that conservatism comes to intelligence only by assuming the radical attitude, and *solving* man's experience, while radicalism comes to maturity only by assuming the conservative attitude, and *respecting* man's experience.

Accordingly, mature radicalism may be defined as that which embraces the highest virtue of conservatism, without sharing its limitations, or at all losing its own distinctive character. Now, it is toward this ripe stage that radicalism in America is rapidly tending,—that is, so far as the problems of religion are concerned, for with respect to some others the same cannot, perhaps, be said.

Let me illustrate this ripeness by an instance drawn from the field of theology. There has been in Christendom a doctrine of the Holy Spirit,—one of the cardinal doctrines of the church. To radicalism a hundred years ago this doctrine was arrant nonsense. Fifty years ago it still suggested little more than a juggle of words in the dogma of the Trinity. To-day religious radicals are affirming the intercommunication of the spirit of humanity with, and its fructification by, absolute Spirit, in a manner which to the very partisans of the old doctrine seems overweening. These radicals tell us that in all ages this faith has been the ineffable solace and the exhaustless invigoration of man's soul. Perhaps their statement is not always guarded and limited with sufficient care, for such things will happen: but the instance is very significant, not only as it illustrates a general tendency, but as it shows the extent to which this tendency has been already productive.

For this recognition is central, axial: radicalism remains eccentric until it arrives at this. As there could not be an astronomy, were not the necessary laws of man's understanding one and the same with those laws which govern the movements of worlds; as there could be no true philosophy, were not reason in man of like kind with universal reason; so could there be no religion in the high sense, no divine liberation of the soul, wherein freedom and obedience are identical, were not that to which man's obedience is due sovereign *in* him, sovereign *with him,* not merely *over* him. And I have often thought that if one would get the key to Carlyle, he must not neglect what I venture to call the great man's failure at this point. Let one read Carlyle's lecture upon Mohammed, his eulogy on the Book of Job, and kindred passages scattered through his writings, and it will appear that this noble writer's ultimate conception is that of an omnipotent will, going only over man's head, and requiring unqualified submission and service. Cannot one find in that the admiration of autocracy, which has grown upon him all his life? How should not a prevailing will seem to him the highest thing on earth? How should not he conceive it the chief duty of men in general to find out some one to obey, some one to typify for them the pure autocracy of the universe? It is true he dislikes a stupid obstinacy; but his point of view remains. Prevailing Wills, he thinks, ought to prevail: it is only dogged Wont's that he disesteems.

Is God only *above?* Is man only *beneath?* Were it too daring to say that the *religion* of God is implied in that of man, the faith of the Eternal in the faith of humanity? Was it a mere shot into the air, that old Hebrew notion of a covenant between God and man, by which both were bound, and in which they were made one? Or was that notion the outward and anticipatory figure of a truth which language even in our day is little able to express, especially since modern nominalism has made such havoc with the little competency to pure thought it ever had? A covenant or contract is the community, the *becoming one,* of two; but beginning at a definite time, and limited to express particulars. Suppose this becoming one to be not a mere act of will, but a fact of being, realized or made virtual in man in proportion as he becomes indeed man; suppose there is this implication in the soul of that which comprehends, orders and sustains all; it will follow that in the highest kind of obedience man obeys nothing external to his own being, and yet obeys that which is strictly universal, not limited by his *particular* being, nor even by the same total of particular existences. Obedience, then, will be accomplished, not by the subjection of all which he is to that which he is not, but by the subordination of his *particular* self to that absolutely universal Spirit, which is neither included in him or foreign to him.

The nominalism* of the time has left no sense in words which permits them to suggest clearly what I would say. It is an unhappiness of radicalism that it has as yet next to no language for its master-thought. It can do little more than accumulate the old symbols, hint-words, figurative and approximate expressions,— the covenanting God, the Holy Ghost, the Muse, the Christ, Immanuel, Jehovah speaking audibly to Moses, Ahura-Magda answering the questions of Zarathustra, Chrishna becoming man and instructing Arjuna, the Mentor of Telemachus, the goddess giving laws to Numa, Themis inspiring the judge. In all these and in many more of like kind,—for the history of man is full of them,—it finds hints of a truth, whose identity no difference of names and shades and degrees of depth and clearness can disguise; and knows this to be the truth of truths for man. Language must obtain new capabilities, such as Hegel—not, it is thought, with entire success,—has tried to give it before radicalism can say what in the heart it already knows clearly. But its thought is clear enough to determine the spirit in which it shall investigate human experience. It studies in man not man alone. It aims to make that experience intelligible by discovering in its grand facts their principle, their reality in consciousness; while it finds ever implied that Unnameable, Adorable, whose infinitude and eternity are pictured in space and time, the Being of all existence, the Principle of all thought.

The uses of this labor, if it can be at all well done, must be great.

* Some of our readers may well need to be reminded that nominalism is the doctrine, according to which all general names are names of nothing real. The word *man,* for example, is said to denote nothing which has a real existence. Here are this, that, and the other—*man,* we are compelled to say; but it is maintained that in defining them by that general term, we define them only by a fiction of the mind, concocted for purposes of convenience only. Thus in saying, "This is a man," we are defining the real by the unreal; with entire truth we could only say, "this is this!" Of course, any word, such as spirit, intended to denote a pure Universal, must be the merest shadow of shadows. The reasoning by which this doctrine is supported is faithfully represented by statements like the following: *No particular man is not a particular man, but man in general: There can be no general reality, for if there were, we should find it as a particular object!* One is inclined to inquire whether he is not dreaming when he sees an able writer on logic, like John Stewart Mill, putting forth this sort of argument in the most entire good faith.

I will try and indicate two classes of them.

In the first place, a refreshment, an invigoration, as from quaffing cool, flowing waters in the desert. To find the unity of your heart with the heart of another is ever a happiness. Other and *not* other,—it is the sweet of friendship, it is the honey of love: very dead indeed is he who is dead to this. But in that other to come near the eternal One, the Unity that is not numerical and merely for itself, but whose oneness is for all *others* whatsoever, and by which alone they have power to be,—that is to attain the ultimate felicity of life. For this it is that all men are seeking, and seeking the more earnestly the more deeply alive they are. At present, we have said, they look for it mostly in facts that are farthest removed from man. But what was it that Thoreau sought and found in the fern and cross-bill, the Maine woods, Cape Cod and the Atlantic ocean? Only fern and cross-bill, wood, water and sand? He found a certain infinite suggestion, a far-off hint of the One-in-all, eternal Nature, which is ever near; and by this was re-created continually in a new and finer image. He grew upon it as few men have grown. All else was but as the dried stubble of last year's fields, compared with that which could afford him this creative exhilaration. Somewhat of like kind animates all modern science, and constitutes, though mostly without its own knowledge, the real reward of its labors. "O Being, Being," it says unconsciously, "blessed to be near thee." Yes, blessed, though it be only by the mediation of cell-germs. But when the Bibles, the divine half-articulate cry of the human soul, the grand melodious imaginations, whose echo never dies, the sacred *nexus* that has made families, cities, societies, the genius of humanity by whose virtue thought, belief, the unseen, has become for it a veritable *ground,* solid as the bases of the everlasting hills,— when all this is meditated in a like or yet better spirit, then this wrinkled Tithonus of a world will have found youth in its years, the blessing of youth without its inexperience.

Again, such studies will have for us an express instruction, making explicit much has now hidden itself deeply, beyond the ken of many, in our life, and showing us the scope and significance of the principles we acknowledge. In the early life of the race much is merely potential which afterwards is demonstrated. Newton's thought was potentially in the scientific mind from the beginning, and was prophesied of by the first impulse to find phenomena in thought. This is well understood. But it seems less understood that much which is now unconsciously implied in thought, and concealed by its very nearness, was once on the surface. We can again bring it to the surface, and make it explicit in our minds, by attending to it in history. We recover our own consciousness by the study of a more primitive experience. I will try to make this clear by illustration.

In the Roman family,—which, by the way, was not limited by blood relationship,—the father not only received all the earnings and administered all the property, but had the power of life and death, so long as he lived. That has at first an unpleasant look. But take a key to it. The family was distinctively a religious organization, with its own sacred rites and symbols,—a "family worship," which was not all a mere reflection from the meeting-house. It was a knot of relations, with religion as the binding principle; and this bound so closely that individual responsibility was swallowed up in the common responsibility of all for each and each for all. The unity of this sovereign principle was represented in that of the father's person, and considered as insepar-able from its representative form. For this is the law of all primitive thought,—that a principle, though necessarily felt in itself, is seen, recognized, only in its symbol. Given, therefore, a principle whose special function is to make the unity of many, its representative must be a unit. Hence monarchy.

Looking at these facts intelligently, we find them first of all affirming religion as the principle of social unity. This is ob-scurely felt to be so doubtless in our day; but this view of its function was nigh getting lost; and a conscious restoration of it to this import would sweep away much that now encumbers us, and renew the strength of much whose feebleness is the weak point of modern civilization. Secondly, the facts tell us that authoritative power is properly representative, *not* of individual wishes and wills, but of a universal principle, which individual wills are bound to obey; and an application of this thought would be to restate the political theories of the modern world.

Again, Tacitus tells us in the Germania that among the primitive Germans it was permitted only to the priests to pass penal sentence, or to impose bonds or inflict stripes; "as if," he says, "it were done not for the sake of revenge, or at the bidding of a leader, but only in obedience to a divine behest *(non quasi in pœnam, nec ducis jussu, sed velut deo imperante.)* Is it unnecessary to remind the modern world that condemnation can be passed and punishment inflicted upon no man, save by the exaction of a sovereign divine principle, which demands this homage at our hands? Not to selfishly provide for our own safety, but to reaffirm our allegiance to justice, this piece of duty is to be done. Obscurely we all feel so; but the fact was getting overlaid with civil forms and with theories which only pit the self love of society against that of the culprit.

Once more, Mr. Maine, in his excellent work on "Ancient Law,"—which would be more excellent, had he brought to his facts any adequate philosophy,—calls attention to the fact that in Homeric times all authoritative judgments between man and man were esteemed "themistes," that is, immediate emanations from Divine justice into the mind of the judge. We can find the meaning of this explicit conception in the implicit hidden persuasion of our own hearts, if we will look for it there: but the modern world was in danger of forgetting, that civil judgments and laws are not the product of certain mechanisms, the jury and the ballot box; while Mr. Maine himself, one of the wisest writers in his line who has taken up the pen in modern times, seems to regard this instance as indicating a fictitious element found in all primitive thought, and while, again, powerful reasoners, like Mr. Mill, are evaporating the Right itself, the soul of all law, and the inspiration of all authoritative judgment, into prudential opinion.

An interpretation of history which proceeds in the way I have tried to suggest,—that is, which finds in special facts universal principles, immanent in the being of man, or constituting rather the essence itself of his spirit,—will be replete with express instruction; yet even these uses may be surpassed by those first named. What an echo, what a resonance, it would afford the faith of our souls! We touch the stops on the key-board of our own hearts, and the world itself is the organ-pipe, and the whole vast breath of humanity is the wind that blows through it.

Here, then, I find the attitude of that which I have ventured to call the higher and maturer radicalism. Its aspiration is to discover the unity of man's visible experience with his living intelligence, the unity of Spirit embodied with Spirit thinking and feeling.

In order to set off this position more clearly, I shall contrast it with two grades of radicalism, which are in my estimation immature, though in different degrees.

The first of these may be distinguished as that of the eighteenth century. Its fundamental assumption is that the recorded experience of man is essentially opposed to reason, and that to deliver oneself from all respect for it is the beginning of wisdom. I select as its types Rousseau and Voltaire.

Rousseau began with a suppositious state of nature, in whose name he made war upon all civilization. All the grand architectures of humanity, cities and societies, temples and arts, worships and laws, were to him mere aberrations and delinquencies. And his state of nature—what was it? A state of utter individualism, egotism, wherein man was a nude self and nothing more, without even an anticipatory stretch of sentiment to anything beyond. He stripped off from his "natural man," along with worship, religion, along with society, duty; he cast away that sense of kindred with the Infinite, which makes man's life sacred in his own eyes, and that faith of fellowship which is the alembic of Nature to distil the ichors of duty and nobility; he stripped man to bones, and then said, not, "This is what we *are*," but "This is what we *ought* to be." Charles Lamb's—or was it Sidney Smith's?—fancy upon a hot day of taking off his flesh and sitting in his bones, had been anticipated, but in entire gravity and with a yet more heroic denudation in view, by this philosopher.

He made this agreeable fancy the basis of his political speculation. Primitive rule is always despotic. Why? We have already hinted at the reason. It is because man has the sense of a sovereignty over his life so soon as he has any human sense at all; because he feels that this sovereignty abides in a universal and therefore unitive principle; and because, seeing principles, as the primitive man always does, only in symbols, embodiments, he cannot discriminate the unity of the sovereign principle and that of its representative. Had Rousseau brought reason to the interpretation of experience rather than to sheer antagonism with it, he would have said, "Authority abides in a universal principle, Right Reason, say, which can be only *represented* by individual men, but, as we now may see, can be represented by *all* in whom right reason is a dominant force"; and so saying he would have given republicanism a perennial basis in thought, and forwarded political theory by a century or two, instead of confusing it for perhaps a longer time. But he must needs think the spontaneous experience of man a fanfaronade of fear, fraud and delusion; he must denude him of all this in order to find his proper being; the result was that he could conceive of man no otherwise than as by nature a nude self, and of society only as an artificial joint-stock corporation, wherein rule is concocted out of the collective self-will and self-interest of the stockholders. It is a conception of human nature and of the phenomena of society which on all sides is doing unspeakable mischief to this day.

Voltaire busied himself much about religion. What was it to him? Why, as a mere cold notion about *a* God somewhere, *le fruit de la raison cultivée,* a product of the opinion-factory, he was ready to furnish it with a ticket of admission to good society,—to give it a "character," as the servant girls say. As an original and originative principle, sovereign, productive, creative, he felt compelled to deny it the favor of his countenance altogether. But thus it is found in the experience of humanity, and as such he could only make it the butt of endless ridicule. I will cite a passage from the *Essai sur Les Mœurs et L'Esprit des Nations,* wherein he describes its genesis according to his way of thinking.

"In order to learn how all these worships or these superstitions got established, we must, I think, follow the movement of the

human spirit abandoned to itself. The half-savage people of a
hamlet sees the fruits which nourish it destroyed; an inundation
sweeps away some huts, or the lightning burns others. Who has
done this mischief? It cannot be one of the citizens, since they all
suffer alike. It must therefore be some hidden power. This has
maltreated them, they must appease it. How shall this be done?
By rendering such services as one offers another whom he desires
to please, by making small presents. There is a serpent in the
vicinity, probably the serpent was at the bottom of the business:
they offer it milk near the cave where it lurks; it becomes sacred
to them henceforth; they invoke it upon going to war with a
neighboring village, which on its side has also its chosen pro-
tector."

Not to notice the amazing agility with which he skips over all
sorts of gaps, we may ask, can anything be more curious than the
process by which he learns what has been "the march of the
human spirit?" Is it by studying the earliest records with penetrating sympathy, until the faint vestiges they afford of primitive
belief become clear? Far enough from it; he despises the spontaneous experience of humanity so confidently, he is so assured it
could be nothing but an absurdity, that he has no question of his
own correctness when he has invented a sample verified by absurdity. As a Chinese juggler will pull you roods of ribbon, as
much as you like, out of his mouth, so our radical philosopher,
when a quantum of primitive religious history is wanted, needs
only to put his hand to his mouth, and out it comes.

But there are a few words in the above extract which deserve
especial attention. He tells us what unhappy things befall "the
human spirit *abandoned to itself.*" These words give the key to
his mental position. Of any interior guidance, of any divine structural idea involved in this spirit to be evolved by it, of a noble
native significance therein which *will* find for itself signs, he does
not dream. The acorn "abandoned to itself" is not abandoned by
guiding nature, and knows how to become an oak. The earth
"abandoned to itself" manages to find its way without any appearance of groping, and comes about, I am told, with surprising
constancy and accuracy. But the human spirit "abandoned to

itself" is abandoned indeed, and makes the acorn an object of envy in the comparison!

Voltaire's misinterpretation of experience is partly caused by, and partly causes, a like misinterpretation of man's being. Each must needs involve the other; fountain and stream correspond. The grand operative principles of the being of humanity, the grand operative elements in history,—he sets up *la raison cultivée* as in natural opposition to both. To-day, radicalism would be likely to err, if at all, in the precisely opposite direction, forbidding reason even to discriminate between natural energies, but confounding them all in one general and implicit acceptance. An extreme instance of this has been given by a strange man of genius, Mr. Walt Whitman.

Again, when men are no longer content to make nonsense of spontaneous belief, a second degree of radicalism may arise, and has in our century arisen, which is still partial, though less flagrantly offensive. Its fundamental assumption is that this experience is to be interpreted without having recourse to anything but the understanding. One would say that religion can only be interpreted religiously,—that the principle itself must explain its manifestations. These philosophers, on the contrary, bid it stand aside; its intervention would, in their opinion, vitiate the interpretive process; "we should then explain history by our personal feelings." Exclude the principle; then pass over its manifestations to the understanding to be accounted for: that is the adopted rule of procedure.

For example, the fathers of the Indo-European race in looking up to the sun and sky saw there somewhat which compelled them, in the attempt to name these objects, to say *God*. They meant to name what they saw; in doing so they gave expression, as the subsequent history of language shows, to their sense of an Infinite and Adorable: the word that, according to the notion of many now, *should* have signified the physical sky alone, *would* signify Divine Being, and finally went over to that meaning exclusively. This act, moreover, is not without consequences of a very remarkable kind. That first sally of the human spirit, as we know from abundant and indubitable evidence, involves all its productive energies. Just here man begins to be indeed man. There is nothing great in human history, absolutely nothing, which does not assume this primitive recognition as the condition of its existence. It is *conditio sine qua non* of all social construction by which man builds himself up into moral order and amplitude, of all art, poetry, thought, ideal activity. Man sings this, preaches it, reasons it, respires it; for ages upon ages he will not build a house, or light a fire on the hearth, or partake of food, without bringing the act into connection with this; he must, for his own content, associate it with his domestication of dogs and horses, with the milking of cows, with the ploughing of land; he must find in it the reason *why* of all obeying, commanding, community; it is the essence of law, it is the melody of the world to him. The facts of history bear me out amply in saying that without some such recognition there would have been no Iliad, no Athens, no social rule, no authoritative judgment between man and man, no family even, nothing in history which makes it human, nothing in language which fits it to be the vehicle of imagination, sentiment and thought.

Now, the class of radical thinkers in question undertake to give an account of this after their fashion, that is, by setting aside religion in that which it proclaims as its proper import, and then calling upon the understanding to furnish out of its own resources a principle or general fact, into which it may be resolved. The notion of God, they say, arose from man's tendency to make fictitious imputation of his own personality to inanimate objects. Being a person himself, he thought that the sky must be a person, that the sun must be a person, &c. Well, it is quite true that man has a tendency to make the world a mirror in which to behold his own image. The understanding may therefore find its account,— I do not say, may find a full and legitimate satisfaction,—in this explanation: it has got hold of somewhat real, which may seem to furnish a thread whereon the facts can be strung, and a thread strong enough to sustain them. But how far is the religious principle satisfied? So far from being satisfied at all, it is flagrantly affronted. All the deepest economies of civilization, all by which man has become a developed and constituted human soul, originating in, and built up by, a piece of pure unconscious fiction? It is not theology, it is religion in its essence, it is the binding sympathy of every human spirit with the verity of Nature, which is affronted by such an interpretation. I know what a play of illusion there is on the outermost face of things, while there are faculties of the mind,—Fancy, for example,—which play freely in this element, not disguising their character; but who is authorized to say that illusion goes quite under and over the being of man, making him but a show communicating only with shows? Religion, which is certainly *a* principle of man's being, and which, if the testimony of history be not discarded, may be pronounced with confidence its central principle, declares to the contrary; who can, without extreme presumption, give the lie to its testimony? The ground for such a negative is merely this: outside of the religious intelligence we do not perceive the truth which that affirms; which is like denying sight because the ear does not see.

Radicalism making nonsense of human experience in all its deeper elements;—radicalism, again, making sense of it, but a sense wholly unsympathetic with the *heart* of ages past, and wholly without significance for the *heart* of this age:— such seem to me its partial forms. Radicalism so interpreting the spiritual experience of man that its fundamental principles shall be in essence to us what they were to those whom of old they empowered and inspired, but seen now in their free universality, found in every symbol that has served them at all, distinguished even from those which have served them longest and best,—this alone I esteem mature. And this, it may again be said, is already in existence, though its work is mostly to be done. The incompleteness of its actual performance I admit freely; it is just setting forth upon a labor which it will probably require centuries to so far finish that the modern mind shall find content in the result; but the spirit in which this work is to be prosecuted has been already attained.

Why, after all, should there be a speculative radicalism? Grant that it may have uses, its abuses are also acknowledged; and at the best is it not disturbing and alarming? Yes, it is disturbing. It

requires those to think as for their lives, who are busy at somewhat which they like better. It awakens active, painful doubt,
where before was only a slumbering dissatisfaction. It shakes a
passive faith, saying inexorably, almost rudely, "Obtain content
in a higher way, or go without it henceforth." It may ask questions, for which no complete answer is ready, and may breed in
conscientious persons a distressful sense of alternatives, neither
of which seems to them all that could be desired. Moreover, it is
indeed alarming; for it indicates a spiritual crisis which has again
and again proved fatal. To this fact I, for one, am feelingly alive,
and do not desire to conceal it in the least. Why, then, be a radical? Why not make that which has served so long, serve longer?

Ah, my excellent conservative friend, why not put your growing boy this winter into last winter's boots? See, they are not
worn out: pray insist upon it, do, that his foot shall go into them!
No? You do not insist upon it? In the face of high rents and high
taxes, and flour at twenty-two dollars a barrel, and beef at forty
cents a pound, you pull out your hard-pumped purse, and buy
the new boots? There are other things besides boots, necessaries
of life in a far stricter sense, that will get outgrown, if not out-
worn. It becomes a question of obtaining a new outfit, or of going
barefoot; and there are those who think that, as the final cost of
wet feet might prove greater than that of new boots, so a neglect
to provide for the new necessities of growing mind, would, in the
end, turn out to be a piece of bad economy. These are not always
persons who delight in disturbing their neighbors, and making
life expensive; sometimes, on the contrary, they are moved by a
tender and loving regard for those whose rest they disturb, and
whose energies they tax.

But I must try to show more specially what is the present posture of the world with respect to these high affairs; why it is
alarming; and why, nevertheless, and indeed all the more, we
must not think of turning back, but only of pressing forward.

There is a point which no civilization hitherto has passed: one
after another has reached it, and there fallen into decay. It is the
point where its morality,—or, more largely, its spirituality,—is
no longer nourished sufficiently by principles merely *implied* in

special traditions and traditionary symbols. The greater minds may go on, and arrive at principles recognized in their universality; the greater number of minds either linger, trying to squeeze out another drop from the empty bottle, or else fall away into sophisms, egoisms, brutalities. Just when Cicero in his treatise *De Officiis* was giving ethical law something in the nature of a universal statement, Rome was dissolving in utter rottenness. Just when Socrates and Plato were in thought, placing moral truth on its own eternal basis, Athens was smitten with incurable disease; and when, later, Demosthenes was giving his orations an ethical breadth and energy, found in those of no subsequent political orator, to my knowledge, until the day of Edmund Burke, the city had already but one heaven, the theatre, and had debased even that. The nations of the earth have been able to appreciate principles only in symbols, from which they were not distinguished, and able to make progress only while they believed themselves simply reciting a definite past. When the gap opens between what they think and what they remember, and when, freed from traditional bondage, they seem ready to enter upon a larger life,—in that moment of opportunity their vitality is exhausted, the knees shake, the cheek turns pale.

This period, hitherto thus fatal, has come for the Western world. It has come by no man's will; it will depart at no man's desire. I do not wonder, still less do I mock, at the instinct of self-preservation which leads many to recoil, and seek a renewal of the primitive forms of faith. But in every such time this expedient has been tried, and in every case it has failed. Athens could put the cup of hemlock to the lips of Socrates, but it could not thereby put health into its own veins. Had it tried to follow him, it *might* have failed no less, for many of those who made the attempt, ran into barren and inane speculations; but what *might* have happened upon this road, *did* happen upon the other; Athens had thrived upon the old unquestioning implicit faith; but could not thrive upon it longer, when question had at length arisen.

With the ultimate questions we are now face to face, and though the eyes be shut upon them, the questions are, and are known to be, still there before us. When the Roman nationality was of like age with our own, the Roman people were acting under the influence of implicit persuasions, concerning which no one knew even that question *could* be raised. They had no more thought about religion than about gravitation, but were as simply, and unreflectingly, and undoubtingly submitted to the one as to the other. Moral, social, and political obligation had never been put far enough away to be recognized as matter of theory. Both religion and social obligation existed for them in undistinguished unity with fixed symbolical forms which they regarded as simple indissoluble facts, like night and day. How different is it with us! For two centuries it has been recognized, for example, that political obligation must be found and vindicated in its principle, if it is to be maintained. And what a conflict, or rather chaos, of theories the modern world has been witness of! Hobbes and Filmer, Locke and Rousseau, Hegel and Carlyle, Fourier and Brigham Young, Come-outer and Bible-Communist,—and who knows how many more?—all have their say about it; and the end is not yet. Pure moral obligation is equally in question, and the various theories upon it equally at odds. Of religion no less may be said; indeed the confusion is here greater than elsewhere. And the change of attitude is here general, comprehending all, those who resist change only less than those who would promote it. Conservative and radical are but shades of the same. The old Catholic believed simply in "Holy Church"; the modern Catholic, Friedrick Schlegel, for example, believes in the *principle* of religion as taught and nourished *by* the church. "The Bible *is* the religion of Protestants," said Chillingworth. The Orthodox Protestant of to-day believes in religion as merely *defined by* the Bible. No one identifies religion now with that by which it is supposably sustained and defined; the relation even in the mind of conservatives is not one of identity, but one of association. And in this alone a profound change from the ancient way of thinking is implied. When some go on and inquire *what* is the association between religion and Church or Bible, whether transient or permanent, partial or total, they only enter an opening made in all minds. So soon as it is known that the principle is one fact, the symbol or instrument another, no prohibition, no resistance will prevent inquiry from going further. Others will not be content to assume the principle, and to inquire concerning its relation to books and institutions, but will ask what it is, or if it be anything, *in itself*. The tendency is inevitable: the old time has gone irretrievably; new mental necessities have arisen: they are mental *necessities:* to resist them is vain, to ignore them infatuated.

Had the matter been in my power, as it could be in that of no man, I should not perhaps have dared to bring about this state of things. But there is One who has taken the responsibility; and now we *must* do our duty in the premises.

Preceding civilizations in like circumstances with our own have been rescued, if at all, by succors from without. When Greece and Rome fell into decay, they were saved by a cross movement, which brought in, on the one side, the fresh life of the Germanic races, and, on the other, a religious inspiration implying the loftiest spiritual ideas, but ideas strictly embodied in symbolical forms, and developing themselves according to the laws of primitive faith. No such succors await us. No virgin Germany is on our borders, and the world has seen its last Messiah. Religion and all the principles that nourish civilizations must now appear to us in their universality and their pure significance, or,—the alternative is one that I do not love to contemplate as possible. This is my mature and sober judgment, springing from no restlessness, no venturesome heat of blood, no predilection for untried things, but from a survey of the case, which did not begin yesterday, nor only last year.

This it is which makes the need of a radicalism, and of a radicalism such as has never existed before,—able for the first time in history to sustain and inspirit a civilization. I am not *sure* that we are yet capable of such. Many of the phenomena which formerly indicated decay in like situations, are re-appearing now. The luxury of decadent Rome, the passion for pleasure of death-smitten Athens, theories which resolve duty into self-interest, authority into self-will, and religion into rhetoric, are all here, in London, in Paris, in New York and Boston. A metaphysic which seeks to extinguish intellectual ideas by showing them as mere nominalisms, mere fictions borrowed from sensations, renders aid and comfort, often unwillingly, to the practical egoism which negates all moral ideas. This has been seen before; we know what came of it; and its appearance in our day suggests serious meditations.

Nevertheless I think that what should be, now at length can be,—that sovereign principles, conceived of in their universality, can indeed be for us what they never were, nor could be, for earlier times.

For we have one inestimable advantage. The conception of universal law, grasped with difficulty by the greatest of the ancients, has now become common and popular. Men in the street speak of the law of gravitation with the same sense of reality they have in speaking of a stone wall. Moreover, they cannot help calling it a law of *Nature,*—cannot help supplying in thought a living, everlasting matrix of all laws. That conception of universal law, connected inevitably, however furtively with the idea of absolute, self-sustaining unity, separates broadly the modern from the ancient world. It is one of those thoughts which make epochs. Already it has penetrated into every part of modern life,—it ploughs with the farmer in the field, labors with the mechanic in the shop, sails with the seaman, is a constant factor in the plans of merchants, the calculations of economists, the thought of legislators. Already, too, it has proved a most powerful, and must, I think, prove an irresistible, solvent of the old symbolical faith. Were it in this respect only a decomposing force, there would indeed be ground for grave apprehensions. But if this resistless agent can be made to serve, and with its entire efficacy, all which it might seem to menace, then our gratuitous fears have named that danger which is indeed security and resource. And this, in my judgment, is the true view of the case. This thought makes the possibility of that new time, which was never possible before. Just this enables us to state universal principles, and in doing so to keep perfectly *en rapport* with the popular consciousness. True, the conception of regulative law is not identical with that of architectural or organific principles, like religion, but it is analogous, and affords the Radical Archimedes a fulcrum for that lever, which is, perhaps, at last indeed to move the world.

Strong be the heart, abiding the purpose, brave, modest, and temperate the spirit of those who are to toil at the task of centuries! Free from petulance, from captiousness, from a polemic disposition, from schismatic irritability; without haste and without halt, without controversy and without compromise; sincere as gravitation and sunshine, simple as truth, tolerant as charity, and ever the more tolerant the more resolute and pious in their lofty industry; let them work from the whole past and for the whole future, but in a spirit which, transcending all limits of time, makes this fleeting present, in the heart of it, eternal.

EPIC PHILOSOPHY

Homer begins the Iliad with "Sing, GODDESS," as if not himself, but a divine being, were the true poet. Shall we suppose that his invocation is merely formal? that it is consciously addressed to Nothing? To do so were to appreciate ill the simplicity and sincerity of Homer. Were it not also to misinterpret the law of all language? Words are never empty formalities at the outset; it was only a veritable meaning that made them. Men do not go about consciously giving names to nonentities. As well suppose a living body to have come into being without the action of any organizing force as persuade one's self that language is originated without belief. Words, like men, may grow old and die; but only by sincere, vital action are they born. It is true that defunct vocables sometimes have their Hades here above ground, wandering about as shadowy semblances of their former selves, neither well dead nor yet alive. But Homer belongs to the young world; and his words are not merely living, they are in excellent health, with red blood in them, and a bloom on the cheek. When, therefore, he says, "Sing, O Goddess," one may be sure that the invocation is no piece of perfunctory compliment, but that his heart keeps pace with his tongue.

Upon whom does he call? The question may be asked with interest, for there is in this part of the old Greek mythology a profound significance, a fine soul of meaning, which remains true for us, and will be true forever, however its forms may prove transitory or grow strange. The "Goddess" is the Muse,—

North American Review, October, 1868.

the Muses considered as one divinity. The Muses, again, were said to be daughters of Zeus and Mnemosyne, or Memory. It will be no waste of study to inquire into the significance of this parentage, and with Homer's devout appeal in mind.

Zeus, in the old Hellenic conception, is the eternal One, the unitive, sovereign genius of being. The physical meaning of the word, we are told, is *sky*, the pure heaven, changeless, all-embracing; but by a deeper and truer meaning it denotes the inner divine sky of the soul, rounding in, with its translucent, indivisible unity, the divided opacity and discord of time.* "From One all things proceed, and into the same are resolved," says Musæus, as quoted by Diogenes Laërtius. Zeus is this One, but rather in the moral sense, that of rule, than in the more metaphysical sense, which Musæus seems to have in mind. It is the testimony of language that man uttered his impression of this comprehending One when he first said *sky;* and since such an object must have been among the earliest named, we can trace that supreme recognition to the very dawn of his conscious being. All-comprehending, all-reconciling spiritual unity,—it is an import which the soul enshrines from the first and forever. And this is the Homeric Zeus, progenitor of the Muse.

On the other hand, Mnemosyne, Memory, symbolizes the sum

* All strictly primitive words seem to have at first a like twofold significance, physical-spiritual. It is the trick of lexicographers to represent the physical meaning as primary, the higher sense as only secondary and superinduced. Let us test this procedure in a single instance. The original sense of *rectus* is said to be *straight;* the secondary sense, *right*. We turn, however, to the root, *reg*, and find that the nearest word to this, formed immediately from it, is *rex* (regs) , a king, or straightener in the strictly moral sense. Could evidence be clearer that the moral meaning was in the word from the first, at the root of it, and that, in making it a mere afterthought, the lexicographer has followed, not the indications of language, but his own whim of opinion? I cannot but anticipate a sure determination of the fact, one day, that man is a speaker only as he is a spiritual being; pure spiritual sensibility joined with a lower kind of impressibility to produce root-words. At first the words are held as common property by the two producing factors, nor is their twofold character for a long time, it may be, explicitly recognized. *Zeus* meant originally, I suppose, both a physical object, and a spiritual reality signified by that object; but to the first namers this meaning was strictly single, not double. When reflective discrimination began, and the word, instead of being divided in itself, and made to bear two widely distinct meanings, like our word *heaven*, went wholly over to the higher, the indication is that this import was the more powerful in it from the start.

total of such things as memory is concerned with,—incident, accident, event, whatever *happens*. In wide contrast, therefore, to the peace of eternity, she images the storied variety and conflict of time, the world of things eventful,—of multiplicity, diversity, contrariety, contention, the surface-world of Nature and man, with heterogeneity and mutation for its inseparable characteristics.

Thus in Zeus and Mnemosyne we have, on the one side, the universe in the everlasting peace and rest of pure unity,—on the other side, the universe in the character of dividedness, changefulness, with a myriad of diverse features and conflicting energies, here playing through a colored phantasmagory of magic mutation, there yawning in chasms of hate, set against itself, crashing in upon itself, blind with contending passion, black with tragic fate. From these opposites the Muse is born,—from these as at once opposite, and yet joined, made one in spousal love.

The Muse, then, is that symphony of existence which arises from the conjunction of these two terms, Spiritual Being in its essential pure oneness, and the world of finite character and action, of diversity and evanescence, the world of time. This conjunction is Music,—"music of the spheres," in the Pythagorean phrase: an imagination peculiar to Pythagoras only in form of statement. It is upon this melodious Voice of the All that Homer calls devoutly, and of which he would be but the reporter or secretary.

Here we lay hold upon the prime fact by which he stands as the type of poetic genius. To him it is existence itself that is tuneful. Through the diversity of characters, the conflict of passions, and the whirl of events, the divine secret of the world *sings* to his soul.* The impassioned, it may be infuriate, tossing, warring, woe of time gives, as he deems, but the notes, out of which the Spirit of the All makes up its eternal harmony.

* Virgil, on the contrary, regards himself only as the singer. It is true, that, after announcing himself as such, he makes a formal invocation to the Muse, but misses even formal propriety in doing so. For he does not pray the Divinity to pour for his ear the melody of existence, nor even to exalt his soul and make it melodious, but only to apologize, if possible, for the strange conduct of the Olympians: *Mihi causas memora:* Let the Muse, since she visits in that family, tell what set on Juno to pursue with revenges that remarkably nice man, my hero.

That antique imagination may be embraced with serious modern conviction. Zeus and Mnemosyne symbolize still the two opposites, of which poesy is the wedding festival. Whoever truly sings, be it "the sweet psalmist of Israel" or Greek Æschylus, the author of the Book of Job or that of the Excursion, sings their espousal. The universe is unity; being rests in spiritual peace and poise forever. The sky is never clouded; only the earth is clouded. Nevertheless, there is the constant antithesis to this wholeness and repose,—antithesis expressed in ten thousand shapes, and pushed with such inexorable energy and excess that we wonder how the bands of eternity do not burst, and suffer the world to welter in immitigable craze. Oppositions and emulations arise, multiply, rage, gain appetite by what they feed on; countless tribes of creatures live only by slaughter, created to kill; existence sprouts all over in horns, fangs, tusks, claws, while from its horrid alembic venoms, hates, envies distil, and drip, drip upon its own blistering heart; hungry pestilences devour nations,—then, like the boa, retire and sleep into new hunger, that they may return to new feast; "the earthquake smacks its mumbling lips o'er some thick-peopled city," or the volcano binds about it, while yet living, a shroud of fire; strife is around man, and strife is within him; the lightning thrusts its blazing scymitar through his roof, the thief creeps in at his door, and remorse at his heart. Who, looking on these things, does not acknowledge that man is indeed fearfully as well as wonderfully made? Who would not sometimes cry, O that my eyes were a fountain of tears, that I might weep, not the desolations of Israel alone, but the hate of Israel to Edom and of Edom to Israel, the jar, the horror, the ensanguined passion and ferocity of Nature? But when we would despair, behold we cannot. Out of the conscious heart of humanity issues forever, more or less clearly, a voice of infinite, pure content: "Though I walk through the valley of the shadow of death, I will fear no evil; for Thou art with me." Sometimes, when our trial is sorest, that voice is clearest, singing as from the jaws of death and the gates of hell. And now, though the tears fall, they become jewels as they fall; and the sorrow that begot them wears them in the diadem of its more than regal felicity. We, too, rest in the rest of

Being; the changeless axis is here, it is in our souls; and around it all the movement of existence becomes orbital.

Eternal rest, endless unrest,—rest and unrest, it would seem, of the same universal whole. There is comprehending unity, that nothing invades, nothing eludes; there is yawning chasm that seems to go through the world, cleaving its very heart. Every globule of existence spins between these irreconcilable opposites. And yet they are not irreconcilable, for they *are* reconciled, though it be ineffably.

Now it is this tossing rest, this multiple unity, this contradictory and contending identity, that makes the universe epical; and to represent this within practicable limits, embodying in human speech the enticement, the awful, infinite charm of that mystery forever resolved and forever remaining, is the grand task of the epic artist.

The poet is the restorer of wholeness. He can strike the universal chord, that of identity, or spiritual unity. But he does this, observe, not by confounding distinction, blurring characteristic, hiding difference, explaining away contradiction, but, on the contrary, by displaying them. No one adheres with a fidelity religious like his to special character, finite fact. Individual feature and complexion, the peculiar expression of all objects, the circumstance and finest edge of all events, are, as it were, sacred to him, and come forth from beneath his pen with an exquisite, loving exactness of rendering. He will give you form, color, manner, gait, garb, tone of voice, measure of stature, tune of thought; minute he will be as Nature herself, nothing small to him which is characteristic; his very human condition he will, as it were, forsake, to spring with grass-blades and hum with bees, to ripple with the ripening wheat and pass in the shadow of flying clouds, to dance with sunshine on the sea, or join its sprite-like hide-and-seek among quivering leaves; sorrow, too, and dismay he will depict as with a kind of love,—tempests that rage across the green fields of humanity, clothed in night and whirling along boughs rent from the tree of life,—frosts that descend untimely upon vernal years, to leave their blossoms shrivelled and all the glory of their garniture gone forever; and by this chase of diversities and celebration of contradictions he will bring out the refrain of the living whole, the repose, the unity, the infinite content of being.

Contrast this procedure with that of the mere generalizer. The latter spares himself all this delicate and subtle exactitude, very likely thinks it trivial. Betaking himself to generalities, he evaporates one generality into another more diffuse and vague, and, by an incessant elimination of feature, arrives finally at a statement the most general possible. At best he has attained only congruity, not consanguinity. His thought holds together, suppose, in itself; it does not bring souls, natures, together; it does not awaken the sense of a universal kindred, wherein the one immortal heart is felt to beat.

Even the naturalist, patient, tireless observer, faithful by his good-will to Nature in her speciality and her unity alike, can draw creatures into association only by mere points of outward resemblance, as two kinds here by a likeness in the hoof, two kinds there by a similarity in the hide, again two kinds by approximation in the shape of a scale. There is a catalogue of superficial resemblances, not community. The poet does not thus go on merely to enumerate points of external peculiarity and resemblance; he, on the one side, delineates the individual thing in the very feature, color, and aroma of its special being, yet, on the other hand, keeps up the interior conversation of each with all. Not by dead similarities, but by the living, flowing fellowship of heart-language, do the unlikes of voiceful Nature blend and symphonize in his thought.

Mr. Ruskin censures a dictum of Sir Joshua Reynolds, to the effect that poetry deals only with what is general and permanent, to the exclusion of transient particulars. The eloquent critic brings forward good instances, with which Wordsworth offered him an abundant supply, to show, on the contrary, that the poet has an inevitable eye for minute traits and evanescent expression. The truth is parted between them. The poet sees the varying surfaces of Nature, and feels in them her constant heart. By a delicately true portrayal of what is most limited and transient, he appeals to a sentiment universal and perennial. Playing with the play of Nature, flitting with winged fancy through all the variety of her manifold forms and changing hues, he yet feels in all, and by the magic of melodious suggestion can make others to feel, that inner identity, that unceasing, ineffable return into oneness, which in the hidden sanctuary of existence is a joy of espousal forever. It is the ringing of these marriage-bells of Nature that is the music behind the words of his verse.

To be cordially sensible of an illimitable kindred, which, moreover, is not only boundless in scope, but divine in kind, purer far and richer in every beautiful claim and blessed response than any blood relationship,—is it not a surpassing delight? But the felicity comes to the last, finest edge, when one may enter into this immortal fellowship without loss of individual character, and, speaking there only his own vernacular, may join by means of it, and with no foreign nor provincial accent, in that language of the heart of humanity wherein was never yet a confusion of tongues.

Man is a stranger in the world, looking on with remote, unrelated eye, till the Muse make him at home there. This, touching upon all that seems most shut up to itself, most set apart from the spirit and sympathy of man, awakens a surprising refrain of fellowship in his breast. Now he lives a life not bounded by the limits of his individual constitution. It is as if an invisible system of nerves ramified from his breast, with a pole in every passing shadow, in every star, in whatsoever has form of being or seeming to the sense. Once that this is rightly addressed, his own being is reflected in all, claimed by all; his voice has an illimitable echo; his heart blends its beating with the vast rhythm of Nature; everywhere are relation and response; from sun and moon look down glorified human faces; wood and river teem with half-humanities, that sway in the trees and slip in the tide; from the lifted mountain-tops, and from the waste grandeur of the reticent, never-covenanting sea, comes a language at once theirs and his own; the bladed grass claims kindred from beneath his feet, and the shadow cast by a stone on the moor moves him with some deep home-feeling, as if it were inscrutably inwrought with shadowy memories of the cradle and the mother's lullaby.

The poet can touch these nerves, and give sympathy the happiness of that unmeasured scope. But he can thus touch them, observe, only at their poles on the surfaces of Nature. Of this a sufficient suggestion is given by the economy of the human body. The brain itself is insensitive; its feeling, at least its pleasurable feeling, is found at the fingers' ends, at the surfaces and extremes of the body. So it is that this universal heart in man is to be happily awakened only at the fingers' ends, the farthest reach, of its manifold relationship. Hence it is that the purest poetry is most objective. This touches the heart healthily, where the nerves of imaginative sympathy come to the surface. Introspection, on the contrary, invades the system, and strikes the nerves midway, hence is unhealthful and painful.

It is only in the sense of unity with the whole that the heart finds peace. Chasm is brutal. Yet he who seeks unity otherwise than in the diversity of Nature and movement of life, he who seeks it by prying and intrusion, finds, not a charmed repose, but only sickness. Nature sings to him who respects her secret, and who only by a reverent remoteness comes near; and he who sings to others will scrupulously keep up the polarity of life, displaying identity only through the medium of peculiarity.

Take as an illustration Burns's "To a Mouse." The "wee beastie" is represented to the life, its habit and condition given without varnish.

> "That wee bit heap o' leaves an' stibble
> Has cost thee mony a weary nibble!"

Leaves and stubble, got by nibbling: this is a veritable mouse, no transparent sham, like Dryden's "Hind and Panther," which are seen at a glance to be no more than a pair of cut and dried theologues masquerading on four legs, whereof two are evidently broomsticks. But while a mouse, it is yet man; and the poet only brings his delineation to ripeness, when he says,—

> "Me, thy poor earthborn companion
> And fellow mortal."

The outward circumstance retains its distinction, the hearts touch and beat together, and we have a truly poetical situation.

Emerson's "Humble-Bee" furnishes an illustration that will bear even closer inspection; for the external peculiarity is shown yet more pointedly, while the interior sympathy is not less, though suggested with a delicate reticence that adds to the charm. The painting is so minutely and exquisitely exact that I have sometimes said, should Nature one day lose the breed of bees, and forget what they were, she might recover the type from this model. Yet who reads without feeling that the humble-bee is one of us?

"Yellow-breeched philosopher,"—

it does not come jarring in, but belongs there; and because this open stroke of sympathy—in which, however, the humor still hints at distinction—is consistent with a piece of painting so objective, we have here a poem in the right sense of the word.

A like effect is reached, when a peculiar human character is so pictured that we at once perceive its remoteness from ourselves and feel it all in ourselves. The more entire, isolated, unapproachable, the more poetic its impression, if only it be so depicted that to every stroke of the delineation our hearts vibrate response. The more peculiar it shows itself, the more does it awaken in us the sense of our community. This is poetry.

It may be said, then, that poetry is the expression of comprehending spiritual unity by means of that which opposes and apparently denies it. This definition, however, is here only provisional. I hope soon to substitute for it another, which, while embracing this, shall be more adequate. At present let us obtain with precision what is in this.

First, let it be observed that the character of things which is opposed to their unity with the soul must not be in its own place denied. Even to disguise it there is to make its subsequent identification with the heart ridiculous. Dress the mouse in jacket and trousers, as we sometimes see monkeys in the street, then say, "Fellow mortal," and the by-standers burst out laughing. Set the bee to discoursing on fate and free-will, and "yellow-breeched philosopher" loses its tone of fine sympathetic humor, to become a sorry jest.

Observe, secondly, that the separation of objects from the heart of the poet and of man is maintained by one order of apprehension, while the identity exists only to another. The one is bluntly, stubbornly, indomitably maintained by the prosaic understanding; the other is melodiously affirmed by the imagining heart, eternal priest at the marriage altars of Nature. Moreover, it is the interest of imagination that the prosaic faculty should hold its ground, yielding never an inch. There can be no espousal, if there is no duality,—no making one unless there are two. The sense of spiritual community *plays over* somewhat which contradicts it; and it is this playing over which constitutes the poetic act. The imagination abhors confusion, though it craves community. It leaves finite objects, merely as such, to stand by and for themselves, refusing all cordial kindred with the spirit of man; and then, in nevertheless making fellowship between them and the human soul, it shows these objects to be capable of such fellowship only in quite another character than that which is proper to them as *things* merely. I will illustrate these points by a stanza of description taken from Wordsworth:—

> "The sylvan slopes with corn-clad fields
> Are hung, as if with golden shields,
>   Bright trophies of the sun!
> Like a fair sister of the sky,
> Unruffled doth the blue lake lie,
>   The mountains looking on."

Well, this is fine!—the understanding would say. Are we to *believe* that the fields have put on the corn as a suit of clothes? or that the said patches of corn, while having that sartorial character, are also captured shields, which the sun has hung up to commemorate his victories? or that the sky and lake are a kind of Jane and Nancy in the same family? or that the mountains really do look on? No; so far as the understanding is concerned, these statements are made only to be disbelieved. To it they are sheer untruth, and are meant for untruth. The understanding is pre-engaged to dispute, to deny, to repugn them altogether. Just that is a part of the programme; and to leave it out would spoil the performance. Did not the statement infold its own contradiction on a lower scale, and thereby obtain the opposition of the prosaic understanding, like the opposition of the viol-string to the bow, it were not poetic truth. To say that Peter is clad, that Jane and Nancy are sisters, or look as if they were sisters, and that Hezekiah looks on, might be to affirm what is entirely credible; but such truth is not poetic truth, for the reason that it does not address itself to spiritual credence. In order that imagination and spiritual apprehension may be reached, there must be that "play over" we have spoken of,—therefore somewhat over which, and in contrariety to which, the play goes on. Thus the great privilege of the spirit to find the whole world kin is freed from confusion with any such community as the prosaic mind can recognize.

I have thus far spoken only of poetry; let it now be said that I have constantly had in view the being of man, regarding this as the poem of poems,—fast locked to any metaphysic which does not approach with a key corresponding to its poetic quality. In the being of man, in the universe of God, there is that "play over." It is, indeed, the grand secret; he that finds it out reads the Sphinx's riddle, and may save his soul alive. Finding it out perfectly, he will know what Spirit is; and until one knows that, does he in the highest sense know anything?

In order to clear up this matter, and prepare the way for further exposition, I wish now to establish a primary scale of degrees, that we may see definitely what is over, what under, and the validity of each in its own kind. And to invite a vigorous attention, I may say that we have now come to the hinge upon which all turns.

Nature as *thing* is Force and Form, no more. Scrutinized to any extent, it will exhibit only these characters, fixed force and form.

To the world of things corresponds in man the perceptive understanding. This finds in things a thing,—character, if one may speak so,—finds, that is, their special determinations, and the consequent isolation of each thing in itself. It is, we might say, a brace between things, to keep them forever apart, without interior communication. It sees every object—ox, grass, hill, river, stone, man—as only itself, utterly locked up in its special identity.

Becoming scientific, however, the understanding not only discriminates, and specially identifies, but finds connections, and *looks* toward unity. But the unity is on the same level with the diversity, and is therefore only partial. There is unity of form between man and a fish, as both are vertebrate animals; there is diversity of form, as the one is a mammal and the other not such. The community of the two, and the special, isolate identity of each, are alike of form, and are therefore mutually limiting. Unity, accordingly, is never attained. The scientific intellect is more full than the ordinary perceptive understanding; but it works within the same limits, has the same kind of recognitions. It recognizes form, force, the constancy of force, and, lastly, as its highest perception, the *form of force*. What we call "natural law" is, of course, simply force formulated, that is, constant in measure and definite in character. Gravitation, electricity, chemical affinity, do not differ as *force,* but only as *forms* of force. Force and form, then, constitute the whole character of Nature in one aspect; and to it in this aspect the prosaic understanding corresponds.

Accordingly, the understanding can never, in any adequate manner, say *God*. It attempts often enough, with stretched mouth, to achieve that grand enunciation, and often supposes the feat accomplished. But its God can be only some particular object or force, supposably an immensely great thing, but after all only a *thing,* one thing among others. Of late some of its officers are making bold to say that no such Thing is discoverable. "God?" some Lewes will say; "what force or form of force is it? Is gravitation God? Is chemical affinity God? If neither of these, what force, then, and where is it?"

Suppose I answer, that God is *in* those forces, and in all others?

"In them?" he may reply; "how in them? how in gravitation? *As* gravitation? Then he is gravitation; and we have two words for the same thing. As somewhat other than gravitation? But what? Do we discern in gravitation anything but itself?"

"But there is somewhat which makes it," I plead.

"Makes what?" he will say. "Makes stones fall? Gravitation does that. Is there a making behind this making? Well, double, triple, centuple, if you will, the *makings,* all we come to is that stones are made to fall. There is a force which has this character; and wherever it is, the character of it is the same. Though the note of hand be indorsed by a hundred individuals one after another, the value of it remains the same."

"But," I say, making a last effort, "God is the unity of all forces."

He smiles provokingly. "You mean, perhaps, that he is that correlation and mutual convertibility of forces of which we are beginning to learn. Truly, I give you joy of a God so substantial!"

I leave the *savant* in possession of the field, easily victorious. It should be frankly confessed, that, as by no peeping and prying and inferring among the fiddle-strings can we discover the genius of the composer, so by no inspection of the formulations of force do we obtain the smallest glimpse of infinite Spirit.

Here we are, then, locked utterly into the limits of finite Nature. Can we, after all, make escape? I do not inquire whether we find in our own breasts a hint of spiritual comprehension and freedom,—we undoubtedly do find such; but it is said that this subjective impression, being contradicted by everything else in the universe, must be suppressed as mere private prejudice or illusion. Some indeed bravely refuse, and pledge their faith to the testimony of "consciousness"; the other party smile superior to "consciousness" none the less; the contestants find no common ground. We will therefore face the difficulty, and inquire whether it is possible to discover a road leading from Nature to Spirit, and *to Spirit as in itself* ALL. I think it can be found, and without any tedious groping.

Be it observed, then, that Nature has another character, very different from the one just noted,—the character, namely, of

Sign or Expressiveness. To the primitive civilizers of humanity it is scarcely known otherwise than in this nobler character. Everywhere the first grand sallies of the human mind overleap the fixed constitution of things, and alight upon somewhat of a higher order, which the world of things *suggests*. Is it not to this overleaping that all human speech is due? Man looks upon an object, and between it and the eye there springs up a felt poetic significance, which, before reflection has come to complicate mental action, is no sooner felt than it issues by a responsive sign, a word. Spontaneous naming is the act of identifying an object with its poetic significance, declaring that the thing *is* what it signifies. Only while the expression or suggestion of objects is taken in entire good faith as their reality is man a producer of root-words.

In the case of words which convey distinctively a moral, metaphysical, or spiritual import, this repose upon the sign-character of Nature is obvious. *Spirit* is *breath; right* is *straight; wrong* is *crooked,*—wrung, turned forcibly aside; *light* is *truth* or knowledge,—"the light which enlighteneth every man that cometh into the world" (the Parsees are said to worship fire or light, that is, they worship what it signifies, as Christians also do) ; *heaven,* too, is God,—"kingdom of God" and "kingdom of heaven" we say indifferently; *warmth* is *love; coldness* is *indifference;* and so on: it were easy to multiply familiar examples,—and I seek no others,—to the weariness of the reader.

But I believe, still further, that man's ability to name physical objects in the directest manner depends no less, though less obviously, upon their sign-character. Were they to man, as to the dog and ox, mere force and form, he would respond to them, in the animal fashion, by the forces of his organism only, by appetite, aversion, anger, fear, and the like. The aspect of green grass excites only the stomach of a cow: here is the mere relation of finite to finite; and accordingly the creature opens its mouth, not to speak, but to bite,—not to utter the object, but to swallow it. Man, on the contrary, sees natural objects as picture, suggestion, significance, and speaks them because to him they are speaking. How could he represent them by signs, did they not present themselves as significant, and as veritably present in their significance?

"Day unto day uttereth speech, and night unto night showeth forth knowledge." Verily, statements so noble as this, coming to us from a far-off antiquity, might tempt one to think that the primitive poetic mind of humanity took off the cream of truth, and left its skimmed milk to science. But can we not perceive that day and night are indeed and forever voiceful? Speech runs and ripples over all the surfaces of Nature: here in grand affirmative tides, Amazons and Missouris of significance; there in vast, perpetual eddies of reverse meaning; again in whirling and dancing equivocations, evanescent half-expressions, with which only the flitting instability of fancy can keep pace. Speech breaks out as from an inner heart in things, and wraps itself as a many-colored mantle about them, hiding what they are in what they suggest; insomuch that the understanding must search as with a candle to discover beneath that glorious disguise their fixed and specific character. Science, coming late and with labor, tries to lift the mantle, tries to divest Nature of her garment of meaning; but one fold falls down as another is raised; only by endless pertinacity of industry and wide combination of effort is the *thing* at last denuded, and seen as it is in itself.

Half the world is now busy in this labor. "Off with it!" men say; "off with that garment of suggestion wherewith Nature clothed herself to the untaught intelligence of humanity!" As the work goes on, there are huzzas mingled with moanings, complainings, reproaches,—huzzas over notable progress achieved, complaint that so great a labor needs now to be done. The first men did us a mischief, it would seem, by permitting Nature to assume that array of significance. Had things been seen from the start as things really are, then what toil and difficulty had our age been spared! But those men, perverse, must go and be "theological," or "metaphysical," or the like: *hinc illæ lachrymæ*. The greater, however, the glory of our age, when, despite these needless hindrances, it peeps and pries, until at length the world of things appears without disguise. We complain, but still more do we exult. The great enterprise prospers; off it comes, that pictured array; the Thing lies bare!

Not quite, however. Seen *only* as it is in itself, the world of things is not yet, nor, in my judgment, is likely to be. Never yet was there a mind dry and prosaic enough to behold any object in the mere light of the understanding,—to see in a horse, for example, only anatomy and physiology. To Dryasdust also, even to that portentous specimen of the genus, the Dryasdust of science,—Herbert Spencer, say,—the neck of the war-horse is indeed clothed with thunder, the Pleiades have sweet influences, the zephyr whispers, the storm roars, morning blushes, the sun rises rejoicing, night is vocal with solemn suggestion, and the blue heaven more, much more, than some gases and an optical illusion. Let Mr. Spencer do his best to see in Nature, as he says, only "force," it will be to him also a language, will *speak* to his sensibility. Let Briareus use all his hundred hands, the mantle of meaning will fall down, and with its lettered folds wrap the heart of the Titan himself.

For by the Word the worlds were indeed made, as the Scriptures say. "And God said, Let there be light, and there was light." Was; for light itself is but a shining syllable, and darkness another, that shines only in the breast of the speaker, not outwardly; and all the universe exists, word-like, only for and through its expressiveness. By the Word, by the perpetual act of Spirit giving expression to its inherent import,—which is its substance, itself, for Spirit is Absolute Import, self-affirmed,—the worlds were made, and do exist. Because Nature is spoken, it speaks; because it speaks, the spirit of man, kindred with the eternal Word, may espouse in Nature its own import, and evoke the representative world of uttered thought and feeling.

The imaginative intelligence recognizes in visible existence this character of Sign, and reads off from it a significance for the soul. *Force* and *form,* says the understanding; *import,* says the poetic intelligence. This *is* thus and so, reports the one; this *means* thus, announces the other. The former regards the finite world as substantial, and as asserting only itself; the latter regards the finite world as denying its own substantiality in behalf of that which it signifies.*

"As denying its own substantiality," I say. How is that? I hope the reader will say, How is that? and will say it with a purpose to be pointedly dissatisfied, unless the question be answered clearly and precisely.

A sign, observe, is necessarily the sign *of that which itself is not.* It exists only to say, "I am not IT," and in doing so to point effectually toward that which *is.* As the finger on the sign-board is not the road or city, as the spoken word *man* is not man, but only sound, so is it with all signs whatsoever: they point wholly away from themselves, being in themselves nothing to the purpose; they are there only for the eye to pass over; and, considered with reference to their real purpose, their entire being is a mere flitting away and vanishing into that which they suggest. Plainly, that which is meant by a word is the real thing. Plainly, a word, by the fact of having a meaning, implicitly denies that itself is at all the real thing. The meaning made the word, holds it in possession, and is all the being of it. The significance is the substantial fact; the sign, by the very fact of being such, professes itself the contrary. If now we venture to apply to the universe this easy and plain discrimination, all the difficulty will be in the venture, none in the application. Two and two are still neither more nor less than four, be the figures written in hundredths of an inch, or from Labrador to Cape Horn. Making bold to write our figures large, we may say with some confidence that the natural universe, as Sign, only spoken into being, and having its being only in its meaning, *denies its own*

* Swedenborg sought to establish a science of significances, a science of Nature on that higher degree. Hence the gulf which separates him from the ordinary man of science. The latter is engaged in supplying what, with reference to the import of Nature, we must call its *grammar;* he looks to the classification and syntactical relation of its etymons or elements. Now Shakespeare and Nature alike, merely as parsed, are void of meaning: we arrive at an order of arrangement, and at nothing more. Swedenborg sought not merely to parse, but to read; he assumed a meaning, and attempted a scientific exposition of it. I am not of those who think his success perfect, or other than very imperfect; sometimes it is only the dignity of the enterprise which forbids one to laugh. On the other hand, one must own that a grammar of the cosmos, were it complete, would not be sufficient. To do Lindley Murray on that scale is to work at a large task indeed; but though one parse the universe, is it enough merely to parse?

substantive existence; the meaning of it, not itself, is the real Fact; it is but a pointing, as of an index-finger, to that which indeed *is.*

What does it say *is?*

When one reads a word, considering it *as* a word, what does he implicitly affirm? Or what does the word itself, by the fact of being such, imply? It implies, and he who reads it implicitly affirms, Mind. Only from Mind could words issue; only to it are they expressive,—that is, indeed words. When the natural universe appears as expressive, a manifold sign, a language, it affirms Absolute Mind, Spirit. Only from this could a universal significance issue, only by it be embraced. If Nature mean anything, Spirit is what it means. And so the human race has thought; its apprehension of this truth is embodied in the confessions and litanies of all ages.

Now to read the world as a language, finding in it an import for the soul, is the essentially poetic act. We have thus arrived at the final definition promised: Poetry is the free reading up and down from Nature to Spirit and from Spirit to Nature, each seen in the other. The outward feature of Nature and life must be preserved, with the finest, most delicate exactitude, that we may not read in a blurred type; and yet in all the soul must find its own immanent secret.

The understanding, meanwhile, holds out sturdily against all this. Its business is to paint the index on the guide-board, that this may be there for that traveller, the spiritual imagination, to go by. Its utmost stretch is to observe that the traveller does go by,—that, looking on the sky, for example, the untaught man has cried, "Dyaus," "Zeus," "God," making a sign of it, and flying infinitely beyond. But it can never verify this enunciation, nor indeed can believe in it; and, trying to give some account of that passage, it will strain a point and say, "Rhetoric." This, too, is liberal of it, extremely liberal; it has grown to be a highly polite and tolerant understanding, when it gives the name of rhetoric to that passing by; before arriving at these handsome manners, it had bluntly said, "Nonsense."

Has it now been made clear what poetry is? And has it also

been rendered apparent, or at least credibly indicated, that the conscious being of man is itself, in the sense explained, a poem? If so, we may proceed to consider the epic in particular, antici- pating that epical truth will be found not only in books, but in the fact of the universe.

We already know that the epic will represent comprehending spiritual unity, and beneath this its apparent contradiction. We know also that the latter will be made to suggest just that which it seemingly contradicts, and so to negate its own negation. This is the character of all poetry; but what distinguishes the epic?

Its primary distinction is, that here the scale of the drawing is strictly and explicitly universal. Existence in its full breadth is the ground; the import of life in its full depth is the theme. Here are to be the ultimate poles: the pure Infinite, in contrast and correlation with finite Nature,—the sovereign, perfect con- sciousness of man, in like contrast and correlation with the most poignant contradiction supplied by his natural experience.

First, the unity is here that of Being itself, absolute Spirit. It is not merely a relative and subjective unity, that of mouse and mountain daisy, beggar and king, with *me,* but the pure One, which in oneness comprehends all. The oneness is, indeed, *the* oneness,—the One to which, in the highest sense, there is no Other,—absolute solvent, that liquefies all, englobing worlds like drops of dew, cosmic dew of suns and stars, mist of milky ways; and which, having pictured itself in Nature, whispers in the enchanted heart of man, I AM.* First, then, the eternal Zeus, rest of all hearts, community of all natures. No epical thought or genius has man without a consciousness of this perfect, universal Identity, this all-embracing sky of the soul.

Let this point be emphasized. What sort of epic were that wherein this ultimate import of the spiritual consciousness should not nobly and expressively appear? The sort of epic which is made such only by the title. The world has seen such, but could not keep them long in view. The Genius of the Whole

---

* It is peculiar also to the epic that this Unity is made explicit, represented ob- jectively, while in the drama proper it remains implicit, felt, not seen, a light to enlighten, but no sun visible. Compare Homer and Shakespeare. The *Prometheus* hovers between the two.

is somewhat necessary to the parts, be it in a tree or in a universe, and so in a poem which attempts to sing the perennial character and relations of man's life.

It is not a little curious to see how the grasshopper intelligence of Voltaire skips about this prime requisite of the epic in his *Essai sur La Poésie Epique*. That he should attempt such a topic is laughable. Few men have been more skilful to break a jest; but here he was broken upon one. I once knew a youth who fancied himself a musical genius, because, having not the slightest ear for music, he was never to his own apprehension out of tune. At sight of a note he could promptly produce a noise; and though, to compare small things with great, it was like Milton's gates of hell grating harsh thunder, yet the innocent creature, not being deaf, as the hearers wished they were, never doubted that he was melodious, since beyond doubt he was vocal. I was reminded of him by reading the "philosopher" of Ferney upon the Epic; for never, perhaps, was a very clever man more incapable of following on the track of an epic imagination, or less aware of his own inability. He perceives that in Homer the gods appear; whereupon he briskly announces, that, in order to an epic, the "marvellous" must be introduced. Now the marvellous, merely as such, has no more a place in epic poetry than in science; nor, indeed, does it find place in any form of noble literature. The blank gape it produces is in the mind just that vacant O, that annular eclipse of intelligence, which the moon-mouth would indicate by the shape it assumes.

The Olympus of Homer is his holding-ground in the heavens. Therein he casts anchor, and so rides out the storms of time in security and peace of heart. He would have "marvelled" to find himself without it, and adrift on the sea of events. He sings first of all that which sings itself in him, the great faith of his soul.

Homer has, indeed, a keen sympathy with that which, perhaps ironically, is called "real life"; and therefore is able to paint it with an almost matchless precision and verisimilitude. He is heroically faithful to Mnemosyne. Here is her whole story, told without euphemism. Here is, now the struggle, and now the stupor of passion, now the rolling resistless tide, and now the

sudden eddy and refluence, of courage,—rivalries, too, mixed
irresolvably of noble and ignoble, honor and infamy, spun into
the same thread; here are the ebb and flow, the toss and whirl,
the interlacement, the twisted tangle, the blind and blurting
conclusion, of actual life. Here also is the charm of feature and
picturesque detail; individual action stands out in boldest relief,
individual portraiture is lavished, while to all this is added the
effect of diverse costumes, tongues, manners: the details, handled
in a way less masterly, were bewildering in their multiplicity;
and the picture, but for its breadth, would be motley in the
crowding of colors and contrasts. But the artist is at his ease with
much as with little,—always the master. And yet, were this all,
the Iliad would not be a poem: it were only a wondrous piece of
photography.

It is that Olympian repose with which Homer is able to over-
arch this field of action, it is that peace of the All which he
makes to breathe about the storm and change of man's little
world, that shows him a poet rather than a photographer, Homer
rather than De Foe. As his terrestrial observation is wide, genial,
and exact, so the faith of his soul, its hold upon celestial Unity, is
sure. To both he is just, and to each in its place and kind. And
the objects of both, though opposite, blend in harmony; and the
greater, though not only greater, but *all*, does extinguish the
less; and the less, though it remains in vigor of feature and ruddi-
ness of strength, *passes* while it remains, and only the One-and-All
is. Thus his picture became a glass wherein the men of his time
saw their life with more than mortal vision. There the visible had
become ideal, yet retained its character; there the invisible had
become apparent, yet nowhere had broken the lines or blurred
the feature of actual experience. There the tempest of our little
life was seen rounded in with skies of everlasting calm: partici-
pants in the divine secret, the mortal beholders looked on and
saw with new-informed eyes the cerulean circumambient eternity, as now it condensed its viewless burden into our whirling
cloudlet of time, and anon drank it off into its own transparent
peace.

I confess we can no longer see the same perfectly in the same mirror. To us the Iliad is not, cannot be, a pure epic. Homer's faith is not precisely that of the modern world; we are able to follow him throughout only, as it were, by sympathy prepense. That "majestic, deathless head," whose nod once shook the world, and was the end of controversy to gods and men, is now subject to the dispute of any too ready tongue, sovereign no more. But the eternal Zeus lives under another name, or without name; Greece and Ilium we have, like the poor, always with us; the epos of existence remains; and Homer's speech needs but a translation into that diction which is behind the words, to become ours.

Have we sufficiently dwelt upon the first grand requisite of the epic? Is it clear that this celestial unity must appear in the written poem, because in the being of man that sovereign import plays forever over the discord and disunity of our outward experience? The matter has, indeed, been treated slightly, but I will suppose that enough has been offered on this head. Let us, then, turn the leaf.

That unity must have its opposite; the nature of poetry, as we are aware, requires this. The opposite, too, must in the present case be no trivial one; the play-over of Absolute Spirit should be worthy of it. The eagle does not display his strength of wing by merely flying across a ditch that a grasshopper might leap. Show us a chasm yawning all the way from east to west, wide as the world; and when the genius of the universe shall cast over that an arch whose keystone is the zenith of eternity, it will do somewhat. Of this consummate act the epic poet is to make us witness.

Every epic artist represents, as antithetic to the unitive genius of being, *the infernal,*—that is, sheer moral inversion, sheer head-down of moral order, the one thing with which the soul cannot be directly reconciled. Moreover, he wellnigh seems to give this abhorrent thing full possession of the field. "I read in Homer," said Goethe, "that properly we enact hell here below." Is this a true reading of Homer? And if so, does Homer read the world truly? I think that in both Goethe and Homer it is a true reading.

Goethe's statement is, indeed, one-sided; and he perhaps betrayed his own limit, while illustrating his penetration, in making it. He himself is a little lame of the right foot. His Mephistopheles is a lovely devil, *cap-à-pie* like a West Point cadet turned out for parade,—*magister artium* in his kind, compared with Milton's Titanic undergraduate. Here Goethe is perfect; but the sovereign term, the Zeus, he does not manage so well.

Yet his statement about Homer can hardly be impeached. What is the situation described in the Iliad? It is this: the crime of a coxcomb has bound two noble nations by the loftiest public sentiment of antiquity, the sentiment of national honor, to the work of mutual destruction. The occasion of their sanguinary struggle is a deed they alike despise, a deed of which the fit notice were a hearty kicking to the culprit. And yet just that in each which dignifies and adorns their humanity it engages to the pitiless destruction of the other.

Is it said, that honor, rightly understood, engaged them to nothing of the sort? It would not in us; in them it *did* so; nor could they disobey its mandate without moral collapse. Hector says, the Trojan women, not to speak of the men, would despise him, did he decline the combat, odious to him as it was. I think it apparent that the nation which had yielded would have seen all the bands of order dissolve in the caustic of contempt.

Highest enslaved by lowest, and compelled to rivet and renew its own bonds,—that is the spectacle. What is intrinsically good, beautiful, noble, made not only to serve evil ends, but even to accept and consecrate the service,—that is the hateful situation which Homer places before us.

Does it seem that the dilemma might have been easily escaped? There is the very bite of it. So easy to escape,—and impossible! In Shakespeare we find the same. How easy for Cordelia, by two words, to save her father and herself the misery that ensues! Easy,—and she *cannot* utter them. It is her true, honorable love that forbids; it is the voluble hypocrisy of Regan and Goneril that compels her love to make its own misconstruction. The ease, and yet the impossibility; the nobleness that immediately makes the impossibility; the ape's hand that behind all manipulates the dead-lock: there, there is the poison of it.

Know we of nothing similar in actual life? Have we never seen petty interests, petty strifes, spites, jealousies, envies, of no more importance than the spit-spat of belligerent tom-cats, roping in worthy natures with abhorrent bands, that multiply and tighten till the anguish is intolerable?

Thackeray's she-catamount of a "campaigner" can hunt Colonel Newcome to his death. What signifies her caterwaul, pray? He knows that it signifies nothing, and he dies of it; the contemptibleness of the torture makes it only the more torturing.

A politician rises in Congress, and proposes a compliment to the shillalah invasion of Canada. Honorable men, who despise the motion, feel compelled to sustain it; the election at New York is at hand, and such a resolution once offered, they dare not vote it down. In other circumstances, a war between England and America might easily have arisen from this move in the small game of an individual anxious to wipe out his "Know-Nothing" record; and when it had arisen, the purest patriotism in the land would have been driven, with loathing stomach, to sustain its country's quarrel. History, indeed, is replete with instances— and did we see it behind the curtains, more instances would be known to us—wherein the noblest sentiments of humanity have been harnessed beyond help in the dirt-carts of sordid interest, while pitiful tricksters, men who would sell what soul they have for a crossed sixpence, and cheat Mephistopheles in the bargain, hold the reins, and goad them on.

It is such a case from which the incident of Homer's story is drawn,—a case of moral head-down in the worst shape it could assume to the mind of Grecian antiquity. The great master does not hide, he is at pains to display, its hateful features. By the avowed and intense revolt of Hector's soul from the work his hands must do, the abhorrent constraint of the situation is made to the last degree biting. And that nothing might be wanting to the keenness of the contradiction, the Trojan prince is shown to us, not only in his valor, his magnanimity, his sense of justice, but also in the tender nobility of his domestic life. Andromache comes before us, queenly, devoted, in all the pathos of wifely love; while the babe, drawn to the father, shrinks away from the warrior, to suggest the last rebuke of that dreadful strife. Meanwhile, in contrast with this beautiful picture,——the noblest touch of tenderness that has come to us from the old Hellenic world,—— Paris has signalized anew his luxurious infamy, and made the occasion of the struggle, odious enough before, seem intolerable. And yet Hector must go to the field and to his doom, and Andromache remain behind, helplessly awaiting her doom, and doomed Ilium also abide her day.

All that follows upon the main situation is painted with the like pitiless fidelity,——pitiless only in fidelity; for deep, tender compassion is in the poet's soul. Hero after hero comes forth, uplifted with all soaring thoughts, godlike in bearing, glorious in form and in renown; then before our eyes he goes down; we see him clutch the earth in blind agony, we hear his armor clank over him,——his only knell. Nothing is explained away; and the pathos reaches its acme in the stern, stern words, "all-ending death." The poet cuts off his understanding from all succors,—— breaks down the bridges behind him. Only by a transcendent process does he escape into repose. The will of Zeus is accomplished: that is all. To Homer this *all* was enough. To the author of the Book of Job it was enough.* A deep sea in which to cast anchor! We in our day like shallower waters.

Why is it that Homer selects the sentiment of honor to be thus enslaved? Because he has the keenest sympathy with it. In his eyes it is noblest, best; its enslavement, therefore, shows most strikingly that moral inversion he wishes to display. Nor is he alone in this procedure; other epic poets have done the same. Dante is pre-eminently the poet of Love: read the story of Francesca, wherein the pathos of the Inferno culminates, and you find him distilling from the honey of love a cup that he swoons but to taste. Milton is the apostle of Liberty: in the

---

* It is true that at the end of the Book of Job a kind of offset is got up. But we may observe, that, in representing this pay-off appreciable by the understanding, the poet—if he wrote the conclusion—falls from poetry to prose. The *poem* was already complete.

Paradise Lost he has opened the heavens to show us the impulse to just this, Liberty, turned toward the pit, and drawing after it one third part of heaven's host. Goethe's noblest trait is his intellectual devotion, his worship of Truth: it is precisely this that in his half-epic betrays Faust. In the Ramayana, a supreme emphasis is laid upon truth in the sense of veracity, respect for the plighted word. Describing his hero, Kapila says: "This illustrious prince could willingly renounce life, fortune the most opulent, desire the most dear,—but the truth never." Now it is just this, respect for the plighted word, that brings about the catastrophe of the poem.

Somewhere in his picture, and generally in the foreground, the epic artist casts in this quintessence of contradiction, this ink of indelible darkness, Worst from Best,—all the juices of sweet life going to feed cancers. Moreover, the higher the art and the grander the genius of the poet, the more resolutely does he leave this terrible fact in possession of its proper field. In the Ramayana, those who had fallen in the war against the demon were, after the victory, magically restored to life. That is impure art. In the Iliad, death has his prey undisputed, and tragic fates pursue even the living. This is the manner of the master.

Worst from Best,—is it found only in poems? The stout common sense of Theodore Parker led him to say that Religion may become prince of the devils. Whence was the inquisition generated? It was bred out of the Beatitudes and the song of the angels, "Peace on earth, good-will to men!" What is wourali poison, in which South American Indians dip their arrows, compared with the envenomed conscience that even the spirit of Christendom has secreted? "We enact hell here below!"

In the epics, then, of men, and in the epic of the Supreme Poet, there is somewhat with which the heart of man cannot be reconciled, nor should be reconciled, since it is antithetic to moral order and unity: when man does not abhor it, he has forsworn his own nature. What, precisely, is this *somewhat,* this Satan ever going to and fro in the world, this serpent always lurking in garden? Let us see whether this thing can be accurately defined. Having learned its nature,—if, indeed, to do so be possible,—we may further inquire whether the epic idea of the world can be seen as comprehending, commanding it, and evoking melody from it. And if the attempt be daring, and our space for exposition brief, all the more must precision be sought; nor will a little formality in the statement, if it help toward precision, be esteemed inexcusable.

1. In the world of the senses and of science all goes by law, the savants tell us. Granted: force has definite characters and constant measures; in measure and character alike it is invariable. All there goes by law: by what kind of law, however? By a law that is absolutely and everlastingly indifferent to any thought which man derives from his spiritual being, to any sentiment, any ideal desire or purpose of the soul. You would have a house, wherein to enshrine the sanctities and felicities of domestic life: what cares gravitation for your wish? These Romans would build a city; Michel Angelo would lift St. Peter's dome: gravitation enters into no complicity with such desires; inexorably, stolidly faithful to its own business, it holds down the rock in the quarry; whoever will get a block of it away shall sweat for it. Well, the builders outwit gravitation, making it help them lift the stone, and put it in place, where the stolid tug of that force shall serve their design: it is outwitted, that is all; not in the least has it been won into sympathy with a human purpose. The forces of Nature, as they do not change to approach, so cannot change to elude, the design of man: get the wind of them, and they are captive. Now, as the soul has, through the body, a foothold in Nature, and commands immediately a certain amount of force, it is enabled to take natural law by surprise, and bring it to obedience. But in obedience it is remote as ever, maintaining the same impassive, unconquerable indifference to all that the soul imagines or intends. As with gravitation, so with all natural forces: even when serving the most vital uses, they are infinitely far away from man's thought of use. Oxygen rushes into the lungs, when they create a vacuum: it is but rushing into a vacuum. It combines with the globules of the blood to recreate life; to further decomposition would suit it as well: growth and decay, life and death, man's gain or loss, pleasure or anguish, are

to it quite the same. Thus it happens that man, as a worker in the realm of finite Nature, must always work among and upon forces that are no less than infinitely removed from any sympathy with his spirit. The world serves him, but does not know him even when it serves.

2. In using these forces, man puts himself somewhat in their power. We lift the roof, but lift it over our own heads: gravitation has no respect for the heads; its business is to draw downward, which it attends to assiduously, not considering who or what is beneath; and it holds the roof in place, I must repeat, only as it is outwitted. When the earthquake comes, comes its opportunity; and now men fly the houses they have built for their security. Moreover, for purposes of use we must set free agencies that were not active before, that we can never be sure of our ability to control, and that, despite their services, ever continue terrible to us. Fire, for example, is a demon that man has conjured up. It is needful, indispensable; we must take it into our houses near the cradle and the couch, must sleep with it for housefellow, knowing all the while that it is an untamable demon, never a whit domesticated by its long intimacy with man. Now fire is not bad; but the burning of the house, for which it is at any moment ready, were an evil. The burning of the house, and the fall, perchance, of the flaming roof upon those it was designed to shelter,—despite all the glosses of optimism, a plain man may take leave to regard that as indubitably an evil.

Here, therefore, is an evil, yet no evil principle. There is a gap between human ends and natural means; and evil—physical evil only as yet—is incidental to it.

3. Man is not only *in* this world of forces thus indifferent to every thought of his spirit, but, as an organized creature, he is himself composed of such forces. Yet more, they assume in him a new and peculiar intensity, becoming sensitive, and rounding into an Ego heated with immeasurable desire. Nevertheless, these forces, though as an organized nature he is compounded of them, belong to that world which is forever infinitely remote from the pure thought and ideal desire of his spirit. The relation of himself as spirit to himself as organized in nature is the same

with the general relation of man to force in the external world. Hunger and thirst are no less indifferent than gravitation to all that the soul believes and loves. Temperamental force has its own orbit, moves by its own springs, knows only its own ends. Indispensable utilities are exacted from it; but it transmits them, as a mail-bag does letters, without knowing what is in them.

Thus the soul must not only work upon, it must also work by means of, an alien material. This material, moreover, is not passive, it is *force,* fiercely intent, impersuasible. Accordingly, the soul can accomplish nothing, it is annulled, until by an efflux of virtue it takes possession of the field; while only by a continuance of the same energy does it keep possession. Even in victory and supremacy, it may not retire and sleep: its authority is dead, its victory vanishes, in the moment that it ceases to act and to overcome. It is a sovereign whose subjects are all rebels at heart, and become such in act the moment it does not make upon them an overmastering impression. They are rebels, not by any concerted antagonism to the regal principle, but because they are wholly moved by an intention of their own, which is alien and indifferent to spiritual ideas.

4. The soul, in building up its own architectures, and preparing its own repast, must make immaterial fire, must liberate demons in its own organic household, and so newly imperil itself. For the better culture and discipline of mankind, it establishes Property,—an institution which rests wholly upon an ideal basis: instantly it creates cupidity, a very terrible demon indeed, hungry beyond measure, sometimes in its rage of appetite devouring entire civilizations. What a raising of chimneys, called courts of law, there has to be! What anxious binding of the demon with precedents, statutes, legal forms! Despite all which, it will sometimes break bounds: and, indeed, when is it not breaking bounds, committing trespass, doing indescribable mischief?

The soul, again, builds the state, to incarnate therein, as in a larger body, the spirit of community: at once it sets free the love of dominion,—fire again, and a fire that makes horrible conflagrations. The desire of power and sway is not bad; the debt to it of civilization is immense, immeasurable; never was there a great ruler or statesman whose breast did not brim with it; and only at far-distant periods of time do the Timoleons and Washingtons appear, who possess it largely without being possessed by it. Often has it wrought prodigiously, when Goodness lay asleep, wrapped in sweet dreams; and history on many a page

> "Tells how the drudging Goblin sweat
> To earn his cream-bowl duly set,
> Till in one night, ere glimpse of morn,
> His shadowy flail hath threshed the corn
> That ten day-laborers could not end."

Nor, on the other hand, is it good; for in itself it has no moral quality whatsoever. But a force destitute of all moral character, which nevertheless must be brought into the closest intimacy with moral interests, and even fanned and stimulated in their behalf, has in it capacities of evil.

The soul builds churches, architectures to house a thought higher still; and again it makes fire; and this time may make the very fire of hell, bigotry, conscientious hatred, holy cruelty, lying for God, tyranny that not only oppresses, but makes in its victims a hunger to be oppressed. And once more we have to say, that the force thus brought into action is in itself neither good nor evil, though of both good and evil it is vastly capable. Fire,—it may kindle fagots about the martyr, and blaze abroad to devastate entire centuries and civilizations, or may genially warm the hearts and households of believing ages.

Finally, this Ego of ours,—this also is demon, is fire. The Spirit makes it: never could mere organic force become conscious, and say *I*. But the Spirit makes it as the intensest conceivable antithesis to its own pure, including universality. *I*,— what a portentous exclusion the word implies! It shuts out all the universe beside itself; indeed, to the egoistic apprehension pure and simple, *I* is universe, is god. A wonderful thing is this particular, limited Self. It is *ec*centric centre,—pure partiality in the state, and with the sense of perfect wholeness. It is Spirit inverted or reverted from its comprehending, universal self-identity, to sustain its own intensest contradiction, a purely limited and excluding self-identification. This special Self is demon all and only. Not good, it is yet here as the strong caryatid to sustain a spiritual consciousness, which is God's surpassing work of art. Not bad, it is nevertheless a caryatid whose head is not kept under without pains, and that at best seldom fails to put a wry face upon his labor.

Fire is not bad; but the burning of the house, which despite all precautions may happen, were an evil. Egoism is not bad; but its exaction and forage upon the soul, which in some degree are sure to happen, are an evil. When the forces of finite Nature turn the virtue and providence of the soul against itself, then there is evil, devil. Devil is not a person, it is not even a thing or a force; it is simply an effect incidental to a particular form of relation. With finite Nature, fixed, resolute, inexorable in its finitude, the soul must make an intimacy, to which intimacy Nature can never respond by the faintest blush of sympathy; natural forces will seek forever, must forever seek, to carry away in their own line whatever comes within their reach; and when they succeed in appropriating and bringing into their own line of action the virtue of the soul, evil appears. The epic poet represents this most terrible incident of the Spirit's engagement in Nature,—the soul pulled overboard by the fish it was drawing in,—the soul caught in the mesh of its own mechanism, ground in its own mill.

If, now, the foregoing exposition be at all correct, it will appear, that, though there is no evil principle, though Satan is the boldest of impersonations, implying some temerity of rhetoric, yet the Satanic, the infernal, exists nevertheless. Disease is no entity; but epilepsy and lockjaw are quite real.

On the other hand, the epic "play-over" must not be forgotten. Evil is real, but it is not commensurate with man's being. Man is properly supernatural; the soul is above all its experience within the limits of finite Nature, and

"Though round its breast the rolling clouds are spread,
Eternal sunshine settles on its head."

Accordingly, I find two opposite classes of theorists, who, severally following, though in contrary directions, a linear and prosaic logic, arrive at a forced conclusion on this matter. The one party, beginning from below, and perceiving evil to be real relatively to the soul as engaged in Nature, reasons to the eternal from the temporal, and asserts a supernatural Satan, conceived of either as a person or a state of existence. The other party, setting out from man's supreme consciousness, wherein he feels the serene eminence of his spirit over Nature, reasons downward, and declares that even within the limits of Nature evil is not real.

The latter opinion seems to have been adopted with a degree of enthusiasm by the Emersonian school in America, though of Mr. Emerson himself one may rather say that he has shown a marked predilection for it than that it is sustained by him as a fixed dogma. The chief argument for it is an undeniable fact, namely, that evil is often reconverted to use. But were this always the case, evil would not lose its proper character. At sight of somewhat with which it cannot be reconciled, the soul is stung, and newly incited. Well, why is it stung? Whence the provocation? It is the sight or the experience of somewhat odious to the soul that stings. If we say, "This so-called evil is made to serve a use, therefore it is not evil; whatever is is right; the soul can and must be reconciled with it,"—where are we? Let us shun huddled thinking.

Asafœtida is the best of antispasmodics; it does not therefore smell the better. Esteem me not narrow-minded, if I hold my nose. The philosopher tells me, indeed, that only devil knows devil,—that only because I am cousin-german to asafœtida does its odor offend me. Perhaps so; it may be, that, were the nose regenerate, it would find only frankincense in fœtor. I humbly confess such grace has not been given that organ. Be it to my shame or no, I must distinguish between scent of heliotrope and scent of carrion-flower. I follow my nose as my fathers did before me. Nor in truth do I propose to be shamefaced before Philosophy in doing so. Offence is offence, make the best of it. Evil is a thing good to esteem bad, good to be offended at, good to keep the cork on. Like ipecacuanha and tartar-emetic, it is useful only as it creates nausea and is intolerantly rejected by the system.

It is said further, that Good has a vast power of assimilation, a chemistry that nothing can wholly resist. This also is true. As in the physical world the organific force will masticate quartz and porphyry, gnawing away at the frozen adamant of mountain crags with teeth harder and more capable of self-repair than those of rodents, and solving all with the alchemy of eupeptic life, until it has given the earth flesh, has clothed this with the garniture of field and forest, and digested this again into animal form and motion, so the higher genius that works in humanity to dissolve and to organize does not live upon spoon-victual alone, but has teeth to cut platinum, a stomach to digest poison, and an art out of pus and gangrene to make the vigor of dancing feet and bloom of dawning beauty. Eyes that are not sick will see this without spectacles, and sound minds will be apt to emphasize it. But let us not say too much, and be like cowards who betray fear by voluble affirmation that there is no danger. Good has diamond teeth,—and it needs them! Poor logic, to say, that, because it has this masticating and digestive force, therefore all is food for it, artistically prepared by some cosmic Blot, and that what seems odious is only pepper-sauce, a sharp condiment to provoke appetite.

In fine, the universe will not be spun out in one thread, and turned to prose. Our nice mental machinery can do much, but cannot do that; and this new-patented method of optimism fails like every other. It does good work of the kind, but the poetic truth of existence will not be caught on the smooth-turning spindle.

The opposition of good and evil is never to be explained away. But this opposition is itself prosaic, if only in itself considered. To deny it is fatal to epic truth; to remain only in it, the captive and jail-bird of Nature, is no less fatal. Evil, and good *as merely opposed to evil,* belong alike to the soul only as standing in organic connection with finite Nature; but the soul's true being is not in Nature, it is in Spirit, the self-affirmed, eternal, indivisible Import, into which Nature, as sign, evermore resolves itself. To the bird as walking the wall exists, and is impassable: the bird takes wing, and the wall, though solid as ever, becomes for it no wall. But man at once walks and flies,—walks and works on these levels of Nature, yet by his true substantive being soars and circles in the divine ether; and here, in unity with the One-and-All, he is himself the sky, which rounds in and contains in harmony his natural experience. In his breast is enshrined this exceeding great mystery,—the infinite separation of Nature from Spirit, the perfect poetic comprehension of Nature by Spirit. A mystery, nay, a very dust in the eyes, to prose thought, it is far otherwise in the *being* of man, as in the universe of God: here it abides in poetic clearness forever,—so clear, that the voice of it, when it comes to speech, can be no other than a voice of singing, to which only melodious numbers and concord of sweet sound afford a fit expression. The universe rings with it like a bell; and the heart of the poet, being *whole*, also rings silver-clear; and in the deep heart of humanity a poetic thought is perennial, though in general it is shattered on the lips.

From the height of its perfect consciousness the soul looks down upon the imperfect *quasi* world of Nature; and seeing itself involved there, yet not involved,—locked into those limits of inexorable finitude, yet above them, including them, resolving them into that breath of Spirit which sings while it passes,— it has the sentiment not only of a Whole, but of an epic Whole, including within its flawless unity the intensest contradiction.

We are now prepared, let it be supposed, to attempt a final survey of this epic Whole, this Iliad of existence, placing its grand features in their true relation to each other. Only from the summit of thought and consciousness can such a survey be attempted sanely; we must therefore begin and end with the all-comprehending Unity, with pure Spirit.

1. Man has the consciousness of Spirit in its integrity, whole and the whole, nothing if not all. He knows this, and, as knowing, is one with it. Never can it be known as *other* than that by which it is known; if another, it is no longer *the* One, but only a particular existence. Tell me not of *a* God, one being particularized among others, though great or greatest. John Stuart Mill

kindly explains, that, though it be ridiculous to speak of *the* Infinite, *the* Absolute, yet God may be infinite in a particular way,—infinitely just and good in the sense of being entirely just and good. His infinite is merely unmixed quality. In the same sense a spider is infinitely a spider, if it be all and only spider. Should the creature ever be afflicted with a doubt about the propriety of catching flies, the spiderly nature, becoming mixed, would fall from infinitude. Infinite in the sense of pure quality is perhaps as good an infinite as positivism admits of; but I quite agree with Mr. Mill in thinking it ridiculous to call this *the* infinite.

The infinite of Spirit is not to be caught in a cobweb. The ambitious broom of positivist logic will neither sweep it down from the dark corners of the understanding nor sweep it together from the floors of phenomenal Nature. What it is we may a little conceive thus: though there were a myriad of perfectly rational minds, there were but one Reason, *and each of them were it.* The consciousness of reason is an integrating consciousness; in it there is a unity, not numerical, but intrinsic: multiple in manifestation, it is not divided, nor in itself multiple, but ever identical. Spirit is reason, and more than we mean by reason distinctively. It is not only integral, but is active, eternal, absolute integration. As there is not only a possible rest *in* motion, but also a rest *of* motion,—as, for example, in orbital movement,—so there is a unity, not only *in* multiplicity, but *of* mutliplicity,—a unity of comprehension and embrace, which, though it contain contradiction, yet does indeed *contain* it, and therefore remains itself unbroken. The consciousness of this it is that the human race has confessed so often as it has said *God.* There is no night there; there all limit is swallowed up, freedom and necessity become one and the same; there the jars of Nature blend in the tune of the eternal Whole, and the clash of oppositions is felt to be sustained by the very unity which they seemingly oppose. "The will of Zeus is accomplished": it is the keynote which to every note is a key. Spirit is; and he is Spirit who is conscious of it, and he the voice of it who hears its language. Spirit is, the everlasting Only, only and all, playing over opposition, yet never opposed; abiding ever in itself, yet not aloof; dwelling only with itself, yet housing the universe.

2. Nevertheless, in precise antithesis to this, there is the world of finite Nature, also assuming to be all, and indeed complete in its way,—no escape from it, when once you have accepted its level and law. It bears, however, this ear-mark of imperfection, that the essential character of it is to be excluding. Excluding: every particle of matter shoulders away every other;—every square inch of space says, as it were, to universal space, "Stand off!"—every moment of time fixes itself between the two eternities of time, denying them, saying, "Of time I alone *am,* I, the present moment!"—every force, so much as it acts, negates all other force. It is a universe of exclusions,—purest conceivable opposite to the including simplicity of Spirit.

What then? We have a dual world: Spirit and Nature standing in irreconcilable opposition, each, it should seem, excluding the very possibility of the other. Yet as Spirit is whole and the whole, or is nothing, dualism kills it. And, indeed, many in our day espouse the cause of finite Nature to this extent, saying, "Spirit *can* be no more than a fiction of speech, since for it as a reality Nature leaves no room." True, Nature has no room for it. Here is a difficulty, which to a prosaic speculation is, and must remain, insuperable. But the bolt turns to another key.

3. We have seen that this self-asserting finite Nature asserts itself only to the same ear which itself makes, to the finite understanding. To the higher poetic intelligence, it is only Sign, only Language. As such, it declares itself to be in and of itself *nothing*. A word,—for what is it here? To be somewhat in itself? No, but expressly to be nothing in itself. It is a word only as, vacating itself, pointing away from itself, denying its own substantiality, it simply and unequivocally *stands for* somewhat which indeed is, namely, an import existing in the mind. The world, then, as Sign, denies its substantial existence, vacates its own pretension to reality, and affirms what is not itself, affirms a significance whose unity and substantiality is Spirit.

It has been said, but will bear saying again, that to this significant and therefore ever-vanishing character of Nature all human speech is due. So all mythology, all theology, comes of the impulse to render that language which Nature is into the language man uses. Poetry, painting, every fine art, is a fine art for the reason that it elects the significant impression of Nature as the real fact of it, while the so-called useful arts regard Nature only in its lower character, as force. Whence the charm of land-scape painting? It is always inferior to that which one may any day see from his doorstep. The charm of it is this: it presents Nature as *only* picture, only significant show, without its outdoor pretension to substantiality,—presents Nature more as what it veritably is. Hence mere *facsimile* painting, which foists upon the picture Nature's habitual disguise of its true character, is but mock art.

4. Having thus affirmed Spirit, then shown finite Nature as apparently denying it, then again shown the same Nature as confessing itself a mere sign of that which it seems to deny, we come to an act which concerns us human beings very nearly, but of which there seems to be in the streets of our cities little notice taken. I have never once seen mention of it on the bulletin-boards, nor found it in the column of news.

Spirit issues in person, in the person, that is, of humanity, upon this scene of finite Nature; *accepts the fiction of its substantiality;* and even so, upon these hard terms, extorts a confession of its presence and quality. Here, then, it is in the militant state, a warrior in armor, overcoming a hostility that never abates, compelling a confession ineffably alien to the lips that utter it.

Spirit militant, Spirit accepting the fiction of Nature's substantiality to conquer it on its own level,—this is the moral life of humanity. With this "accepted fiction" under the feet, we cannot wonder that our life should divide itself into the irreconcilable opposites, Right and Wrong, God and Devil. A contradiction is involved in such a state of existence; the contradiction will appear, and make itself felt, sometimes to the utter anguish of the soul.

Here the soul conquers, but always with costs; here it endures

defeat, but in defeat still conquers, if its quality has been signalized. No other business has it than to say effectually, I AM:
achieving this, though in dungeons, at the stake, on the cross, it
is victorious.

Partial defeat it ever does and must suffer, optimism to the
contrary notwithstanding. "All is well," am I told? Yes, the All
is very well, undoubtedly. One gets fresh intelligence of that
fact in his own breast now and then, and pipes his little note
of rejoicing accordingly. But is this taken to mean that all *goes*
well? that in the line and on the level of outward events there
is perfect process? that the moral life of man involves no contradiction, in the midst of which the soul must strive and suffer?
that we may lie on our oars and trust the tide of events to take us
to port? Enough, O, more than enough of this! In the line of
events, as related to the moral life of humanity, there is, there
can be, no perfect process on the earth: the very conception of
our existence forbids: We chant, with a sweet imbecility, "the
good time coming": it is ever coming, and never come. Some
say that the golden age has been, and some that it is to be; but I,
that all events are cheap and all times tawdry,—that only the
soul is golden, and that the shine of this metal out of the dust-
cloud of history is the true result.

Here is the field of the tragic poet. He causes the soul to show
itself and to shine from out the utmost darkness and devilishness
of events. The one is helpless and inextinguishable; the other
victorious and without honor. The soul suffers every conceivable
defeat, and is godlike still; the law of events follows its own
fatal course, making no clear distinction between good and bad,
and is seen in its proper under-foot character. Thus, Shakespeare
in his grand tragedies will give us scarce a crumb of comfort, so
far as the course of events is concerned. Iago, indeed, ends his
iniquity with his death: who is consoled? who cares? You crush
the snake that has just fleshed its fang in priceless honor and
innocence: well; it was but a snake. Iago dies; but Desdemona,
Othello!—who talks of a balance struck? Or who in this presence
will proclaim the "good of evil"? What good? Snake number two

is more likely to be regenerate? St. Snake is somewhat less beautiful to me than the creature uncanonized. Anything, if you please, but Satan in a state of grace!

I thank Shakespeare that he gives no hint of these suspicious compensations. Out of wrong done and suffered the soul has shown its quality: this is the true result. All the grandeur of the great poet's genius is found in this, his habitual manner of representing life. Had he stooped to patch up events, pretending, after the fashion of the novelist, that the significance of life is found in *their* course and result, he would have stooped indeed, and been no longer Shakespeare.

Spirit by issuing upon this scene of things brings moral good to a world which before was but a system of forces, incapable of moral character: by the same act it makes the possibility and the *general* (not particular) necessity of moral evil. It does so by placing the virtue of the soul within reach of the energies of the finite world, "laws" of Nature, organic impulses and desires, —huge polypi, that throw their long tenacious tentacles about all that comes within their scope, and know not what they devour. Thus the Hebrew "God of battles"—the unity of Spirit in the militant state—says, "I, God, make good, and I create evil." Does this sound harsh? But is it not true? Are not moral good and moral evil correlative opposites, each of which forever wars upon and forever implies the other? Does not the soul make both, the former by its intrinsic quality, and the latter by the situation it accepts? As the human providence which evokes the element of fire makes it possible that any house may burn and certain that some houses will burn, so spiritual virtue, by creating moral good, enables the characterless energies of Nature to attain the higher, though abhorrent quality of evil.

But the divining sense of humanity has touched the ultimate truth of this situation with a precision yet more admirable. Spirit militant, appearing no longer as the "God of battles," but as the suffering Prince of Peace, the crucified God, meekly enduring, in the consciousness of an infinite resource, all the utmost despite of Nature,—never yet has a nobler or *truer* imagination inspired the worship of humanity. A great injustice is, indeed, done this perennial poetic truth, when it is *Calvinized* into prose; yet what an appeal, even so, has it made to the heart of man! Let the form change as it may and must; but let the grand imagination remain, for the tragedy of the world has this extent; and Æschylus and Shakespeare and every greatest poet has touched it most nearly just then when his genius was at the supreme height.

The strictly moral consciousness is dualistic, not integrating; for beneath its feet is an assumption contradictory to the eternal quality of Spirit, namely, the assumed substantiality of finite Nature. Hence it dwells in a divided world, whose ultimate terms are God (the warring or suffering God) and Devil. But optimism pretends that the moral consciousness is unitive and entire. It blinks the underlying contradiction, and therefore must seek to persuade us that "the Devil is not so black as he is painted," and indeed is not of a black complexion at all, but is only a serviceable angel in soiled linen,—grimed with necessary labor, and none the worse for not appearing in holiday clothes. I freely make over my share in this charitable judgment to those who can find a use for it, and freely confess that a more limping, one-legged thing is not known to us than a purely moralistic theology which sets out with denying the necessary dualism of morals.

5. But the old religionists permitted themselves to speak of *mere* morality, as if there were a consciousness in man and a truth in being that transcended morals, though without invalidating them. Were they utterly deceived? Has humanity no consciousness, has being no character of this transcendent kind? Are right and wrong the supreme words?—wrong, however, being inscrutably wrung back, and so brought, as it were clandestinely, into the line of right. Epic imagination, whether as found in written poems, or as speaking in all the higher spirituality of mankind, affirms a sovereign Unity, which, indeed, becomes moral by descent into the limits of finite Nature, but which is in itself, as Hooker said, "not only one, but very oneness," while in oneness it includes, and is, all. Let it be permitted me to speak as I can, and without reproach, of this Unspeakable,

happy if the words shall in any manner or degree hint what the best of words will never more than hint.

It may be read in epics, and as their supreme import, necessary to render them epical, that Spirit, even while provisionally accepting this finite Nature as substantial, and issuing upon it in the militant character, remains not the less and forever in itself, in the consciousness of its pure, eternal integrity, unbroken by the dividedness of time, untouched by its tumult. This One to which there is no Other, while yet it does not exclude, but embraces and houses all multiplicity and diversity,—is it not the "open secret," always inaccessible to the critical understanding, while to the adoring heart and spiritual imagination it is not only accessible, but is alone to them in the deepest sense native? Inexplicable, indubitable, not to be solved only because itself the universal solvent, it is the mystery of eternity, yet is mysterious only to the prosaic mind, while only through its infinite reconciling presence is finite Nature itself other than an affronting mystery to the credent and poetic soul. This is the blessed *play-over,* beneath which, and yet within which, all the fortune of life, all the struggle and process of existence, go on, and into which they evermore vanish, to appear in vanishing and to die in renewal, as words sink and are lost in the import that creates and sustains them.

An indestructible consciousness in man, fundamental fact of his being, makes him a participant in this oneness, this wholeness, this perfection of Spirit in itself. Spirit as engaged in Nature,—it is Sarpedon, son of Zeus, warring, stricken, perishing, lying gory on the battle-field; Spirit abiding in itself,—it is Zeus poised in Olympian peace, and in himself containing all. Sarpedon falling, dying, the victim of Nature; Zeus immortal, hurtless as the blue heaven, and embracing Nature as the sky the earth;—the one is the passionate experience of man, and the other is his pure, integrating consciousness. But the latter is his consciousness, not merely as *his,* and subjective, but as veritable, substantial, the indivisible consciousness of Spirit, existing only because Spirit is, one and indivisible,—the eternal fact impressing itself with the sense of its own infinite reality.

It follows from all the foregoing that man's being is a scale of three degrees. On the lowest, he is only an organized nature, a mote or molecule in the immeasurable system of things; a little learning the trick of it, a little and a little better able, from age to age, to take care of his small peculium; getting to be at length, from a mote, an insect, and humming so as to be heard, O, yards away! On the degree above this, far above, he is moral, engaged in the battle without truce between good and evil; at issue with others and with himself; finding a law in his members warring upon the law of his mind and bringing him into captivity, till he cry, "Wretched man that I am!" Here he may have noble battle, but never peace; always there is a Hannibal in his Italy, or the Gauls are gathering on the border; and he is still bound by the necessities of the conflict in the rare hours of his triumphal march. On the highest degree, he is one with the One-and-All. Here, as from the height of eternity, he looks down on his small fortunes in the world of time, and by all that he there suffers renews and intensifies the consciousness of his eternal security and sovereignty in God.

It was the door into this supreme consciousness that the Christian evangel, particularly as represented by Paul, unbarred and threw open to the access of mankind; the doctrine of "salvation by faith," though its dryness now parches the tongue, began the epopee of Christendom, and gave the key-note to the largest symphony in which the imaginations of nations and ages have as yet joined. This consciousness, though not at all denying, but, on the contrary, admitting and using, what is beneath it, declares itself alone veritable. Spirit only is; all else appears, and is not. And here one cannot help asking by what fine luck it was that Hellenic tradition made Homer blind; that which he sang he saw but as a picture within his breast. For so the eye of absolute Spirit sees Nature and the natural experience of man as things by itself imagined, airy nothings with a local habitation and a name.

The epic poet sets off all the worst that the soul can suffer in Nature against that higher impossibility of its suffering at all. He gives himself the divine pleasure of beholding this troubled, tumultuous *quasi* existence as it vanishes momentarily and forever into the peace and perfect comprehension of Spirit in itself. That engagement in Nature, and yet an everlasting ease and delight of self-rescue out of Nature,—the perpetual play-up of finite life out of itself and into the infinite as its truer self, while Spirit in its divine play-over stoops to the world, and, stooping, remains infinitely above, and seeming to acknowledge another than itself, makes that apparent *other* an instrument through which to blow its eternal affirmation, I ONLY AM;—this is that symphony of being whose choirs are solar and stellar systems, and whose notes and numbers are individual lives, while in each note the tune of the whole, the tune of eternity, presides, and the Symphonist himself is present. And in finding this, we find the epic interpretation of human life.

SOCIAL IDEALS

There are great common or social ideals which arise in the world, are diffused, gain supremacy, and remain, it may be, for many centuries, ruling men at the very roots of their souls. The coming of such into existence and power is perhaps the most important kind of event that ever occurs on the earth. Compared with this, the rise of a kingdom like Prussia, or of a republic like the United States, is, to speak moderately, an event of secondary importance. Such an advent there was in the rise of Christianity; and all that Christianity has done in the world, all its effect upon minds and morals illustrates the power of a common ideal to make, unmake and transform. If you would understand the past, study its ideals; history is unintelligible without them. If you would know your own age, study the "spirit of the age," its ideal, that is. And especially if there are tokens that we live at the opening of a new epoch, when ancient ideals are dying, and another sovereign, not of the same blood, is coming to the throne, an inquiry into the nature of the change thus going on must be of surpassing interest.

We do indeed live at one of those turning points in history. From the fourth to the fifteenth century one ideal, represented by Catholic Christianity, but enclosing within it from the eighth century another, embodied in the feudal system, reigned with undisputed sway in the occidental world. Copernicus, Columbus and Luther,—the first giving to the human mind a new heavens,

Index, February 10, 1872. A lecture given in Horticultural Hall, Boston, under the auspices of the Free Religious Association, January 28, 1872.

the second a new earth, the third a new moral poise,—put an end to that period, already disturbed by the crusades, the Black Death, and the flight of Greek learning from Constantinople to the West; and two centuries later,—for profound alterations of the human mind are manifested but slowly,—the guiding imagination of the medieval world was gone and irrecoverable. No sooner had it disappeared than the institutions it had given rise to, and which to a large extent remained,—as always happens in such cases,—lost on the one hand the genius that had made them wholesome, and on the other the explanation that had made them seem reasonable; at once they appeared anomalous, grotesque, monstrous, the product of imposture and violence.

Partly, therefore, through the reaction against these institutions, there arose, to replace the old, a new ideal, that of Liberty. Liberty—what a word to conjure with has that been for a hundred years! And yet during the space of some twelve centuries—centuries that wrought out for us all the elements of our civilization,—it was scarcely, or but faintly, pronounced; even a class of reformers like the Puritans, honest, brave and high-souled as any the world has known, cared not a button for liberty in the more modern sense. Time was that the words "obedience" and "service" made music in men's ears. Then it was the ideal of religion to have no will of one's own; then the proudest nobleman professed, and made it matter of pride, to "serve his fief," that is, his system of relations with all above and all beneath him; then courtesy crowned itself with the title of servant, and the modern gentleman, following the verbal forms of a departed ideal, may still subscribe himself the "obedient servant" of another. Strange!—the title that raw Irish "help" may now refuse as degrading, was once worn as a plume by the very men who made pride a grace, if not a virtue. The "fag" system of Eton, Harrow, Rugby, &c., is a relic, curious to American eyes, of that old world in which service, whether the word or the thing, was not esteemed degrading, but the door to honor. How foreign is all this to what we boast, and without boast may reasonably esteem, as the "spirit of the age!" For good or evil— for good *and* evil—another ideal has arisen; it has dominated civilization for a century, and is only now beginning to be displaced by a second, of which also, in its turn, I shall have occasion to speak.

The ideal of liberty has its bright side and its eminent use in modern civilization; but unhappily it was formulated in a spurious way,—chiefly in the last century and by Jean-Jacques Rousseau; and in this vicious shape has come down to our age. The doctrine that thus got into vogue was substantially as follows: That each individual has by gift of Nature an unqualified property in himself; that he is born to be absolutely his own master, and to dispose of himself at his own sovereign pleasure; that his individual will is therefore his proper guide and supreme law; that this natural liberty, so called, has but one limitation—it should be so adjusted by each to the like liberty in others that he may enjoy his own without encroaching on theirs; that government is a purely defensive expedient, designed to secure to each his perfect possession and disposal of himself, and that it borrows the right to accomplish even this limited task only from the voluntary consent of the individual parties to it.

This doctrine, it may be observed, would be quite as suitable to rats as human beings. Your rat is quite as much attached as a human creature can be to life, liberty and the pursuit of happiness—would be nothing less than absolute owner of himself, would make his private inclination his supreme law, and dispose of himself at his own sovereign pleasure; and rat government, could these assiduous rodents arrive at such, would undoubtedly be designed to sustain each in the liberty so dear to him. That order of doctrine, however,—spawned in Europe, not America, and made public in Europe at a time when Massachusetts was as loyal as London to the British crown,—was to be imported into this country, and to have a notable career. To please and propitiate Virginia, Thomas Jefferson was chosen to write the Declaration of Independence. Jefferson, who as late as November 29th, 1775,—five and a half months after the battle of Bunker's Hill,—wrote thus in a private letter, "Believe me, dear sir, there is not in the British empire a man that more cordially loves the union with Great Britain than I do"—a "love" that included allegiance to the British crown,—had in the months intervening between that November and the June following blazed out as a political philosopher of the newest school. Seizing the opportunity to air his neophyte faith under auspices so uncommon, he proceeded, after the fashion of his teachers, to select certain ordinary descriptions of self-interest, common to rats and men, to endow these with "inalienable" rights, and to announce that civil society exists to no end but to assure the said rights of self-interest. This screed of doctrine became a resource, and was much endeared to many good men, during the struggle against slavery; it is now a sacred scripture, much more sacred to numbers than the scriptures commonly so-called. One might compare it, in its actual relation to the spirit of the nation, to a dry bone underground, around which the rootlets of a vine have wound and woven themselves in a myriad-fold complexity of filaments; the vine could well live and flourish and bear fruit without it, but cannot be disrupted from it without injury. Every community has its dry bones so embraced; and, whatever the rude agitator may think, the real thinker knows that it is a serious business to meddle with them. But when in the hollow of the bone poison is hid, and the rootlets have penetrated to it, and the leaves begin to wither and the fruit to rot by effect of it, then the time for root-pruning has come, and the knife should be taken in hand. The feeding roots of this nation have now, it is manifest, struck through to the poison in Jefferson's doctrine. This doctrine is to-day furnishing the logic of "free love," and, if the premises be admitted, an *unanswerable* logic. It is propagating to-day a putrid ferment to destroy not only the most sacred of social institutions, but the very grounds of social duty.

Under these circumstances, everything admonishes us to return and resume the sober, constructive spirit of Washington, Adams, Jay, Hamilton, Ames, Osgood. During the gallant, but alas, ineffectual struggle of the Federalists against Jacobin politics, Rev. Dr. David Osgood of Medford, Mass., delivered a number of political discourses, so replete with sound judgment and just sentiment, and marked by so high an order of grave eloquence, that the author was honored with a share in that secret, cowardly vituperation which Jefferson poured out so prodigally upon the best men of his time. That certificate of character should entitle him to remembrance. Over this, Jefferson's style of political speculation triumphed in what he himself vaunted as "our second great revolution, not inferior to the first, that of 1800,"—a revolution of which himself was the hero and himself the eulogist. The hour has arrived when we should reverse the triumph, and, instead of finding a foundation in isolating self-interests and rights of self-interest, should find it where eternal wisdom laid it, in connecting and commanding obligation,— the hour when rat-liberty, or such as consists in pursuing in one's own fashion whatever one esteems happiness, should be recognized as proper only to beasts, and only to the wild among beasts, while it is at once the privilege and the imperative vocation of human beings to put this unequivocally away, that, through the duty of all, and the discipline of all and productive restraints submitted to by all, men may create for themselves a chartered and fruitful freedom, to liberate and empower them in head, heart and hand.

It is undoubtedly a function of civil society to protect individual rights, that is to say, the rights of individual self-love. Had Jefferson said just this, and with the due qualifications, he would, so far, have done well. But in the first place, he ran to an absurd excess by announcing these rights as "inalienable." Inalienable! If the right to life is so, this nation did a murder with every rebel shot on the field in our great civil contest. The right to liberty,— if that is inalienable, the State commits a crime with every thief sent to jail. Not only are all such rights qualified, conditional, alienable, but it is the express office of the commonwealth to affirm personal responsibility by treating them accordingly, extending over them the sovereignty of moral law. Inalienable! The statement is preposterous, and only as practically set at naught by the common sense of the community, can it fail to be mischievous.

Again, it is not the sole function of the State to protect individual self-interest and rights of self-interest; and in restricting it to this, Jefferson betrayed the one exceeding, fatal vice of his political philosophy. Above all that, civil society has a *productive* function; it is to embody and exact the duty of all men to concur in DOING unitedly whatsoever is necessary to an honorable, fruitful, progressive social life,—as, to take familiar examples, in establishing courts of justice, making roads, providing for education, &c. Farther, and more comprehensively, it is to make a field and climate for the virtues of civilization, such as constitute its life-blood, as industry, honesty, chastity and the like. In fine, its grand function is, in duly protecting the rights of self-interest, to hold them in perpetual correlation with the social principles and social duty which are sovereignly imposed upon humanity by its civilizing genius.

Take this point of view, and you have an answer to the disintegrating doctrines now getting abroad; assume Jefferson's point of view, making private rights inalienable and exclusive, and you have no answer but a fetch. Does someone, male or female come forward to cry from the housetops, "Hear, O heaven, and give ear, O earth! my pursuit of happiness is interfered with by the State!" My distressed friend, I would say, if you are not willing to pursue happiness in subordination to social duty, that is, to the great, necessary laws of all human welfare, then are you one of the very persons to whom civil society should supply a will wiser than their own.

But instead of proceeding with mere criticism I will try to sketch very rapidly and briefly what approves itself to my judgment as a sound doctrine,—finding in the end what there is of wholesome and useful in the modern ideal of liberty.

1. Man has, as I often say, a *pregnant* genius, by the law and promise of which he is bound. That is his distinction. Nature has endowed him with the functions of her own maternity; to bring forth civilization, with all the wealth, material and spiritual, that belongs to it, he is brought forth by the universe. That function *gives a supreme law to his being;* all his duties, rights, hopes, with his entire privilege and price as a human soul, are rooted in it and inseparable from it. To subserve that civilizing genius, to distinguish and enforce the obligations implied in it,

and so to make the necessary basis of civilization, government is instituted and civil society exists.

2. The matrix of civilization is social. What we are to each other makes us to be what we are in ourselves. The individual nature, taken strictly as such, is utterly sterile, an inhuman nature,—is what a seed buried in the soil would be, were the sun blotted out of the heavens. Isolate from earliest years a creature born from the loins of humanity, and of the fruition of humanity there will in him be nothing; he can become by his physical growth only a beast, wanting even articulate speech. Thoughts, morals, manners, arts, industries, language, everything that distinguishes human beings, comes of the relation between human beings. Could anything be more irrational than to put all this out of sight in stating the grounds of civil society—to set out with absolute individualism, absolute individual liberty,—to limit social duty to the one point of properly letting each other alone, that each may pursue happiness, rat-fashion, according to his own inclination—and to regard civil society as instituted only in order that the right to be let alone may be respected and sustained? And yet that is the doctrine which, having long dominated in politics, is now coming to be applied to the most intimate and vitalizing of social relations—and it is even accepted by some as the type of true "radicalism."

3. Man being born and bound—bound by everything human in him—to make for himself such a kind of life as he has not by mere gift of Nature, it is important to notice that his first act, at the outset of his human career, is to put his natural liberty away, and to accept in place of it a system of productive restraints and imperative duties, and with these *measured* liberties, always submitted to law, while determined in their measure by considerations of general utility. Natural liberty! Why, the institution of property alone takes the very ground from beneath its feet, leaving it not a spot to alight on. Inalienable natural liberty! And yet every human being born in this community comes into the world to be deprived *in toto* of his liberty of self-disposal for the space of twenty-one years, two thirds the average life of a

generation. One half of all human beings die, and never, by any legal allowance, touch that liberty with so much as the tip of the finger. The first lesson set to each, and the one at which each is kept so long, is the lesson of obedience; and if many were kept at it longer, it would be much better for them. Every child, again, in being taught honesty, veracity, and the like, is instructed to put that liberty away, and substitute for it fixed obligations. You *must* do this, and you *must not* do that, we say; and until he has got that *must* by heart, and learned to make it steadfastly predominant over his natural liberty, he is fit for no liberty whatever. And so it is that all civilization and all culture mean the sovereignty of obligation over inclination, and the submission, rather than the supremacy, of the casual, private will. If, therefore, you wish to get a principle the most vicious possible, take that "natural liberty" for a principle; and if you would turn the world upside down, emptying all civilization into the abysses of beastly nature, reason from that, and apply it with uncompromising logic, as a principle.

The limit of liberty is this: Every man *has* a right to do what *is* right, and no other. We have been told of late that a class of our "sisters," inhabiting certain "filthy localities," have a right to pursue happiness in their own way,—"as good a right" as others to live chastely and decently. The sufficient answer would be that, if it is right for any woman to profane her womanhood, then she has a right to do so; but neither woman nor man nor any other creature can have a right to do harm and wrong, any doctrine of liberty to the contrary notwithstanding. True, that strange judgment was reasoned cogently enough from the original and indefeasible liberty, of which there has been so much and so unwise talk; and one might say to the indignant democratists,—You have prostituted the franchise, and the sentiment is more respectable than the logic which forbids you to do the like by your homes. If every barbarian in New York, because his "natural liberty" must be compromised with, has a right to vote, even though his vote will tend only to sepulchre the city in infamy, then I see not but the said "sisters" have a right to do *their* kind of mischief,—which is perhaps little worse for themselves, while it does not necessarily involve others, and threaten the hopes of the nation, at all in the same, nor even in a comparable degree. I, however, recognize a liberty to do right, not wrong, and to do good, not mischief; and recognize no right to liberty as taking precedence of our common right and duty to make a healthy society, a well-ordered life, a productive and honorable civilization; and any liberty not held in submission to the laws of welfare, and made serviceable toward welfare, is one that has only a vicious imagination and spurious ideal for its support.

4. One has a right, I have said, to do what is right, and to get it done for himself and others. We are bound, every one of us, to put away our irresponsible liberty as beasts, and to put obligation in the place of it; and every life is inchoate save as this is done. How shall it best be effected? Shall the wisest, assembled in Congress, say, determine for every man, and in all particulars, what he ought to do? Yes, if human life will best profit by that. I have no right to desire anything but the best law for my life, and no liberty to reject such law, no matter how or by whom it is got at. But here some considerations of great importance come in, and here we reach the wholesome side of the modern ideal. Social regulation, it has been discovered, may be overdone, while too much of it makes barrenness rather than fertility. In the first place, there is an important class of actions not properly under the control of the will. No man can rightfully choose what he will think; and in the degree that he attempts to do so, his mental action becomes vicious and destructive. Thought is not thought unless it is a law to itself. The practical recognition in modern times of this truth, though partial as yet, has been of incalculable profit to civilization, and is rightly regarded as at once a token and means of progress. Again, the corporate community is fallible, it also like the individual; and when all the ignorance and barbarism of the land is held to have the same title with knowledge and civilizing mind to political function, the amount of fallibility exhibited by it is likely to be liberal; a certain frugality of civil regulation is therefore discreet. Farther, general and peremptory rules can never be flexile and

adaptive enough to anticipate all the fine elections of character; an excess of them would therefore tend to suppress character, converting men into animate machines. Once more, spontaneity is precious. Spiritual, like physical, productivity is inseparable from it; room must be made for this, ample room. Hence social regulation, effected by government and law, is sane only as it is wisely sparing,—making thorough work indeed so far as it goes, but carefully not going too far. The modern mind is much impressed with the need of that wise abstinence; and so far its ideal is good.

On the other hand, suppose one should deny the jurisdiction of the corporate community altogether, and make that of the individual exclusive; suppose he should lay it down for an absolute and universal principle that each is privileged to determine for himself, and in all particulars what is right. That were wild. Men have a life, a welfare, a productive function in common; they exist as moral and intelligent human beings, they have articulate speech even, only through the effect of their relations, their interdependence, their social complexity; and the last violence is done to the truth of Nature by him who would regard each of them as rounded completely in his separate self, and endowed with an invincible independence. There is no such independence; *inter*dependence is a first law of human life; and it is only by the recognition of this, and the regulation of it, and an ordered integration of society, that the productive function of humanity is otherwise than abortive. We *must,*—Nature has said that we must,—have fixed common understandings, fixed for all, and obligatory upon all, in order that the soul of any man may have its proper fruition. There can be, therefore, no right of a jurisdiction exclusively individual—no principle in Nature to that effect.

No exclusive jurisdiction, then, of the social body, and none of the individual. Either of them practically asserted as exclusive would make human nature barren and prohibit civilization. What then? The jurisdiction must be composite, partly social, partly individual. With respect to our broadest and strictly necessary relations of interdependence, it should be conceded to the corporate community; while with respect to all others, where the interdependence is less strict, and to which invariable rules could not well apply, it should be assigned to the individual. In general, the best modern sentiment inclines to say,—Leave as much to the discretion of the individual as may be without compromising social integrity and health. Spontaneity is so valuable, so essential, to the finest essays of genius and the ruddiest energies of enterprise and invention, that to make ample room for it is the part of wisdom. We hold, therefore, that it is well to simplify the functions of civil society, and by getting just enough done thoroughly, surely, seasonably, to make it safe that the conceded jurisdiction of the individual should be liberally extended. But just in proportion as social powers are yielded to mindlessness and barbarism, this liberality becomes unsafe; there must be more governing in quantity to make up for the defect of quality; the functions of government are at once over-done and insufficient; and a fluctuating, confused, desultory mass-despotism sprawls over the whole field of human action, covering all, and usefully occupying no part of it. Are there no signs of a tendency to just this in our community? Such a plethora of laws, and never enough effect of law! The statute books bursting with fulness, and private usurpations grown to enormity! Interferences with what should be the allowed liberty of individual action, such as no European people would endure, and the right effects of civil order too imperfectly attained! Our democracy is like a full bowl in unsteady hands, always slopping over upon floors and garments, and giving us in that way a great deal too much of its contents, while for this very reason it never brings enough to the lips. Our reformers, some of them, wish to vote everything, and run to the ballot-box as a little boy to the imagined omnipotence of his papa, to ask for all things, possible and impossible; and meantime with continued excess, we have continual deficiency.

Time now to rectify our ideal. To do so, one truth, one grand truth, should be recognized; all men are justly bound by the end for which all men exist, to wit, an honorable, productive, progressive life. That fact goes before liberty; it is true *princeps*.

Our "wagon is hitched to a star." Jefferson, Paine and Company undertook to cut the traces, and make the wagon "free."

Bound by that end, all men are bound to the means, adjustments, principles and applications of principles necessary to its realization. Of the things thus necessary, the two first and broadest are strictly correlative; first, social law, social integration,—as necessary to the end for which man is created as individual existence even, and to be reasoned from, as ordered by, its own principles; secondly, the spontaneity, the initiative, of the individual. Neither of these without the other; neither to be borrowed from the other. As the effect of their just correlations honorably maintained, there will come an *upward* liberation, which consists in man's higher use at once of himself and of what the world offers him for use—in the flowering and fructification of his life. That liberation, that flowering and fruiting of his life, that higher use of himself and his conditions, is freedom, *real* freedom. For this the State exists, and for this the conceded jurisdiction or "liberty," of the individual exists; both for their uses, both for the same use, and both by the same right—the right, duty, imperative vocation, of man to bring out of his life the just fruit of it.

Now, all this has been pushed aside. We have been beguiled into setting up individual "natural" liberty, as an exclusive, absolute principle—against the primary law of social interdependence, against the commanding obligation of that high end for which man is created. So isolated, this liberty becomes beast-liberty, rat-liberty. Everything, however, it is thought, must hinge upon that. And because it is no true human principle, the doors are tumbling off their sham hinges, the tempest sweeping in, and we a nation of Mrs. Partingtons trying with busy broom to sweep the tempest out: quite in vain; it pours through the halls, through the rooms, to the marriage chamber, to the marriage bed; and if we are not to be swamped, it is necessary that we come to a better understanding, beginning with Duty,—social duty, to be socially defined and enforced, for the broad necessary relations of interdependence, and individual duty—duty still—for so much as may wisely be entrusted to that: thus, through duty done and discipline established, we shall arrive at all the richest effect of social integration, while enabling ourselves to secure also the richest effect of spontaneity, by making it not only safe but profitable to allow the discretion of the individual large room and function. Cherish liberty, then; 'tis a treasure; but do not make it a first principle, for then it is no treasure. Duty for the first principle, and liberty only and always under the sovereignty of Obligation.

But we have another ideal, which also has its good aspects, but which long since began to become spurious by excess, while in the doctrines of the International Association, it is just now arising in a shape of the last extravagance to claim supremacy in the modern world. It is the ideal of Equality, which in its excess becomes that of uniformity, or universal sameness—the same function, the same fortune, the same of everything, as nearly as may be, for all. It is plain that the term *equality* has made a vast impression upon the modern imagination, has become one of the magic words, words to conjure with; we roll it as a sweet morsel under the tongue, and it is like wine to exhilarate; the sound of it is music in the ear; it seems to assure the goodness of all that comes under its patronage, while everything looks black and cruel which is dissociated from it. Forty years ago De Tocqueville, in his remarkable chapter entitled, "Why Democratic Nations manifest a more ardent and enduring love of Equality than of Liberty," wrote as follows: "Everybody has remarked that in our time, and especially in France, the passion for equality is every day gaining ground." He speaks of this passion as "ardent, insatiable, incessant, invincible," and ventures the statement, certainly important if true, that the communities possessed by it will sooner choose "equality in slavery" than liberty without it,—will purchase equality, if need be, at the price of "poverty, servitude, barbarism." These surprising words, emanating, be it remembered, from no lover of monarchy, though from one who carried France in the eyes somewhat too much to detect the finer shades of sentiment in other lands, were penned while Red Republicanism was yet in the egg. The brood has been well hatched since that day. If the statement were true then, it is thrice true now. I do not doubt that this penetrating observer saw justly what was before his eyes in his own land; and as little doubt that Renan, in that wondrously prophetic essay wherein before the late war he predicted the down-fall of France, as the necessary result of internal decay, was right in attributing that decay chiefly to the inflamed egotism which will sooner embrace barbarism than frankly acknowledge a superior.

Now this sentiment, though vicious and destructive, implicates a measure of what is true and good. As our admirable Fisher Ames said at the beginning of the century, "Most of the democratic articles of faith are blended with truth, and seem true." (He added: "And they so comfortably soothe the pride and envy of the heart that it swells with resentment when they are contested, and suffers some spasms of apprehension even when they are examined.") There is a sense in which equality of rights ought to be affirmed and maintained. The benefits produced by a system of social order may be, and ought to be, open to all impartially. The right to personal protection, the right to hold property, the right of inheritance, should be maintained for all in the same sense; access to the courts of justice, the use of public schools, public roads, public conveyances, and the like, should be assured to all with the same restrictions and the same freedom. There is a certain public inheritance, a wealth produced by the system of social order, to which of right every citizen is heir on the same terms with every other. Observe, this is no right of every unclean or incapable individual to be reckoned personally the equal of the wisest and best; nor is it an equal right of function in the state or elsewhere, irrespective of capacity and fitness; for all right of function must be conditional strictly— conditioned upon the ability and disposition to make the function serviceable, that is, to make it real *function* rather than obstruction; it is simply a common privilege of access, on the same equitable terms, to the benefits produced by political function, that is, by a system of civil order.

That is the sane, republican doctrine of citizen-rights,—the same for all citizens who do not forfeit them by misbehavior.

There has been occasion to assert it with emphasis in Europe, against a system which, upon no equitable ground, made over the best fruits of civil order to a preferred, hereditary class; and there has been occasion to assert it with no less emphasis in our country, where a provincial prejudice would exclude Frederick Douglass from public tables, forbidding him to take food beside men, not one of whom but were honored to be reckoned his peer. This republican doctrine of citizen rights is as dear to me as to another. Call them equal rights, if you will,—provided always that an enthusiastic, passionate, purblind imagination of equality as universally necessary, and even as a universal fact in nature, does not creep in under that word *equal,* to run away with your wits. Numbers, as everyone may see, have in fact been deported thus from the domains of common sense, and cast away upon the quick-sand-conceit that in the political institutions character and capacity should go for nothing, since, forsooth, "all men have equal rights." Said Fisher Ames—to quote him again:—"If the philosophers among the democrats will restrict the word equality as carefully as they ought, it will not import that all men have an equal right to all things, but that to whatever they have a right, it is as much to be protected and provided for as the right of any persons in society." This, however, was only good sense, while what the "democratic philosophers" craved, and the only thing to content them, was a blown imagination.

The "passion for equality" first over-stepped the bounds of sound sense, and manifested its character as a passion, unreasoning and irrational, by asserting the personal equivalence, the equal personal *value,* of all men. It no longer said simply that citizen-rights, properly discriminated, are the same for all citizens who do not alienate them by misconduct, but quite struck beyond this and said broadly, with Thomas Jefferson, "All *men* are equal." This violent and absurd imagination was at first applied only in politics, and in our country has never gone very much farther. Indeed, and as it might seem, strangely, it was felt to be *true* only in politics. All men are equal, we were told; but even in the minds of those who said so with greatest gusto, this meant only that all are equally entitled to the elective franchise.

For as a man will on Sunday, and in the Wednesday evening prayer meeting, believe fervidly in the dogmas of total depravity and eternal damnation, while for the rest of the week he will perhaps cherish as his dearest friend one of the very persons whom his Sunday-belief proclaims a child of the Devil, doomed to everlasting burnings, so it is with all formalists; they have all their box-truths, true inside the box and not at all so outside. Never was this sectional and cooped belief better illustrated than by the democratists who proclaimed all men equal. The box that defined the space of their "great truth" was the ballot-box.

Rousseau formulated this dogma, as he did that of natural liberty. According to him, we have seen, each man's will is his supreme, only law. Each, accordingly, being absolutely independent, is the equal of every other, just as all perfect circles are equal in the sense of being equally circles. As, therefore, from the absoluteness of the individual will, he argued that no man can owe, or be required to acknowledge, any social obligation but such as he chooses to make for himself, so from the personal equivalence of all, he argued that each is entitled to an equal function in the state with every other. This conceit became that of his nation, and with this it is that the modern career of France began.

And here it was that opened the contrast and chasm between French democracy and our ancestral republicanism. The latter, as represented, for example, by its illustrious martyr, Algernon Sidney, had the infirmity to choose plain, sterling good sense as against inflated imagination, quite false to be sure, but then so big and so enticing to heads of a certain quality! Sidney says: "That equality which is just among equals is just only among equals; but such as are base, ignorant, vicious, slothful or cowardly are not equal in natural or acquired virtues to the generous, wise, valiant and industrious, nor equally useful to the societies in which they live: *they cannot therefore have an equal part in the government of them;* they cannot equally provide for the common good; and 'tis not a personal but a public benefit that is sought." Our ancestral republicanism had an honorable purpose to make citizenship, under the conditions of good behavior,

a ticket of admission to the benefits of a sound social system; Rousseau, and France with him, flew away from this good ground to perch upon a crazy conceit instead; and Jefferson, spreading his new-found French wings to the airs of a great occasion, flew to the same roost.

Limited, for the most part, in our country to the field of politics, though always growing and encroaching, as such moral fungi will, this conceit, this imagined equilibrium of egotism, had in France at the outset the aid of a passionate reaction from old manners and institutions, has had a longer period there than here, and has not been resisted by a characteristic sobriety of mind in the nation. There it has for some while prescribed the customary attitude of men toward each other; and the result is a moral atrophy, a dry-rot of the higher sentiments, a debility of character, an impoverishment of natures through their mutual relations, a death of discipline at the root, a destruction of authority, a shrinking and shrivelling of capacity, and incapability of any better alliance than such as may be found in the lumped egotism of classes, and in fine, a deterioration of the national spirit more rapid than was ever seen in history before,—all of which may serve for a warning, and cannot fail, one would say, to warn none but those who are blind and deaf and dead to instruction. France has beautiful capabilities,—the brightest, most vivacious genius, the most charming manners, in the world; and I could do anything sooner than exult over her misfortunes; but to be bewitched with spurious ideals was her first misfortune, upon which the others have followed; and one must take his instruction where it is offered.

"By no weak pity might the gods be moved"; and man, though moved by pity, should at least not suffer it to blind his eyes.

All those effects might have been anticipated. A nation is not in a good way if it does not invite and nourish superiorities by grateful recognition, and by offering them a proper field and function; but a nation jealous habitually of them, habitually intent on making a bad climate for them, purchases the mediocrity it desires. A nation filled to the lips with an impassioned, intolerant conceit of equality does just this; and is punished by obtaining what it imagines, actual equality, to wit, an equality in universal littleness. France has gone a long way in this direction. During the war she had no general, and after it no statesman. She has passed through her great struggle without showing one trace of great character—unless a certain elevation and amplitude of mind in the writer, Renan, furnish a solitary exception. Admirable littérateurs she has; but even in literature her best is burnished silver, not gold. Meantime, the levelling passion, having always for its ideal an equilibrium of egotism, destroys all that gives depth, fertility, richness to the social spirit,—reciprocal reverences, reciprocal, glad recognition of special superiorities, honorable, fructifying exchanges of deference and obedience, and the like. The "three reverences" of Goethe are precisely and pre-eminently what this spirit cannot endure; and therefore it cannot endure that which above all ennobles character and gives dignity to human life. The nation, accordingly, has continual agitation without silent, long-breathed, fruitful activity— that "distressing small motion," of which De Tocqueville speaks; and its life is likely to be polarized, as that of France has been so largely, between the narrowest, disintegrating egotism and the painted quackeries of sentimental politics. A peculiar aversion to discipline becomes a national trait, because discipline implies obedience; and if the individual must obey, he will by preference obey someone whom he does not at the same time feel painfully compelled to respect,—some little man, easily seen to be a pigmy perched high, easily felt to be an "equal," or else one who, if possessed of ability, atones for it, and reduces himself to the required level, by defect of character. The representative of public authority must maintain himself either by purchased adhesion and military force, like Napoleon III, or by pouring out floods of flattery upon caitiffs, with Trochu, whose fulsome eulogies of troops that got under fire only to scamper away were exacted by the "passion for equality." It is to be observed that the one general who had the manliness to rebuke insubordinate and cowardly regiments, compelling them for a moment to feel their beloved equality pretty thin stuff, was murdered the moment the communists got him into their hands. And the communists had to reassert their sense of equality by shutting up their own leaders in jail once a fortnight,—Assi, for example.

It is the last result of this spirit that genuine, sterling self-respect becomes an all but impossible virtue, being displaced by that self-conceit which lives only in comparisons. Self-respect, a sentiment without which men were of no more worth than frogs in a pool, is wholly simple and positive, like the growth of herbage or the shining of stars: it does not feed upon comparisons, is incapable of envy or mean jealousy, and is nourished rather than depleted by its association with deference and reverence. Nothing is more foreign or more fatal to it than the spirit which says, "I am as good as another, and will never acknowledge a superior"; it dies before that base self-assertion can go from the heart to the lips.

I remember the powerful and significant impression made upon me years ago by Toschi's engraving from the St. John and St. Augustine of Correggio. The apostle, a little elevated above the others, is instructing him; his face radiant with intelligence and benignity. Augustine stands with his head slightly bowed, listening with ear and soul. His serious, noble countenance expresses profound reverence, purest thoughtfulness and incorruptible self-respect, not opposed and contending, but united to make by their union the indivisible majesty of character and manliness. He receives every word as the coined gold of heaven's truth, yet does so with a mental poise and self-possession no less than perfect; and his vast docility lends itself with untold enhancement to all that which makes his spirit masterly. No upstart conceit there to squeak, "I am as good as you!" One imagines how that noble aspect of the man would be cheapened and degraded by the slightest access of this self-assertion, jealous and pert. And partly, it may be, because this is quite wanting, there is no arrogance of superiority in the face of the apostle,— no line there to say, "Stand apart, I am better than you." The conceit and blurt of equality, the arrogance and exclusiveness of caste,—of neither is there a vestige.

It occurred to me while looking on that picture why it is that the modern artist must leave men aside, and turn to the landscape, in order to produce what may finally affect the beholder. A noble form of human relation can no longer be imagined with artistic clearness and simplicity. The typical modern must be "independent" to be manly, indocile to be sincere, and jealous of superior qualities to preserve the equalizer's substitute for self-respect. The passion for equality, after debilitating all productive social principles, has swarmed like a plague of moths upon the human mind itself, to prey upon its blossoms. Well for Correggio that he was not born in modern France! He would probably have found in himself a genius to paint only horses, boar-hunts, or spectral impossibilities, like those in which Gustave Doré revels with the pencil and Victor Hugo with the pen.

But every ideal, genuine or spurious, must of necessity go on developing itself, to bring forth all of good or of evil there is in it. Thus that of Catholicism is compelled, even in its decrepitude, to produce new dogmas, new pretensions, more and more alien to sincere modern intelligence. So in the present instance: the ideal of equality, long since become spurious, advances upon itself, rejects its own past, develops new designs, and becomes more exacting and intolerant as it becomes more extreme. It has of late generated the demand for an artificial, constrained equalization of conditions, to be established and maintained at the expense, and to the utter displacement of all liberty whatsoever; and a powerful wide-spread organization, vaunted publicly in the present Congress, as comprising "the leading minds of all civilized lands," has arisen, and is secretly, inexorably at work, to effect that purpose. Time fails me, however, to discuss this branch of the subject. In one or two remarks your patience will perhaps indulge me.

This equality has no room, and knows that it has no room, and means to have no room in fact, for liberty, whether the natural liberty of Rousseau, on which I set no value, or the chartered and fruitful freedom of individual action in civilized communication, which every man ought to value greatly. Now it is well known that Jefferson in his famous preamble put equality before liberty; probably, however, it is not generally known that his first draught of that paragraph revealed his point of view more explicitly. In that first draught he expressly represented the right, not only to liberty, but to life itself as borrowed from and contingent upon, his great first truth, equality. He wrote thus: "We hold these truths to be self-evident: that all men are created equal and independent; *that from this equal creation they derive* certain inherent and inalienable rights, among which are life, liberty and the pursuit of happiness." The right to life "derived" from natural equality! He drew his pen through that; but there must have been a strange speculative bias in the man who could indite such a statement at all. It was a bias, however, in what was coming to be "the spirit of the age"; and this spirit, continuing and producing itself, has already become in some quarters a Turk that endures no brother near the throne.

With good enough warrant, too, if the "great truth" of equality be indeed a great truth. Suppose we had been fervidly saying for a century that all horses are equal,—proclaiming this as the grand fact about horses. Well, one day a fellow rides up to my stable (I have none), takes out my blood horse, puts his own half-hipped, spavined nag in the stall instead, mounts and coolly rides away. I have him arrested for robbery; whereupon he proves from my own lips that all horses are equal, therefore that I had suffered no loss! A just lesson for a loose tongue, I should say! Somewhat in this fashion it is that the new equalizers have taken up the talk of democratic politics, to proceed upon it in dead—and killing—earnest. I imagine them addressing the astonished democratists on this wise:—

"Equality is a fact in Nature: you confess it such: we are about to make it a fact of civilization. Think no longer to put us off with mere ballot-box equality; that little game is played out; we have been at school for a century, and are not to-day the green heads you gulled so easily once. You baited your hook with *liberty,* and caught your gudgeon; we know the smell of the bait now, and are not the gudgeons you take us for. You got up for us a little, special, formal equality at the polls, as an expedient to cheat us out of the real thing; you did cheat us, to our shame be it said, but see if you can do it again! All men are equal of right; we have sworn that they shall be so in fact. They can be so

in fact only if conditions are equal; and conditions will be made
equal only when personal liberty and private property are done
away,—only when the *collectivity,* centred in an efficient head,
shall own everything, dispose of everything, prescribe everything,
take the weanling from the cradle, put the defunct into his grave,
and between cradle and grave appoint him his place, function,
provender and all the rest. Understand then, once for all, that
we do not care for your democracy, would not give a pin to
choose between one and another of your systems of government;
all of them throw a tub to the whale, and all do it with the same
interested design; and we—we no longer swim in those waters."

This in substance is said, and this is but the logic of equality
carried to its conclusion. In this spirit it was that a leading com-
munist of Paris, hearing talk of liberty, said with cool scorn,
"Liberty, what have we to do with that? It is equality we are going to have, equality, not liberty." In a similar spirit *L'Interna-
tionale,* an organ of the International, said in February last,—I
quote from an article in a recent number of the Edinburg
Review:

"Raspail and Rochefort, however sincere they may be, do not
know the first word of the revolution to which they are march-
ing. They have not even a socialist programme. They would be
socialists, but cannot, because, like all middle-class democrats,
they start *from a point of view absolutely false—that of individual liberty."*

It is not, I repeat, Rousseau's liberty merely that is repugned,
but the liberty of the good citizen to choose his own occupation,
own and bequeath property, and the like. The former is indeed
discarded; and so far well; it is a sign of recovery; but the latter
is discarded with it, and so one extravagance exchanged for another. Only an iron system, wherein each man shall be fastened
down as with a spike driven through him, can secure real equality; and real equality these men are sworn to have.

Well, the democratists have been proclaiming equality, exalt-
ing equality, furnishing tools to Tammany, or to a swarm of
adventurers, out of their faith in equality, seeing in the light of
their great truth, equality, how indispensable to the common-

wealth are the wisdom of fools and the virtue of scoundrels; and now if they shall have to drink of the beer they have brewed, I, who like the beverage as little as they, and have earned it less, shall observe the consequent wry faces, not without a certain grim satisfaction. Besides, I feel myself in a degree indebted to those crazed heads. They are bringing to the test this loose talk of the modern world, and not an hour too soon. Enough of painted half-truths, held up to glitter and entice, but in application deftly slipped aside into some special sphere, where it is supposed that we may safely indulge that sort of sincere make-belief, of which human beings, conservative or radical are more capable than could be wished; enough of these, and thanks even to the insanity that forces upon them the test of an unsparing application. Moreover, these new Mahometans of the International have this merit, exceptional in our times, that they are not fiddling at formal politics. They mean *effects,* these men do; and I, who also mean effects, and have a disesteem not less than theirs for political formalism, with the minds that run only and always in the grooves of political formalism, am half ready, if not more than half, to welcome anything which promises to break the domination of this,—this, that has blinded eyes and tied hands far too long. Liberty and equality, supposed to consist in the privilege of incompetence to be the puppet of knaves at the polls; subjection to "despotism," supposed to consist in living under good and wholesome laws, without going to town-meeting; —if so be that only the satans can sweep these entangling and choking cobwebs away, I submit to the hard necessities of history, and say, "Let the satans come!"

Nevertheless I show you a better way. There is a good liberty, without which life is infertile, sterile, hardly worth having; it is *that* which you democratists are taking away, while you tie us down to a dependence upon barbarous impulses and chaotic natures. There is a generous social equality, which pours out benefit upon a land as the sun pours light—such an equality as led the Puritans of Massachusetts (no democrats they), there in their wilderness, enduring the utmost privation of pioneer life, to endow the politics of the world with the richest gift these have received in the space of some centuries—with the recognized duty, namely, of the republic to educate the whole people: it is this that you are making less, while you press your mechanical or supposititious equality into its place. Daily through affection for a false liberty we are robbed of the true; daily a false conceit of equality, hugest lie ever yet flung in the face of Nature, stints the munificence of republican equity; and meantime each of these spurious ideals is generating its own peculiar craze, the one running to "free love" and chaos, the other to such a system as would make all men but equal cogs on a wheel; and if we are not to wait, as I *will* hope and trust we are not, until craze shall crush craze and sanity arise from their ruin, we have just this to do; to put Duty before liberty and Quality before equality. Through duty and discipline make Freedom, to which the conceded liberties of the State and those of the individual shall alike conduce: be *that* freedom your ideal. On the other hand, say not —All men are equal—in other words, that whatsoever makes worthiness in men is to be thrown out of account; say rather— Worth is the fountain of equity, and that fountain it shall be our purpose for the behoof of the whole people, to unseal.

BIBLIOGRAPHY OF THE WRITINGS
OF DAVID ATWOOD WASSON

BY ROBERT C. ALBRECHT

1851

Confession of Faith of Rev. David A. Wasson, as given in to the
  Council at his Ordination at Groveland, September 4th, 1851.
  (1851?)
"Dr. Isaac Barrow." The New Englander, IX (November, 1851),
  498–510.

1852

Religion Divorced from Theology. A Farewell Discourse, Preached
  before the Congregational Society in Groveland, August 29, 1852.
  Boston: Thurston, Torry & Emerson, 1852.
"Lord Bacon." The New Englander, X (August, 1852), 333–374.

1853

Sacrificial Religion and Spiritual Religion. An Installation Sermon,
  Preached before the Groveland Independent Church, May 1, 1853.
  Boston: Thurston, Torry & Emerson, 1853.
"To Wendell Phillips." Liberator, XXIII (May 20, 1853), 89. (Letter.)
Report of a speech at the New England Anti-Slavery Convention,
  Melodeon, Boston, May 25. Liberator, XXIII (June 3, 1853), 95.

1855

Letter of transmittal and copy of a speech given at the New England Anti-Slavery Convention, May 31, 1855. *Liberator,* XXV (June 22, 1855), 98–99.

"The Goal of Life." *The Christian Examiner and Religious Miscellany,* LIX (September, 1855), 187–203.

Ancient Feasts and Modern Famine. A Sermon Preached before the Worcester Free Church, Sunday, Dec. 2, 1855. Worcester: Baker, Trumbull & Barnes, 1855.

1856

"Mr. Wasson's Farewell Sermon." *Liberator,* XXVI (April 25, 1856), 68.

"Explanatory Letter." *Liberator,* XXVI (September 5, 1856), 148.

The Universe No Failure. A Sermon, Preached before the Worcester Free Church, Sunday, Nov. 4th, 1855. Worcester: Charles Hamilton, 1856.

1858

"The New World and the New Man," *Atlantic Monthly,* II (October, 1858), 513–531.

"Sacrifice." *Christian Examiner,* LXV (November, 1858), 313–332.

"All's Well." *Atlantic Monthly,* II (December, 1858), 861.
Reprinted: *The Radical,* III (November, 1867), 147–148. David Atwood Wasson, *Poems* (Boston: Lee and Shepard, 1888), pp. 124–127. (Hereafter, *Poems.*) George Willis Cooke, *The Poets of Transcendentalism* (Boston: Houghton, Mifflin and Company, 1903), pp. 169–172. (Hereafter, Cooke.)

1859

"Joy-Month." *Atlantic Monthly,* III (June, 1859), 685.
Reprinted: *Poems,* pp. 128–129.

"Seen and Unseen." *Atlantic Monthly,* IV (July, 1859), 57.

Reprinted: *Woman's Journal*, XII (July 16, 1881), 225. *Poems*, pp. 130–133. Cooke, pp. 166–169.

1860

Letter on the death of Theodore Parker. *Liberator*, XXX (July 6, 1860), 107.
"Justice vs. Admiration." *Liberator*, XXX (December 31, 1860), 210. (Letter.)

1861

"Fremont." *Liberator*, XXXI (October 18, 1861), 166.
Reprinted as "Deliverance," *Poems*, pp. 92–93.
"Rest and Motion." *Atlantic Monthly*, VII (May, 1861), 525–541.
"Time's Household." *Atlantic Monthly*, VIII (October, 1861), 846.
Reprinted: *Poems*, p. 73.

1862

"Light Literature." *Atlantic Monthly*, IX (January, 1862), 86–88.
"The Sword in Ethics." *Christian Examiner*, LXXII (January, 1862), 1–22.
Review of *The Anti-Slavery History of the John Brown Year; being the Twenty-seventh Annual Report of the American Anti-Slavery Society, N.Y.*, New York, 1861. *Christian Examiner*, LXXII (January, 1862), 139–140.
Review of Charles K. Whipple, *Relation of the American Board of Commissioners for Foreign Missions to Slavery*, Boston, 1861. *Christian Examiner*, LXXII (January, 1862), 140–141.
"Ease in Work." *Atlantic Monthly*, IX (February, 1862), 241–244.
"Individuality." *Atlantic Monthly*, IX (April, 1862), 424–429.
"Hindrance." *Atlantic Monthly*, IX (May, 1862), 607–610.
"Originality." *Atlantic Monthly*, X (July, 1862), 63–67.
Report of sermon. *Liberator*, XXXII (October 31, 1862), 175.

1863

"Mr. Buckle as a Thinker." *Atlantic Monthly*, XI (January, 1863), 27–42.

"Buckle's Treatment of History." *Christian Examiner,* LXXIV (January, 1863), 61–76.

"The Law of Costs." *Atlantic Monthly,* XI (February, 1863), 241–250.

"Defiance." Boston *Commonwealth,* I (April 10, 1863).

Reprinted: *Poems,* p. 83.

"Love against Love." Boston *Commonwealth,* I (April 10, 1863).

Reprinted: *The Radical,* II (April, 1867), 476. *Parnassus,* ed. Ralph W. Emerson (Boston: James R. Osgood, 1875), p. 83. (Hereafter, *Parnassus.*) *Poems,* p. 78. Cooke, pp. 172–173.

"Royalty." Boston *Commonwealth,* I (April 10, 1863).

Reprinted: *The Index,* n.s. II (September 29, 1881), 145. *Parnassus,* p. 198. Mrs. John T. Sargent, *Sketches and Reminiscences of the Radical Club* (Boston: James R. Osgood and Company, 1880), pp. 403–404. *Poems,* p. 82. Cooke, pp. 173–174.

"Thoreau." Boston *Commonwealth,* I (April 17, 1863). (Poem.)

Review of John Stuart Mill, *On Liberty,* Boston, 1863. Boston *Commonwealth,* I (April 24, 1863).

"Shall We Compromise." *Atlantic Monthly,* XI (May, 1863), 649–655.

"Courage in Belief." *Christian Examiner,* LXXIV (May, 1863), 383–400.

"Phrenology and Philanthropy." Boston *Commonwealth,* I (May 1, 1863).

"Size of Brain." Boston *Commonwealth,* I (May 8, 1863).

"To the 54th Regiment of Massachusetts Volunteers." Boston *Commonwealth,* I (May 15, 1863).

Reprinted: *Poems,* p. 84.

"Letters in Reply to 'The Argument for Slavery.' " Boston *Commonwealth.* "I. Diversity and Unity," I (June 12, 1863). "II. Ethnology and the Negro," I (June 19, 1863). "III. Cotton," I (June 26, 1863). "IV. Cotton and Men," I (July 3, 1863).

"To Death." Boston *Commonwealth* I (July 31, 1863).

Reprinted: *Poems,* pp. 110–111.

"A Letter to Thomas Carlyle." *Atlantic Monthly,* XII (October, 1863), 497–504.

Reprinted: Boston *Commonwealth,* II (October 2, 1863).

"Wendell Phillips as an Orator." *Christian Examiner,* LXXV (November, 1863), 396–409. (Review of Wendell Phillips, *Speeches, Lectures, and Letters.* Boston, 1863.)

"Noontide [June, A.D. 1854]." Boston *Commonwealth,* II (November 6, 1863).

Reprinted: *Poems,* pp. 112–115.

"O'er the Sanded Floor." Boston *Commonwealth,* II (November 20, 1863).

Reprinted: *Poems,* pp. 100–101.

Review of Wendell Phillips, *Speeches, Lectures, and Letters,* Boston, 1863. *Atlantic Monthly,* XII (December, 1863), 792–794.

1864

Review of John Stuart Mill, *Principles of Political Economy,* New York, 1864. *Atlantic Monthly,* XIII (February, 1864), 250–253.

Review of William R. Alger, *Critical History of the Doctrine of a Future Life,* Philadelphia, 1864. *Atlantic Monthly,* XIII (February, 1864), 253–256.

"Whittier." *Atlantic Monthly,* XIII (March, 1864), 331–338.

"The Relation of Theodore Parker to Hume, Voltaire, and the Skeptics of the Eighteenth Century." *Liberator,* XXXIV (April 8, 1864), 60. ("Abstract.")

Review of John William Draper, *History of the Intellectual Development of Europe,* New York, 1863. *Atlantic Monthly,* XIII (May, 1864), 642–647.

"The Man for the Hour." *Liberator,* XXXIV (May 27, 1864), 87. (Report of a sermon.)

Review of *The Iliad of Homer faithfully translated into Unrhymed English Metre by F. W. Newman,* London, 1856. *Atlantic Monthly,* XIV (July, 1864) 135–136.

"Character and Historical Position of Theodore Parker." *Christian Examiner,* LXXVII (July, 1864), 1–41.

Reprinted: *Liberator,* XXXIV (July 15, 1864), 116. (Extract.)

Review of Charles Kingsley, *The Roman and the Teuton,* Cambridge and London, 1864. *Atlantic Monthly,* XIV (August, 1864), 252–254.

"Communication." *Atlantic Monthly,* XIV (October, 1864), 424–433.

"The True Basis of Suffrage." *Liberator,* XXXIV (November 18, 1864), 186. (Report of lecture.)

"Ice and Esquimaux, I." *Atlantic Monthly,* XIV (December, 1864), 728–734. "Chap. II. The Ice in Its Glory," XV (January, 1865), 39–51. "Chap. III. Birds and Boys' Play," XV (February, 1865), 201–212. "Chap. IV. Autochthones," XV (April, 1865), 437–448.

"Chap. V. Terra Incognita," XV (May, 1865), 564–572.

1865

"The Theme of Iniquity." Boston *Commonwealth*, III (January 14, 1865). (Poem.)

"Wilhelm Meister's Apprenticeship." *Atlantic Monthly*, XVI (September, 1865), 273–282; "Second Paper," XVI (October, 1865), 448–457.

"Sears on Modern Radicalism." *The Radical*, I (September, 1865), 102–105.

Report of a lecture. *Liberator*, XXXV (November 3, 1865), 174.

"The Duty of the North: A Letter to Rev. Henry Ward Beecher." Boston *Commonwealth*, IV (November 11, 1865).

Review of *The Works of Epictetus*, trans. T. W. Higginson, Boston, 1865. *Atlantic Monthly*, XVI (December, 1865), 761–762.

Review of *Speeches of Andrew Johnson*, Boston, 1865. *Atlantic Monthly*, XVI (December, 1865), 763–764.

Christianity and Universal Religion. Discourse Delivered before the XXVIIIth Congregational Society of Boston, Sunday, November 19, 1865. Boston: Parker Fraternity, 1865(?).

The Radical Creed: A Discourse at the Installation of Rev. David A. Wasson, as Minister of the Twenty-eighth Congregational Society of Boston, May 7, 1865. Boston: Walker, Fuller and Company, 1865.

1866

"Ideals." *The Radical*, I (January, 1866), 177.

Reprinted: *Woman's Journal*, XII (November 5, 1881), 353. *Poems*, pp. 149–150. Cooke, pp. 165–166.

"Letter to E. H. Sears." *The Radical*, I (January, 1866), 385–393.

"To President Johnson." Boston *Commonwealth*, IV (February 3, 1866).

Reprinted: *Poems*, pp. 85–86.

"The New Epoch in Belief." *The Radical*, I (February, 1866), 193–204.

Reprinted: *The Index*, VIII (August 9, 1877), 374–376.

"The Political Situation: A Discourse Preached to the Twenty-eighth Congregational Society at the Melodeon, on Sunday, Feb. 25, 1866." Boston *Commonwealth*, IV (March 3, 1866).

"The Veto Message: A Discourse Preached to the Twenty-eighth Congregational Society, at the Melodeon, on Sunday, April 1, 1866." Boston *Commonwealth,* IV (April 7, 1866).

"Ministering Angels to the Imprisoned Soul. From an Unpublished Poem." *The Radical,* I (May, 1866), 330.

Review of James McCosh, *An Examination of Mr. J. S. Mill's Philosophy: Being a Defense of Fundamental Truth,* New York, 1866. *The Radical,* I (July, 1866), 447–448.

"Delusion." *The Radical,* I (August, 1866), 458.

Reprinted: *Poems,* p. 94.

"Letters to E. H. Sears." *The Radical,* II (September, 1866), 44–55.

1867

"Modern Poetry." *Galaxy,* III (April 1, 1867), 785–789.

"Scipio to the Senate." *The Radical,* II (May, 1867), 574.

Reprinted: *Poems,* pp. 155–157.

Review of John Greenleaf Whittier, *The Tent on the Beach, and Other Poems,* Boston, 1867. *The Radical,* II (May, 1867), 575–576.

"Modern Speculative Radicalism." *The Radical,* II (July, 1867), 641–662.

Review of Ralph Waldo Emerson, *May-Day and Other Pieces,* Boston, 1867. *The Radical,* II (August, 1867), 760–762.

Review of Mrs. Caroline Corbin, *A Woman's Secret,* Chicago, 1867. *The Radical,* III (September, 1867), 56–58.

"Chips." *The Radical,* III (October, 1867), 96–100.

"To S.R." *The Radical,* III (October, 1867), 100. (Poem.) (Included in "Chips.")

"Remarks of D. A. Wasson." *Report of Addresses at a Meeting Held in Boston, May 30, 1867, to Consider the Conditions, Wants, and Prospects of Free Religion in America, Together with the Constitution of the Free Religious Association There Organized.* (Boston, n.d.), pp. 40–47.

1868

"Doubt." *The Radical,* III (January, 1868), 293–299.

Review of John Stuart Mill, *Dissertations and Discussions,* in four volumes. Vol. IV, Boston, 1867. *The Radical,* III (March, 1868), 511–512.

"Two Forms of Absolutism." *Christian Examiner,* LXXXV (July, 1868), 1–16.

"The Secret of Power." *The Radical,* IV (July, 1868), 17–28.

"Epic Philosophy." *North American Review,* CVII (October, 1868), 501–542.

"Silence." *The Radical,* IV (October, 1868), 261. (Poem.)

Review of Daniel G. Brinton, *The Myths of the New World: A Treatise on the Symbolism and Mythology of the Red Race in America,* New York, 1868. *The Radical,* IV (October, 1868), 316–318.

D. W. [sic] Wasson to 'Warrington.' "A Thinker on Free Suffrage." Boston *Commonwealth,* VII (December 12, 1868). (Report of remarks; reprinted from Springfield *Republican.*)

"Being and Nothing—In What Sense They are Identical." *Journal of Speculative Philosophy,* II (1868), 245–247. (Letter.)

1869

"Political Protestantism." Boston *Commonwealth,* VII (March 6, 1869). (Reprint of a report in the *Anti-Slavery Standard* of a paper read at the Third Sunday Afternoon Meeting in Horticultural Hall, Boston, January 31, 1869.)

"Chips. II." *The Radical,* V (April, 1869), 312–315.

Boston *Commonwealth,* VII (June 5, 1869). (Report of second anniversary meeting of Free Religious Association at Tremont Temple, Boston, contains summary of Wasson's remarks.)

"The Plover." *The Radical,* V (June, 1869), 471–472.

Reprinted: *Poems,* pp. 151–154.

"Nature's Politics." *Christian Examiner,* LXXXVII (November, 1869), 295–309.

"At Full Speed." *The Radical,* VI (December, 1869), 458–461.

"The Relation of Social Science to Religion." In *Proceedings at the Second Annual Meeting of the Free Religious Association, Held in Boston, May 27 and 28, 1869* (Boston, 1869), pp. 77–92. (Reprint inserted at the end of *The Radical,* VI (December, 1869).)

1870

Boston *Commonwealth,* VIII (January 1, 1870). (Reprint of column of Warrington [William S. Robinson] from the Springfield *Republican* on Wasson's remarks before the Radical Club.)

"The Confession." *The Radical,* VII (January, 1870), 1–11. Reprinted: *Poems,* pp. 56–71.

Review of John D. Baldwin, *Prehistoric Nations,* New York, 1869. *The Radical,* VII (January, 1870), 72–76.

"Rev. D. A. Wasson on 'Jesus, Christianity, and Modern Radicalism.' Horticultural Hall Discourse," Boston *Commonwealth,* VIII (March 26, 1870).

"To G. L. S." *The Radical,* VII (March, 1870), 230. Reprinted: *Poems,* p. 79.

Review of J. G. Fichte, *Science of Knowledge,* trans. A. E. Kroeger, Philadelphia, 1868; and J. G. Fichte. *Science of Right,* trans. A. E. Kroeger, Philadeplhia, 1869. *The Radical,* VII (March, 1870), 255.

"Explanation Wanted." *The Index,* I (April 23, 1870), 5. (Letter.)

"Mr. Abbot's Religion." *The Radical,* VII (May, 1870), 408–421.

"To Our Only." *Old and New,* I (June, 1870), 738. Reprinted: *Poems,* pp. 76–77.

"The Nature of Religion." In *Proceedings at the Third Annual Meeting of the Free Religious Association, Held in Boston, May 26 and 27, 1870* (Boston: John Wilson and Son, 1870), pp. 28–35.

1871

"D. A. Wasson on 'The Complaint of Labor.' Horticultural Hall Discourse." Boston *Commonwealth,* IX (February 25, 1871).

"Jesus and the Christ." *Old and New,* III (May, 1871), 567–579.

"A Note from Mr. Wasson." *The Index,* II (June 17, 1871), 188.

"The Dangers of Discovery." *Old and New,* IV (November, 1871), 541–545.

"Ought Women to Vote." *The Radical,* IX (December, 1871), 392. (Notice.)

Remarks. In *Proceedings at the Fourth Annual Meeting of the Free Religious Association, Held in Boston, June 1 and 2, 1871* (Boston: John Wilson and Son, 1871), p. 69.

1872

"Jewels." *The Radical,* X (January, 1872), 4–16.

"Social Ideals." *The Index,* III (February 10, 1872), 41–44.

"Paint." *The Index*, III (March 23, 1872), 90–91. (Letter.)

"The Declaration of Independence." *The Index*, III (April 6, 1872), 110. (Letter.)

" 'The True Method of Salvation.' A Discourse by Rev. David A. Wasson, Preached to the Twenty-Eighth Congregational Society, Sunday Forenoon, May 19, 1872." Boston *Commonwealth*, X (May 25, 1872).

"Mr. D. W. [sic] Wasson in Germany.—I. The Germans of Tradition and of Fact." Boston *Commonwealth*, X (July 20, 1872). (Reprinted from the Boston *Daily Advertiser*.)

"Mr. D. A. Wasson in Germany.—II. Will the Empire Be a Great Power." Boston *Commonwealth*, X (August 17, 1872). (Reprinted from the Boston *Daily Advertiser*.)

"Mr. D. A. Wasson in Germany.—III. Heidelberg." Boston *Commonwealth*, XI (September 7, 1872). (Reprinted from the Boston *Daily Advertiser*.)

"Mr. D. A. Wasson in Germany.—IV. Social Economy in Germany." Boston *Commonwealth*, XI (October 12, 1872). (Reprinted from the Boston *Daily Advertiser*.)

"From Germany." Boston *Commonwealth*, XI (November 2, 1872). (Letter.)

"Mr. D. A. Wasson in Germany.—V. The Labor Question." Boston *Commonwealth* XI (November 9, 1872). (Reprinted from the Boston *Daily Advertiser*.)

"Radical Problems." *Old and New*, VI (November, 1872), 599–601.

1873

"Mr. D. A. Wasson in Germany.—VI. The Conflict in Germany." Boston *Commonwealth*, XI (January 25, 1873). (Reprinted from the Boston *Daily Advertiser*.)

"Mr. D. A. Wasson in Germany.—VII. Germany in Winter." Boston *Commonwealth*, XI (February 22, 1873). (Reprinted from the Boston *Daily Advertiser*.)

"Mr. D. A. Wasson in Germany.—VIII. The Riot in Stuttgart." Boston *Commonwealth*, XI (May 10, 1873). (Reprinted from the Boston *Daily Advertiser*.)

"Mr. D. A. Wasson in Germany.—IX. Women in Germany." Boston *Commonwealth*, XI (August 9, 1873). (Reprinted from the Boston *Daily Advertiser*.)

"The International" [International Association of Workingmen]. *Journal of Social Science,* V (1873), 109–121.

1874

"Letter from D. A. Wasson." *The Index,* V (June 11, 1874), 283–284.

"Mr. D. A. Wasson in Germany.—X. German Criticism of America. . . ." Boston *Commonwealth,* [XII] (July 18, 1874). (Reprinted from the Boston *Daily Advertiser.*)

"Mr. D. A. Wasson in Germany.—XI. Every-Day Life And Manners. . . ." Boston *Commonwealth,* [XIII] (August 1, 1874). (Reprinted from the Boston *Daily Advertiser.*)

"David Friedrich Strauss." *Old And New,* X (September, 1874), 378–388.

"Mr. D. A. Wasson in Germany.—XII. The Great Historic Movement In Europe. . . ." Boston *Commonwealth,* [XIII] (October 10, 1874). (Reprinted from the Boston *Daily Advertiser.*)

"Old Catholicism." *The Index,* V (October 15, 1874), 495–496.

"The Modern Type of Oppression." *North American Review,* CXIX (October, 1874), 253–285.

1875

"Mr. D. A. Wasson in Germany.—XIII. The Great German Quarrel. . . ." Boston *Commonwealth,* [XIII] (January 9, 1875). (Reprinted from the Boston *Daily Advertiser.*)

"State and Church in Germany." *The Index,* VI (May 27, 1875), 244–245. ("A Paper Read at the Convention of the American Social Science Association, Detroit, May 11." Report reprinted from the New York *Tribune.*)

"State and Church in America." *The Index,* VI (December 16, 1875), 590–593.

"The Nature of Religion." In *Freedom and Fellowship in Religion* (Boston, 1875), pp. 17–45. (Included in the volume are two fragments, "Humanity's Dream," pp. 370–372, and "Religion and the Social Sciences," pp. 409–411.)

1876

"State and Church in Germany." *Unitarian Review and Religious Magazine,* V (January 1876), 1–28.

"Was Washington a Federalist?" *Woman's Journal,* VII (April 22, 1876), 129.

1877

"Horticultural Hall Lectures. Rev. D. A. Wasson On 'Theodore Parker.' " Boston *Commonwealth,* [XV] (March 10, 1877). (Report.)
"Theodore Parker as Religious Reformer." *Radical Review,* I (May, 1877), 46–73. (Abstract titled, "Theodore Parker and His Critic," *The Index,* VIII (August 16, 1877), 388.

1878

"Because." *Unitarian Review and Religious Magazine,* IX (January, 1878), 11–28.
"The Chestnut-Street Club. Mr. D. A. Wasson on 'Rights.' " Boston *Commonwealth,* [XVII] (December 21, 1878). (Report reprinted from the Boston *Daily Advertiser.* Reprinted December 22, 1878, in the Boston Sunday *Commonwealth.*)

1879

"A Letter from Mr. Wasson." *The Index,* X (January 16, 1879), 30–31.
The Concord School of Philosophy, 1879. "Social Genesis and Texture," "The Nation," "Individualism as a Political Principle," "Public Obligation," "Sovereignty," "Absolutism Crowned and Uncrowned," "Representation," "Rights," "The Making of Freedom," "The Political Spirit of '76." (Lectures noted in *The Genius and Character of Emerson: Lectures at the Concord School of Philosophy,* ed. F. B. Sanborn (Boston: James R. Osgood and Company, 1885), p. xi.

1880

The Concord School of Philosophy, 1880. "Philosophy of History," "The Same." Two lectures noted in *The Genius and Character of Emerson* . . . , p. xiii.

Mrs. John T. Sargent, ed. *Sketches and Reminiscences of the Radical Club of Chestnut Street, Boston.* Boston, 1880. (Contains numerous reports of remarks by Wasson and of two lectures, "Democracy," pp. 26–27, and "Thou Shalt," pp. 95–100. Also contains "The birds are all singing, . . ." (p. 398), part of a version of "May," *Poems,* p. 120.)

1881

"Chestnut-Street Club. Paper by Mr. D. A. Wasson upon Representative Government." Boston *Commonwealth,* [XIX] (February 26, 1881). (Reprinted from the Boston *Daily Advertiser.*)
"Rights." *International Review,* XI (August, 1881), 152–179.

1882

"Theism and Spencerism." *The Index,* n.s. II (January 5, 1882), 314.
"Free Thought and Other Matters." Boston *Commonwealth,* [XX] (January 7, 1882). (Letter.)
"Theism and the Scientific Method." *The Index,* n.s. II (January 12, 1882), 326–327.
"The Alternatives." *The Index,* n.s. II (January 26, 1882), 350–351.
"Last Words about Method." *The Index,* n.s. II (May 4, 1882), 519–521.
"Light and Life." *The Index,* n.s. II (June 1, 1882), 567–569.
"Evolution: A Letter to Mr. Underwood." *The Index,* n.s. III (November 9, 1882), 218–219.
Reprinted as "Mr. Wasson on Evolution," *Journal of Speculative Philosophy,* XVII (July 1883), 318–322.
"Evolution: A Second Letter to Mr. Underwood." *The Index,* n.s. III (November 16, 1882), 230–231.
"Evolution: A Third Letter to Mr. Underwood." *The Index,* n.s. III (November 23, 1882), 242–243.

1883

"A Spurious Right." *Woman's Journal,* XIV (March 31, 1883), 96. (Letter signed "D. H. Wasson" but almost certainly D. A. Wasson.)
The Concord School of Philosophy, 1883. "Herbert Spencer's Causal

328 *Bibliography*

Law of Evolution." Lecture noted in *The Genius and Character of Emerson* . . . ,p. xviii.

1884

"The Two Candidates: An Open Letter to William J. Potter." *The Index,* n.s. V (October 2, 1884), 159–160.
"A Man's a Man for A' That." *The Index,* n.s. V (December 25, 1884), 304.

1885

"Possessor or Possessed." *The Index,* n.s. V (January 1, 1885), 314–315.
"About a Word," *The Index,* n.s. V (February 5, 1885), 377.
"Arnold Upon Emerson." *The Christian Register,* LXIV (December 3, 1885), 772.
Reprinted: Frank Preston Stearns, *Sketches From Concord and Appledore* (New York: G. P. Putnam's Sons, 1895), pp. 128–132.

1886

"Ego upon Abbot." *The Index,* n.s. VI (February 18, 1886), 405–406. (Letter.)
"Subjectivism." *The Index,* n.s. VI (February 25, 1886), 410–411.
"Not So." *The Index,* n.s. VI (March 4, 1886), 429. (Letter.)
"Time." *The Index,* n.s. VI (March 18, 1886), 453.
"The Open Secret." *The Index,* n.s. VI (April 22, 1886), 507–509.
"Carlyle on Happiness." *Unitarian Review and Religious Magazine,* XXV (May 1886), 385–402.

1887

Review of Brooks Adams, *The Emancipation of Massachusetts,* Boston, 1887. *Atlantic Monthly,* LIX (February, 1887), 251–257.

1888

"The Floods. In Memory of John Brown." In Hermann von Holst, *John Brown* (Boston: Cupples and Hurd, 1888), pp. 179–181.

Reprinted: *Poems,* pp. 139–141.

Poems. Boston: Lee and Shepard, 1888.

1889

Essays: Religious, Social, Political, with a "Memoir" by O. B. Frothingham. Boston: Lee and Shepard, 1889. Contains: "Nature the
Prophecy of Man," "Authority," "Unity," "Social Texture," "Conditions of Social Productiveness," "The Puritan Commonwealth,"
"The New Type of Oppression," "The Genius of Woman."

1899

"Light." In *Souvenir Festival Hymns* (Boston, 1899), pp. 29–30.
(Hymn.)

INDEX OF NAMES

331